Table of Contents

The Pleasures of
Computer Gaming

The Pleasures of Computer Gaming

*Essays on Cultural History,
Theory and Aesthetics*

Edited by
MELANIE SWALWELL
and JASON WILSON

McFarland & Company, Inc., Publishers
Jefferson, North Carolina, and London

LIBRARY OF CONGRESS CATALOGUING-IN-PUBLICATION DATA

The pleasures of computer gaming : essays on cultural history,
  theory and aesthetics / edited by Melanie Swalwell and
  Jason Wilson.
        p.   cm.
     Includes bibliographical references and index.

     ISBN 978-0-7864-3595-1
     softcover : 50# alkaline paper ∞

     1. Computer games — Social aspects.   2. Video games —
Social aspects.   I. Swalwell, Melanie, 1972–   II. Wilson,
Jason, 1974–
GV1469.17.S63P54   2008
794.8 — dc22   2008005197

British Library cataloguing data are available

Cover photograph ©2008 Shutterstock

Manufactured in the United States of America

McFarland & Company, Inc., Publishers
  Box 611, Jefferson, North Carolina 28640
  www.mcfarlandpub.com

Introduction

Melanie Swalwell and Jason Wilson

In 1976, Atari released an arcade video game, *Night Driver*, which was an influential creative achievement, but whose audiovisual design, to twenty-first century eyes, might seem abstract or schematic. The flyer produced to promote the game to arcade owners, as well as highlighting certain "profitability features" and operator options, foregrounds specific aspects of the games:

> Now from the Atari stable of high profit-scoring racing machines comes the first game to offer players the excitement of night racing. New *Night Driver* places the driver in the cockpit of their own Sebring type racer. Players select one of 3 tracks, press the accelerator and roar into the night. The monitor displays a twisting, curving road ahead. The harder the acceleration, the faster the track comes at the player. Screeching tires around curves, crashes against road barriers, the whine of changing gears add to the fantastic realism.... New "Blacklight" graphics. The ultimate in realistic nighttime simulation. A unique ultraviolet light illuminates car on screen and instructions on the monitor bezel.... Exclusive Durastress tested solid state reliability ... means your crew can sit back and watch the earnings grow each mile [Atari, 1976: 2; emphasis in original].

Night Driver is promoted here as embodying technological advancements that have particular effects. First, the blacklight technology, sound effects and the on-screen display are all foregrounded as being productive of a kind of "realism." Second, the game's audiovisual aspects are promoted as a selling point for the game; as part of its spectacular pleasures. Third, the cabinet design is promoted for its durability in an arcade setting, and the game is promoted as a reliable, profitable investment for arcade owners.

We begin with the text of this historic flyer for several reasons. We find it significant that these aspects of *Night Driver*—technological innovation, player experience, and business logic — are foregrounded in the advertising to a far greater extent than the "configurative" acts (Eskelinen) that players have to perform in playing the game. Structural features of the ergodic aspects of the game are taken as read, or seen as permeable with the fiction or simulation that the game offers — the player "presses their accelerator and roars off" into a "night" that is present only in the mise-en-scène — while the audiovisual production of the spectacle of nighttime driving is emphasized. It is elements such as the game's production of spectacle, and its potential as a piece of commodified entertainment — elements that might be seen in some quarters as inessential — that Atari self-nominates as the true achievements of *Night Driver*, and what distinguishes it from a host of competing digital and nondigital slot machine entertainments.

The foregrounding of these elements (technological innovation, player experience, and business logic) by Atari strongly resonates with one of the principles linking the essays in this collection: that is, the (re)placing of digital games and gameplay into longer arcs of cultural history and theory. By this we mean that digital games are not *just* games: they circulate as commodities, new media technologies, and items of visual culture, and are embedded in complex social practices. In this collection, we are particularly interested in asking how digital games might relate to the basic assumptions of a broader media and cultural studies. Understandings of the significance of digital games can be enriched, we contend, by thinking them through in terms of contemporary debates in critical theory. This facilitates more complex and nuanced accounts of gameplay and its pleasures. Doing so is not an act of "theoretical imperialism" (King and Krzywinska 4–6), but rather is an effort to enrich our understanding of gameplay. These are not entirely unprecedented ideas, but arguments that nongame media might provide useful resources for studying digital games have been trenchantly criticized. A brief excursus is therefore required to explain and situate these ideas.

The dust is clearing after the pitched battles that characterized the early history of game studies. Just as many early games partook of the twitch and kill logic of the shooter, so some tendencies in early game studies attempted to "clear the screen," of any attempts to understand games in terms of other media. Jesper Juul's shooter game *Game Liberation* clearly expressed the hostility ludologists felt toward approaches to games from already established strands of cultural and media studies. Across levels entitled Narratology, Psychology, Film Studies etc., Juul would have the player destroy representations of entrenched theory (busts of Freud, iconographic representations of film cameras, diagrams of narrative structure) for points. Appropriately, the honor roll of high scores on the website where the game still resides is crowded with the names of prominent ludologists such as Espen Aarseth and Juul himself.

Juul's game is merely the most visible expression of a tendency among ludologists to consider digital games as "remediated games" (Eskelinen), but in a way that ultimately cuts games off from the remainder of a visual culture to which they are clearly related. While the debate and subsequent denials (Frasca 2003a) have focused upon narrative, it went beyond this. When Markku Eskelinen describes cinematic cut scenes as the merest "window-dressing," he not only misreads their crucial role as a reward and a rhythmic element in gameplay — a pleasurable element of play — he also seeks to deny the exchange between games and cinema.[1] When Espen Aarseth suggests that it doesn't matter in terms of gameplay whether or not a player's avatar looks like Lara Croft, he is suggesting a definition and a range of enjoyment in gameplay that is far narrower than that used by players, journalists, and industry professionals.[2] There is a suspicion of visual pleasure running through those arguments that propose seeking an underlying ludological structure in games (*all* games). When Juul himself spends several publications searching for a reified "gameness" in a bewilderingly diverse field of products (2003, 2005), we need to begin wondering what, exactly, is at stake in these investigations: gamers and game designers have, after all, gotten along perfectly well until now without such a definition. (Janet Murray has suggested that narratology's colonization of games is ludology's phantom, its "anxiety of influence," and that narratology is the authority against which this group of scholars has rebelled, thus representing that which "must be repudiated in order for their own interpretation to have meaning" [2005]. Patrick Crogan reads this as the ambivalence characteristic of an emerging field still debating its object of study, that is, as a stage in discipline building [10–14].) We must wonder whether a critic's motivation in providing such a definition can be anything other than an attempt to make proprietorial claims on an entire field of cultural production.[3]

There were clear benefits in shaking the complacency of media theorists who thought that they could unreflexively bring to games critical tools developed in relation to other media (though it is not clear how many attempts there were to do this).[4] However, in attempting to define "gameness" or "ergodicity" once and for all, game studies was entering into a strange Oedipal dynamic with previously established disciplines such as film studies. As pointed out as long ago as V. F. Perkins's *Film as Film*, but more recently in texts such as Noël Carroll's *Engaging the Moving Image*, every attempt to define film as a medium (e.g., montage theory) ends up prescribing what film ought to be — trying to define some films as "uncinematic" — rather than reacting to what film is or has been. This, in short, is because forms of creative practice will always exceed any attempted definitions of them. It is also because no creative practice or enjoyment of it takes place in a vacuum — the "purity" of any medium is constantly, gloriously sullied by the frenetic exchange of images, techniques, and concepts between media and the human beings that enact them. Very quickly, ludologists were seeking to claim that some games (e.g., *The Sims*) were not really games because they did not fit definitions of "gameness." Thus they ironically repeated the mistakes of a discipline that they sought to shut out from the consideration of games.

Focusing on a reified "gameness" partly denies the connection between games and broader cultural histories and theoretical perspectives, connections that can contribute valuably to the maturation of game studies and which we seek to restore here. In providing an account of these turbulent early debates, Janet Murray has called for this period to be left behind, arguing that it is time to reframe the conversation, while making a rather tongue-in-cheek claim to have the last word on this (2005). As a debate that was, from the start, quite bewildering to many humanities scholars, we are only too happy to oblige. Though there have been significant revisions by some theorists (see, for example, Frasca 2003a), and claims of misunderstanding, we recount this debate here not just for historical clarity, but to help situate the significance of the type of work that features in this volume. To extend Murray's call, it is well past time for moving beyond the misleading characterization of all nonformalist work as "narratological." The reduction and oversimplification of complex accounts that are trying to do something different to the goals the so-called ludologists set for themselves has gone on too long. We hope the present collection contributes to such a moving beyond, and a renewed appreciation of the nuanced work of the many cultural, media, and literary scholars who take digital games and gaming as their objects of study.

There is a need for scholarship that pragmatically attends to both the continuities and the discontinuities between games and other (existing and developing) media, not in order to deny the specificity of games as a family of cultural technologies, but in order to avoid the unhelpful dualisms and the hardening of positions that result from the tendency to divorce games from other media to which they are clearly related. Attempting to cut video games off from other media is counterproductive in that it blinds us to rich commonalities and continuities with cinema, television, music, visual arts, *and* predigital games. In seeking complex responses to questions such as: what is a playing subject, or what is it to engage playfully with technology, accounts of engagement with other media can be useful.

As scholars of digital games, the contributors to this volume are concerned to understand a range of aspects of the digital games phenomenon, not confined to the games themselves. Conversely, then, if issues such as the reception of digital games, their deployment in political debates, the relationships of digital strategy games to longer traditions of wargaming, the role of "addictiveness" as a design element in compelling gameplay, and how players learn games are important for a broader cultural and media studies, as they most certainly are, then they ought also to be an integral part of game studies.

Apart from being committed to re-placing games in longer arcs of cultural history and within broader critical debates, the contributions to this volume all adopt a "positive" approach to studying games and gameplay; and a drawing on the interdisciplinary resources of the humanities and social sciences, particularly new media studies.

Much has been made of the claim that games should be studied "on their own terms"; however, this does not equate with essentialism, nor with proscriptive approaches to how one *should* study games. Approaching an object of study "on its own terms" does not necessitate an approach devoid of any concepts, learning, or tools that might usefully aid in explicating its significance (as if such an "innocent" approach were possible). Nor does the use and redeploying of insights gleaned from other media and disciplinary contexts indicate that an object of study is not being studied "on its own terms." The essays in this volume all take what we think of as a "positive" approach to games. By this we do not mean an uncritical, celebratory tone, but a focusing on what computer gaming *is* and what it produces, rather than what others think it *should* or *should not* be or do.

As scholars trained in the interdisciplinary humanities and social sciences, where one is expected to be cognizant of debate in, and working at the intersections of, several disciplines, we well appreciate the richness and complexity that this tradition inherits, as well as the freedom to work disciplinary boundaries in productive, rather than patrolling, ways. There are rich synergies to mine between games and a range of media and theoretical perspectives. Witness the questions being asked by a sampling of authors here, who find advantages in bringing digital game studies into dialogue with an interdisciplinary new media studies, questions regarding the conditions that might facilitate immersion, what it is to be so immersed, and the subjective implications of interactivity; or the consideration of nonstandard uses of digital games — either through actively playing with the rules or through the dissolution of self in the pleasures of seriality and excess. In seeking answers to such questions as these — questions that art historians, film scholars, reader response theorists, and subcultural studies researchers have also asked — the theoretical inheritance of the humanities and social sciences provides much to work with, and enables the nuancing of these debates in game studies. Not only can game scholars draw on these riches, but also the understandings that they put forward will, in turn, inflect understandings and approaches across the range of fields associated with studies of other media, visual, and literary texts.

The major thrust of this volume, then, is to situate games, gameplay, and gaming practices and pleasures within broader contexts of cultural history and theory. Theory has a role to play in unpacking the significance of gaming practices, histories, and modernities. The chapters that follow discuss play in ways that are informed by cultural theory, historical perspectives, an awareness of parallel developments in other media, and the situatedness of play in specific material contexts. While refusing to get sidetracked by the now redundant defending of games as a cultural form, a number of essays critically assess the legacy games have inherited from military, gambling, capital, and scientific research. Together, these essays examine the significance of games for what they can tell us about contemporary social, technological, and cultural change, and of games as aesthetic phenomena.

Apart from a concern with placing games in wider contexts, the other major theme to the collection is gameplay. As a conjugation, "gameplay" brings together two of the most debated terms in Western philosophy. While "game" and "play" are most frequently associated with the work of mid–twentieth-century scholars Roger Caillois and Johan Huizinga, respectively, "game" has, for instance, also exercised the minds of such thinkers as Nietzsche, Heidegger, Derrida, Schiller, Kant, Plato, Huizinga, Bakhtin, Marx (Slethaug), and Wittgenstein. As such, we believe that gameplay stands as a provocative category for the scholarly analysis of digital games. In this collection, we seek to bring gameplay, long a category of valuation in popular games criticism, into dialogue with more scholarly interests. Many of the basic questions that players and reviewers ask themselves are embedded in the essays collected here: what makes a game absorbing? What is the player asked to do during gameplay, and what kinds of performance and pleasure are enabled? What is the role of design? What relationship does this game bear to "the real"? Is this game, in the end, any good? We argue that there is a need for scholarship that thinks in positive terms about what it is to play games, that attends to the specifics of genre and subgenre as well as the types of engagements on the part of players, and that is committed to questioning the wider cultural significance of gaming. Aware that "videogaming" describes a remarkably lively and diverse set of practices and texts, particular description and analysis are required if we are to understand games' engagement of players.

Gameplay is, then, a central element in the study of games as we conceive of it. In review forums like gaming magazines or websites, the term is often used to refer to the experiential qualities of games. For gamers, gameplay is a positive term that is used to refer to the quality of interactions that are coded into a game, including how compelling a particular game's premise is, how challenging its interactions are, and the relation between what a player is doing and what is happening onscreen. A strange mix of maths and art, gameplay is often considered apart from visual spectacle or sound as the distinctive, variable quality of the medium; at others, it is treated as if a magic component, a kind of "x factor." Though its relational qualities mean it is rarely explained (since it can only unfold performatively), gamers know when gameplay has been sacrificed in pursuit of the "Holy Grail" of realism. While high-quality, graphically rich experiences are technically impressive, on their own they do not make a great game, as Mark, a LAN admin, noted:

> Something that you ultimately discover is that there are games that just look fantastic, but they're really garbage to play. If something's missing that gameplay element, it's just no fun at all. You can have the prettiest graphics in the world, but if it's just not a good game, you don't want to play it ultimately.

As interactive media, the experience of playing digital games — "that gameplay element" — is central to their significance. The highlighting of gameplay here indicates the crucial importance of the experiential and the somatic in players' experiences and apprehension of games, an element that has not to date been accorded the prominence it deserves in the nascent field of game studies. As well as being a move evident in the study of other media, Wilson has argued that:

> ... if we simply attend to what happens when we and others play games, we allow the possibility of a new aesthetics of gaming to emerge.... When we realize that what is almost never talked about in current critical work is the body of the player or the nature of machine-mediated play, a field begins to open that might allow us to talk about the uses and pleasures of gaming, and to see its various forms in a wider network of interactions.

Yet the experiential needs to be considered critically. While there has clearly been a historical shift toward direct experience of media and art (something which Wilson's essay in this volume considers in depth), it was Raymond Williams who observed that the meaning of the term "Experience," "once the present participle ... of 'trying' or 'testing' something," that is, of experimentation, had come to have its current association with "feeling" (128). Experience can, as Williams makes clear, serve to entrench already established subjectivities, perhaps just dressing them up in the appearance of experiential immediacy, a point that needs to be borne in mind, we contend, in considering the pleasures of computer gaming (a theme that is taken up by Nicholls and Ryan in this volume).

In this Introduction, we have argued that game studies needs to think *beyond gameplay*. By this we mean to distinguish the concern with gameplay presented here from the already discussed purism that seeks to pare back the essence of what it is to play a game, leaving the pleasures of cut scenes and considerations of avatar embodiments in its wake. For us, this means thinking about gameplay *and* its beyond: it denotes moving beyond a particular,

limited conception of gameplay, rather than leaving gameplay behind altogether.

The scholars showcased here understand "doing game studies" to mean
a range of different things. This anthology embraces these diverse energies
and directions, offering them as an indication of new directions for the study
of games, and more specifically, of gaming pleasures.

Seth Giddings and Helen W. Kennedy do not try to understand play in
terms of a deep underlying structure, but rather they try to understand the
player's relationship to digital gaming's worlds of interaction by training their
analytical gaze on themselves, and their own efforts at learning a new interface. Their piece comments on the drama of mastery that confronts every
player as they learn a new game, or rather, as the player is trained by the game
as multiple agencies become imbricated. There are no level playing fields in
digital gaming. Apart from opening up a new reflexive means for analyzing
play, Kennedy and Giddings's piece uses humor as a tool for understanding,
and raises the crucial question as to whether a playful criticism is the one best
suited to understanding playful cultural forms.

Many videogame scholars have pointed out that the way players play and
use video games often exceeds the intention of designers, and theoretical sum-
maries of the nature of gameplay. Cognizant of players' "bad behavior," Julian
Kücklich's essay asks: how can the issue of cheating be approached theoretically? To date, games theorists have shunned the subject of cheating: it is a
messy reality that upsets structural stories about pure "gameness." But cheats
are a significant feature of gameplay, whose pleasure presumably derives from
the fact that cheating is prohibited. "Cheat guides" on the Internet and in
print show how central cheating is to the social practices around gaming,
with codes and strategies that allow players to go one up on the machine, and
designers' "Easter eggs" all adding significantly to the pleasures of game culture. In this chapter, Kücklich explores these matters, with reference to concepts from literary and media studies and systems theory, to gain new insights
into a largely neglected part of gaming culture.

Joyce Goggin replaces games in a history of modernity, looking at games
in terms of their embodiment of seriality, and thinking about the expenditure and dissolution of self in play. In particular, she thinks about videogames
in relation to gambling. For Goggin, it is the videogame's participation in the
pleasure principle of repetition that firmly connects the digital gaming experience to the ongoing slavish or blissful expenditure of the self in gambling.
The ever-increasing popularity of the videogame as the narrative mode of
choice now compels us to consider a new aesthetic, or a poetics of the senses —
a consideration from which gambling studies have also recently benefited. In
Bataillian terms the experience of intense engagement and subjective expen-

diture (in both videogames and gambling) is grounded in a constant oscillation between winning and losing, the past and the future. It is this dialogic movement that constructs the gaming experience, the gamer, and the text produced by interaction with the game world.

Some of the most enjoyable bodily pleasures of gaming result from the felt sensations of movement in games — improvisation, freedom, becomings. For Melanie Swalwell, moments of players' kinaesthetic responsiveness to games evidences both the closeness and the liveliness of gamers' aesthetic engagements with computing technology, and indicates that there is a need for more nuanced understandings of players' aesthetic relations with game worlds and avatars. Swalwell lays out a Benjaminian account of movement sensations, pointing out the partial nature of the "becoming similar to," and the potential this has for game analysis and theorizing.

Jason Wilson engages with the "archaeology" of gameplay, tracing continuities between the earliest iterations of new media art and the very first videogames. Considering the common goal of artists like Nam June Paik and early game designers like Bushnell and Baer to construct a new form of "participation TV," Wilson shows that across this range of practice, there was a common concern with changing the kinds of information behaviors that were possible in relation to television, and possibly a shared utopianism as well. Wilson's piece argues for a reintegration of critical studies of new media art and videogames.

Also considering the relationships between video games and prior or parallel forms of visual culture is Bernadette Flynn. She draws on a combination of visual and spatial theory to explicate different conventions of representing movement through space in specific digital game examples. Flynn's piece poses a number of questions. How do forms of spectatorship intersect and at times merge with the player's dynamic engagement in constructing the game event? What models might best be utilized to analyze the pleasures of the user's navigation experience? Discussing how the hermeneutics of film language overlap with the agency of spatial navigation, Flynn explores notions of the mobilized virtual gaze and cinematic pleasures alongside older forms of navigation and spatiality from architecture and landscape design.

Patrick Crogan considers a prominent genre — the real-time strategy wargame — in connection with a broader modern project of predicting the future, and with debates in critical theory about the nature of modernity and simulation. The history of the development of wargaming is punctuated by debates about its true value for the military, debates that revolve around the negotiation of the dialectic of calculation and the incalculable — war as planned enterprise versus war as volatile contingency. This chapter reexamines two major themes in the analysis of computer games with respect to these and other major debates in wargaming: the "realism vs. playability" debate, which concerns the form of the game interface as well as the nature and emphasis of gameplay, and interactivity.

Video games constitute an elaborate form of practical discourse on spatiality. Game play is linked inseparably to the way we, as participants in the culture of advanced technological societies, gain orientation and spatial understanding in our navigation of the everyday world. Games do not function as allegories or as poor imitations of the real: games feed back into our understanding of lived space, into the decisions we make as we orient and move in the world of consensus reality. Drawing on sociological and philosophical discussions of the unsettled zone of our social and ontological being by Lefebvre, Soja, Lash, McHoul, Luhmann, and others, Brett Nicholls and Simon Ryan argue that games space constitutes a kind of Thirdspace, a space that is both lived and imagined.

These essays contribute to the project of broadening the context in which we understand games in a number of overlapping and connected ways. Swalwell, Nicholls and Ryan, Flynn and Crogan all consider video games in relation to much broader debates in cultural theory concerning modernity and the nature of aesthetic experience. Giddings and Kennedy and Swalwell zero in on the nature of gameplay, and come away with understandings that emphasize the importance of the body and sociability — players' pleasures — rather than pure "gameness." Crogan, Flynn, and Wilson all think about games in terms of longer and broader cultural histories, and productively connect games with other kinds of visual and interactive culture. Goggin and Kücklich show how videogame play is understandable in relation to practices that exceed a narrow definition.

The range of contributions to this volume do not suggest a move in any one direction that will enable us to come to a final understanding of what gameplay is, but rather indicate that an expansion of the resources, ranges of comparison, and scope of investigation is a necessary prelude to apprehending the complexity of digital gameplay and its pleasures. Although the earliest debates in videogame studies were useful in defining games as an object of analysis, and in problematizing approaches that did not accord them their specificity, these essays suggest that the time has arrived when scholars whose interest in and love of games is informed by their broader cultural and theoretical interests can have a say. We hope you enjoy playing with their ideas as much as we have.

Notes

1. For a discussion of the role of cut scenes, see Klevjer (2001); for a book that convincingly details the multiple connections between games and cinema, see King and Krzywinska.

2. Notable industry insiders such as Ernest Adams constantly stress the importance

of character design, visual elements, and, yes, narrative in game design. See Rollings and Adams.

3. Revealingly, Juul has characterized the recent history of video game studies as a "gold rush," apparently without irony (2005:11).

4. See Frasca 2003b. It is difficult for ludologists to name anyone beyond Janet Murray who used narratology in relation to games, and anyone who has read *Hamlet on the Holodeck* will look in vain for the crude assimilations that the ludologists charge her with.

Works Cited

Aarseth, Espen. "Genre Trouble: Narrativism and the Art of Simulation." In *First Person: New Media as Story, Performance and Game,* edited by Noah Wardruip-Fruin and Pat Harrigan. Cambridge: Massachusetts Institute of Technology Press, 2004.

Carroll, Noel. *Engaging the Moving Image.* New Haven, CT: Yale University Press, 2003.

Crogan, Patrick. "The Game Thing: Ludology and Other Theory Games." *Media International Australia* 110 (February 2004): 10–18.

Eskelinen, Markku. "The Gaming Situation." *Game Studies* 1.1 (2001). 23 March 2007 http://www.gamestudies.org/0101/eskelinen/.

Frasca, Gonzalo. "Ludologists Love Stories, Too: Notes from a Debate That Never Took Place." In *Level Up: Digital Games Research Conference Proceedings,* edited by Marinka Copier and Joost Raessens. Utrecht: Universiteit Utrecht, 2003.

_____. "Simulation versus Narrative: Introduction to Ludology." In *The Video Game Theory Reader,* edited by Mark J. P. Wolf and Bernard Perron. New York: Routledge, 2003.

Juul, Jesper. "The Game, the Player, the World: Looking for a Heart of Gameness." In *Level Up: Digital Games Research Conference Proceedings,* edited by Marinka Copier and Joost Raessens. Utrecht: Universiteit Utrecht, 2003.

_____. *Half-Real: Video Games between Real Rules and Fictional Worlds.* Cambridge, Massachusetts Institute of Technology Press, 2005.

King, Geoff, and Tanya Krzywinska, eds. *ScreenPlay: Cinema/Videogames/Interfaces,* London: Wallflower Press, 2002.

Klevjer, Rune. "In Defense of Cutscenes. "In *Computer Game and Digital Cultures Conference Proceedings,* edited by Frans Mäyrä, 191–202. Tampere, Finland: Tampere University Press, 2002.

Murray, Janet H. *Hamlet on the Holodeck: The Future of Narrative in Cyberspace.* New York: Free Press, 1997.

_____. "The Last Word on Ludology V Narratology in Game Studies." Paper presented at Changing Worlds: Worlds in Play conference (2005). 23 March 2007 http://www.lcc.gatech.edu/~murray/digra05/.

Perkins, V. F. *Film as Film: Understanding and Judging Movies.* London: Penguin, 1990.

Rollings, Andrew, and Ernest Adams. *Andrew Rollings and Ernest Adams on Game Design.* Berkeley, CA: New Riders, 2003.

Slethaug, Gordon. "Game Theory." In *Encyclopedia of Contemporary Literary Theory: Approaches, Scholars, Terms,* edited by Irene R. Makaryk, 64–69. Toronto: University of Toronto Press, 1993.

Williams, Raymond. *Keywords: A Vocabulary of Culture and Society.* Rev. ed. London: Flamingo; Fontana, 1983.

Wilson, Jason A. "Odyssey Renewed: Towards a New Aesthetics of Video-Gaming." *M/C: A Journal of Media and Culture* 3.5 (2000). 23 March 2007. http://journal.mediaculture.org.au/0010/odyssey.php.

Gameography

Game Liberation, Jesper Juul. *M/C: A Journal of Media and Culture* 3.5 (2000). 23 March
        2007. http://journal.media-culture.org.au/0010/liberation.php.
Night Driver, Atari, 1976.
The Sims, Maxis, Electronic Arts, 2000.

1

Little Jesuses and *@#?-off Robots: On Cybernetics, Aesthetics, and Not Being Very Good at *Lego Star Wars*

Seth Giddings and Helen W. Kennedy

S: Who's leading?
H: We're leaderless.... Rudderless!
H: Ooh. Something says that there's something here ... that we need to do.

The two Lego Jedi knights wander aimlessly for a while, barely distinguishable from the crowd of more purposeful computer-controlled Lego Star Wars characters. The "something" appears to be a grate in the floor. It glows with a throbbing blue light that indicates some kind of significance, the precise nature of which soon becomes apparent: glowing objects can be acted on by "using the Force" (standing near the object and holding down the circle button on the PlayStation 2 controller).

Later in the game Helen tries to see if her avatar (now a Lego Chewbacca) can kill Seth's (Lego Yoda). Chewbacca leaps around the screen repeatedly until it becomes clear that Helen should be pressing the square button (fire weapon) rather than the x button (jump) to use Chewbacca's laser crossbow. In scenes with many NPCs on screen it is often hard to work out which avatar one is actually in control of. Moreover it is quite possible for one's avatar to be killed and to reappear without the player noticing for some time that control has been taken from them by the game.

Our case study — a session of videogame play in which both the players (ourselves) and the screen action are video-recorded — is littered with moments of confusion over the game's expectations both at the level of the controls and at the level of overall progression through the game. The notion that videogames are "learning machines" is a familiar one (Provenzo, Gee) and our case study offers many examples of the ways in which we as players learn how to play this particular game. Our hypothesis though is that conventional assumptions that players learn the game system to achieve mastery over it — and that this mastery is the source of the prime pleasure of gameplay — is in fact an inversion of the dynamics and pleasures of videogame play. Games configure their players, allowing progression through the game only if the players recognize what they are being prompted to do, and comply with these coded instructions. The analysis of the pleasures of gameplay must take the respective agencies of the players and the game technologies as central, as well as those between players and the game.

> H: (after a few minutes of aimless wandering and jumping) I think this is the bit where we're supposed to work things out....

The term "gameplay" is ubiquitous in the discussions of game players and game designers, and is commonly identified as central to the particular pleasures and fascinations of games. John Banks notes, however, the elusiveness of the term. It is often missing in academic accounts of video games and videogame culture and yet is simultaneously the quality around which claims about video games as a distinct medium necessarily revolve. Banks suggests that this is a weakness in theoretical vocabulary. Recent discussions within game studies have suggested that the problem is one of methodology rather than vocabulary. Analyzing gameplay is notoriously difficult; players are usually too engrossed to reflect on their experience and researchers studying other players find it hard to get any analytical purchase on their activities (as gameplay is so often characterized by little movement or comment on the part of the players). In this essay we offer one approach, using video and participant observation, to gain some purchase on the intangibilities of gameplay, and we suggest some salient concepts. Though no doubt new vocabularies and methods are needed, we would go further — the intractability of gameplay as a phenomenon is the product of a critical aporia due to the inherent humanist assumptions of the humanities and social sciences informing the development of game studies and new media studies in general. Gameplay cannot be understood without an understanding of the agency of games as technologies.

Lego Star Wars: **the video game (images supplied courtesy of TT Games).**

It is important to note that we are using two senses of the term "gameplay." First, we mean it in the sense it has in the language of game design and criticism, that is, gameplay as ludological form, the ways in which the game engine or assets are coded by their designers in anticipation of the game player's expectations, skill, and attention levels. Second, we are using it to refer to the "event" of gameplay, the synchronic moment of specific players and game in a particular time and space. In coding gameplay in this first sense, game designers are anticipating a range of instantiations of gameplay events, in this second sense.

Starting Points

This study is fuelled by our interest in theories of technology and culture, theories that question widespread assumptions that human agency is the primary object of research and that human agency is the only significant force or determinant in the social world (e.g., Haraway 1991, 1997, 2003; Latour 1992, 1993, 1999). In analyzing this event of the playing of *Lego Star Wars* we found the concept and terms of *cybernetics* to be particularly useful in tracing the flow of control, regulation, and feedback between the human and

Toy Wars (images supplied courtesy of TT Games).

nonhuman elements in the gameplay event. We suggest that the distinct nature of videogame play is generated in the intimate and cybernetic circuit between the human and the nonhuman. Here we mean cybernetics not in its loose discursive sense of "something to do with computers" but literally as the material feedback of information and control between machines and organisms (Wiener). We want to resist firm conceptual differences between technology and culture in general, and interrogate assumptions of the conceptual separation of bodies and subjects from machines and images at the level of everyday lived experience.

Most studies to date of videogame playing itself follow the tendency to concentrate on the social or communicative contexts and practices of new media, studying the contexts and practices that frame and inflect playing (e.g., Alloway and Gilbert, McNamee, Wright, Boria and Breidenbach, Ito). Other studies that begin to address the human-technological circuits of gameplay of central concern to this thesis tend to echo cyber cultural studies (or film theory) in that they work with theories about the nature of interaction and immersion, rather than any observation of actual, lived interaction (e.g., Friedman, Morris, Lahti). While game studies has developed a rich seam of enquiry into the formal structure of video games and their images and scenarios (Juul 2001, Järvinen, and Aarseth, Smedstad & Sunnana) these cybertextual analyses are concerned with the video game as a (dynamic) text or object. Each of these approaches is vital, and they overlap productively. However this overlap is not absolute — there are gaps between them, between ethnographies that say little about the detailed nature of human / media technological intimacy and theories of subjectivity that do, but without the ethnographic concern with the observable, lived experience. These approaches tend to say little about the aesthetic or formal nature of video games as media objects. Cybertextual analyses do the latter, but posit only abstract or notional playing subjects, contexts, and / or events. The study presented here suggests some ways to begin to operate in these interstices.

Video games as screen media texts offer visual pleasures; the attractions of *Halo, Half-Life II*, or *The Legend of Zelda: The Wind Waker* are inseparable from the beauty of their graphics. The event of videogame play — video games *in* play — however instantiates an intimate relationship among players, images, and technologies that is both material and aesthetic: an instance of the consumption of popular screen media and of the '"interactive" use of computer hardware and software. So, while we were concerned to identify the operations and agencies of the game and the game software, we wished to resist studying the game as an abstract form or structure. The pleasures of *Lego Star Wars* cannot be reduced to its status as a ludological form: it is a media object and aspects of the gameplay require knowledge of the Star Wars universe, and of Lego as a toy. Thus our model does not dismiss established notions and analysis of visual / screen aesthetics, but it does cast them as descriptive of only part of gameplay. Any consideration of videogame play aesthetics must consider questions of agency. We wanted in this small study to suggest a method for analyzing the aesthetics and agencies (both human and nonhuman) at play.

We set up a simple exercise: choosing a multiplayer game that one of us (Helen) had not played before and the other of us (Seth) had played briefly, we recorded the onscreen game events via the television screen and our own gameplay and speech with a video camera mounted on top of the television pointing at ourselves. After an hour or so of play the two tapes were captured in a digital editing program and synchronized. The speech and key game events were transcribed and short sections selected for in-depth analysis. The findings of any such study will of course be inflected by the particular game under scrutiny. Our game, *Lego Star Wars*, suited our purposes as it allows cooperative two-player play, thus facilitating — indeed necessitating —

conversation between the players. It is a very forgiving game for inexpert players, as there is little in the way of punishment for avatar death. It is also a very funny game, making numerous jokes about both the Star Wars characters and films and about the game world's construction from virtual Lego. Our method is small-scale ethnography, using video — a micro ethnography. In studying the event of gameplay we are assuming that the videogame "text," the videogame technologies, and the players are all in play, all objects of study, as are the circuits within and between them.

We quickly realized, in attempting to analyze this gameplay, that the circuits of agency and affect were much more complex than expected, and that we did not have the conceptual vocabulary to describe the interactions and agencies we were identifying.

Control Aesthetics

We have for some time been suspicious of widespread assumptions that "interactivity" — particularly in videogame play — is premised on the exercising or extension of human agency. This assumption gives rise to two further problematic positions: first, Sid Meier's much-repeated aphorism that gameplay is "a series of interesting choices" (cited in Juul 2005); and second — but closely connected — the notion that the experience and pleasures of gameplay are bound up with the attainment and exercise of mastery by players, mastery of the game system, perhaps even mastery of the player's own body. We will interrogate both of these assumptions through our analysis of playing *Lego Star Wars*. We are accustomed to think of interactive engagement with a game as one of (human) choice and intervention, yet our study of learning to play a game indicates an inversion of this logic might be more accurate. The learning player does not so much make choices as attempt to work out what the game is expecting them to do; the game trains the player.

Critique of Mastery

Discussions of virtuoso gameplay performance often resonate with the claims made for a putative technological sublime. Images of cybernetic or cyborgian transcendence abound. Banks quotes an Australian game designer in what is a fairly typical account:

> ... It got to the point where I could finish the game [...] in 27 minutes — about 40 minutes if I held the controller upside down. I could literally play the first level with my eyes closed, using only muscle memory! Anyway *Mario Kart*: sometimes,

playing it, I lost all sense of everything except the game. My hands moved without conscious intervention on my part ... I believe the MK "trance state" short circuits this delay not requiring the brain to be aware of something before the hands have responded.

Kushner bestows on game designer John Romero the same transcendent machinelike characteristics: "Romero was so good at Pac-Man that he could maneuver the round yellow character through a maze of fruit and dots with his eyes shut" (Kushner 5). While these accounts are frequently offered in order to make a particular point about the "skill" of an individual in "mastering the interface" we would want to read these accounts slightly differently. From a theoretical perspective concerned with the operations and effects of technological as well as human actors it is possible to turn this gameplay upside down. That is, Romero could play Pac-Man with his eyes closed because the game had thoroughly and completely mastered *him*, it had taught his fingers the precise micromovements needed to fulfill its intentions (continued play), and it had imprinted on his brain cognitive analogues of its virtually mapped game world. The player is mastered by the machine.

We would argue that this machinic language should not only be read metaphorically. Gameplay is an intense event, a set of intimate circuits between human bodies and minds, computer hardware and the algorithms and affordances of the virtual worlds of video games. Early accounts of videogame play were particularly concerned with describing and accounting for these intense experiences (Turkle, Sudnow). On reflection it is telling that tales of mastery are spun from these moments of the technological capture and entrainment of human players' time, attention, and peace of mind.

Nonhuman Agency

Our analysis of our playing of *Lego Star Wars* identified a complex and overlapping set of circuits between the game, its elements, and ourselves. It is difficult to analyze and account for nonhuman agency in the virtual worlds of video games, as this agency is exercised as much through the setting of limits or the offering of activities as it is through establishing rules as such. Even the moments at which the game entities most clearly impose themselves on the player / avatar — for instance, when the latter is killed by an NPC — are so thoroughly legitimized by the game world and its diegetic dynamics that they are invisible in these terms.

We can look to *Lego Star Wars* for a clearer example of such agency, but it is one that requires a little explanation. The game has an innovative two-player mode, in that it does not use a split screen presentation. Rather, both

Chewie and Yoda (images supplied courtesy of TT Games).

players explore a section of the game world together. The levels of the game usually extend beyond the screen, and the virtual camera (controlled by the game, not the players) tracks the players' avatars as they move across or into the space. However, if the avatars move in opposite directions, or if one avatar stays still, but the other moves in the general direction encouraged by the progression of the game, the edge of the screen becomes a dragnet, as if the moving player were pulling the screen with them and the recalcitrant player is caught on the opposite edge of the frame, an edge that now becomes a physical barrier. If this goes on for more than a few seconds the reluctant avatar is left behind, that is, they disappear off-screen, and the virtual camera moves freely again. Control of this avatar is taken from the player, and though it will appear again shortly, the player has to actively retake control by pressing the relevant button.

> H: (Chewie, screen left, standing still)
> S: (Yoda, screen right, floating on his tray, using the Force to switch on lights around a platform)
> S: (moves right toward more lights) Let's see if we can switch all these on.
> H: (legs not moving, but dragged right by virtual camera)
> S: Come on!
> H: (drops off screen right — laughs) sorry!
> (Chewie appears screen right — now controlled by the computer, not Helen, follows Yoda around the platform for a few seconds)

H: (presses "start" button, retaking control of Chewie) I'm back in the room!
   (Helen/Chewie then leaps around the platform for some time, as if celebrating and exercising this regained control)
H: I love his action! It's so fantastically...
H: ... absurd.
   (Helen/Chewie moves off to the right of the screen)
H: Come on Yoda.

It is perhaps an indication of the difficulties of analyzing gameplay in detail that a little process such as this has been explained by us in two hundred words, and yet it can take place in little more than two seconds. Moreover, players learn this feature of the game through their kinaesthetic experience of it — it is the nuances of positioning, virtual friction, and the removal and readoption of avatar control that is felt and learnt.

Cybernetic Aesthetics: Effects and Affect

Videogame play comes into being through a set of feedback loops between players, software, and hardware. Each of these is an agent or actor in the videogame event. What if, rather than privileging the player and the player's agency, our starting position were that these actors are symmetrical — each acting on the other? Both humans and nonhumans are the playful objects here.

In their invaluable guide to computer game analysis and design, Katie Salen and Eric Zimmerman draw extensively on cybernetics as a key term in the analysis of the operations of video games. Their adoption of the terminology of feedback loops and regulators, of negative and positive feedback, is precise and pragmatic — they are explaining the mechanisms of the game, not articulating a cybernetic technological imaginary.

> As a cybernetic system, the rules of a game define the sensors, comparators and activators of the game's feedback loops. Within a game, there are many sub-systems that regulate the flow of play, dynamically changing and transforming game elements [218].

Cybernetic Media

Wiener's cybernetics is a broad model that applies to tremendously diverse relationships and phenomena. In game studies we are of course concerned with a popular media object, and this raises the question of how cybernetics is put to aesthetic effect. Salen and Zimmerman's concern is to explain the construction of a pleasurable gameplay experience, not the technical workings

of software per se. They are explaining cybernetic systems designed to facilitate play. In *WipEout*, they point out, negative feedback loops are mobilized
to adjust the performance of NPC hover cars: if the player is in first place,
the NPC car will accelerate; if he or she is lagging behind the NPCs will drop
back to allow the player to catch up with them. The aim of the *WipEout* system is pleasurable gameplay, in particular "jockeying for position among a
dense cluster of hover vehicles, battling for first place with another racer who
is hot on your tail, or dead ahead in your sights" (220). Feedback systems
"support meaningful play by making the game responsive to the ongoing state
of the game" (221).

This analysis of the operations of *WipEout* in play is a useful example of
what Salen and Zimmerman refer to as "second order cybernetics," that is,
the feedback system under study is recognized to include human agents
(researchers) among its elements. This second order cybernetics must be
extended and developed to fully account for the imbrications of agencies and
their attendant pleasures. By understanding gameplay as cybernetic, issues of
interactivity and player agency are recast in terms of networks and flows of
energy that are entirely interdependent:

> we do not see here two complete and sealed-off entities: the player on the one hand
> and the game on the other. Rather there is an interchange of information and
> energy, forming a new circuit [...] Through the tactile and visual interface with the
> machine, the entire body is determined to move by being part of the circuit of the
> game, being, as it were, *in the loop* [Lister et al. 370].

Avatars, Identification, and Affordances

H: I'm Chewie!
H: You're Yoda! You get to be ... Mr. Wise.
H: Shall I see if you can get killed? [rather than shooting at Seth/Yoda as Helen
     intends, Helen/Chewie jumps up and down on the spot]
 S: (laughing) death by leapfrog!
H: (laughing) you may have the wise words, but I have the fancy moves!
     [until this point Seth/Yoda had been walking slowly around — S. finds that
     using the jump button (×) and the left analogue stick triggers a more energetic
     movement]
 S: I'm just moving the stick a little bit.... And he's flipping out....
H: Woohoo! He's fantastic!
H: Yoda! Calm down!

Much has been made of comparison between theories of the film viewer's
identification with key protagonists within a film narrative and the game
player's identification with the avatar. The argument is thus that the player
may identify more strongly with the avatar because the player controls the

character's movements, decisions, and (depending on skill and experience) that character's ultimate fate (always within the strict limitations and possibilities structured by the game as software). While this has proved a productive theoretical approach it may not fully account for the complex and shifting positions and identifications taken by the game player. James Newman, for example, argues that the player's relationship with the avatar is constituted less by subjective identification and more by a material engagement with the avatar as a software element, "a set of potentials, available techniques, opportunities and capabilities which can be embodied, expanding the abilities of the player and equipping them for the task at hand" (Newman 418). The avatar-player loop is one of the game-in-play's cybernetic subsystems.

Discussing Lara Croft and the *Tomb Raider* games, Diane Carr talks of the avatar as a "vehicle":

> Watching a film may of course involve shifts in processes of looking and identification, but *driving an avatar involves utilizing a console, identification is occupation: literal and mechanized.* This flux in agency is the price we pay to play. When Lara dies her temporary mortality returns the role of subject to her operator. She exerts violence with us, and then she dies for us, over and over [175, our italics].

This is not to argue that players may choose a character out of a sense of identification (and Carr does not dispute the particular appeal of Lara Croft or her role in the successes of *Tomb Raider* as gameplay):

H: I'm Chewie!
H: You're Yoda! You get to be ... Mr. Wise.

The player is delighted to be able to play as a wookie and responds to the other player's avatar in terms drawn from her knowledge of the Star Wars entertainment supersystem. However, while this awareness of, and pleasure in, recognizable characters persists (albeit intermittently) throughout the gameplay event, both players' attention is quickly shifted to the affordances of the chosen characters, that is what can be done with that character within the demands of the game world:

H: Shall I see if you can get killed?

We might argue that while the aesthetic or subjective operations of choosing an avatar (or choosing a game based on its main character) on the one hand, and the use or driving of that avatar as a set of capabilities on the other may seem autonomous, they are articulated — and the nature of this articulation depends on the particular game being played and the specific moment of gameplay within any particular event. For instance, the gameplay design in *Lego Star Wars* demands the transference of agency between avatars and from the player to game and vice versa as essential to progression through the game. R2-D2, for example, has the capability of unlocking doors and so must, at least briefly, be occupied to enter new game spaces. The game forces "identification" on the player. In this instance we are very close to Newman's idea of avatar as capability — our choice of R2-D2 is a pragmatic one based on the specific task/puzzle posed by the game.

In the current example, however, the breakdown of one circuit of control (Helen's pressing of the "jump" button instead of the "fire" button) instantly instantiates another, and becomes the basis of a circuit of kinaesthetic and spectacular affect: Chewbacca repeatedly leaps over Yoda's head to the hilarity of the players:

S: (laughing) death by leapfrog!
H: (laughing) you may have the wise words, but I have the fancy moves!

Soon after this Seth worked out how the Yoda avatar needs to be controlled. Yoda initially walks very slowly, but once jumping (pressing the × button) and changing direction (moving the left analogue stick) he leaps and pirouettes manically around the screen. Again this is very amusing for the players:

S: I'm just moving the stick a little bit.... And he's flipping out....
H: Woohoo! He's fantastic!
H: Yoda! Calm down!

This little event is the product of a set of interfering aesthetic and cybernetic circuits. The "ideal" cybernetic circuit of effect that would successfully result in Chewie shooting Yoda is replaced by a cybernetic circuit of both effect — simple manipulations of the controller triggering jumping avatars — and affect — the pleasure of unexpectedly, and ludicrously, agile characters lead to both hilarity and a brief, improvised "mini-game." Significantly, both effect and affect are generated by and through the cybernetic operations of *amplification*, that is, the tiny (and in this case inadvertent) effort of pushing the × button results in maximal movement of the avatar, and new visual pleasures and play possibilities.

> The dimensions of Lara Croft's body, already analyzed to death by film theorists, are irrelevant to me as a player, because a different-looking body would not make me play differently.... When I play, I don't even see her body, but see through it and past it [Aarseth 48].

While we would acknowledge Espen Aarseth's frustration with textual analyses of video games that are insensitive to distinct forms and practices of the video game, we would argue that the ludic and vehicular nature of avatars is *articulated* with their status as symbolic objects. Again the dynamics of effect and affect are inseparable. As we saw above, much of our pleasure in the affordances of Yoda and Chewbacca in this game lies in the articulation of

Aesthetics and kinaesthetics (images supplied courtesy of TT Games).

the possibilities for movement and action they afford, on the one hand, and in the visual appeal and expectations that come with their status as both familiar media characters and Lego toys, on the other. This articulation of course shifts through the rhythms of the gameplay. In the heat of a battle or the tangles of a puzzle the player may be less concerned with the appearance or intertextual connections of his or her avatar, but at other moments these factors may be primary, and at times the two will be inseparable.

Kinaesthetics

If the aesthetic, symbolic pleasures of avatars are articulated with their vehicular capabilities and their mediation of agency between player and game world, then that point of articulation is often, perhaps usually, their kinaesthetic effects and affects. The motive of the vehicular avatar is of course movement through the game world. Avatars are movement, cursors that scroll the game world past the virtual camera and lead the player's attention into and

through the game world — they drive through the game. Some, such as Lara
Croft and Chewie and Yoda, are constituted by kinaesthetic subsystems: Lara
with her spectacular jumps and rolls, Chewie and Yoda with their similar,
though funnier, gymnastics. Video games as cinematic media are much more
closely related to animation than live action film. Speaking generally, the aesthetics of animation are much more thoroughly concerned with movement
than the narratives, characters, and verisimilitude of live action (Wells,
Manovich).

In the following example, at a later stage in the gameplay event, a kind
of spontaneous and improvised animation is performed by the player/avatars.
Seth worked out how to change characters while the game is in progress:

> S: (initially a clone trooper): [changes into a rolling robot]: Oo! There we go.
> H: (a Jedi): what did you do then?
> S: er ... use the shoulder buttons.
> S: you can turn into one of those....
>   Both players press shoulder buttons and their avatars transform rapidly, cycling
>   through the available alternatives.
> S: ... fuck-off robots with a force-field.
> H: Oo! (laughs) Look at that! Hey hey!
>   Both players select rolling robots and there follows a minute or so in which
>   the robots roll around the available space, occasionally unrolling to fire off a
>   few laser blasts.
> H: have they got anything for us to shoot?

Here progression through the game was suspended while the kinaesthetic *and*
visual pleasures of the robot avatars were played with. Readers who have
played this game will, we hope, recognize something of these (largely nonin-
strumental in terms of game progression) pleasures. The distinct responsiveness of the robot avatars, the fluidity of their animation as they roll into balls,
the synchronization of sound and action as they unfurl and the rhythms of
their laser blasts are satisfying to the player in a way that is hard to describe
or explain.

Little Death

This robot dance marks an interlude (literally, a break in play) in our progression through the game. It represents a brief, yet deeply pleasurable, exploration of the avatar's animation and virtual physics: a moment of semiotic and
kinaesthetic play in the more worklike demands of the game's dynamic. There
are pleasures too then in the abdication of agency: a lack of control or ability to
move unrestricted in the world is not entirely unpleasurable. As Salen and Zimmerman demonstrate, an effective ("meaningful") gameplay event is one in which

A droideka in action (images supplied courtesy of TT Games).

the player and the computer are evenly matched, the game carefully engineering its expectations of the player. Even for players well trained by the game the loss of agency and interpassivity, Carr's "flux of agency," are part of the "loop" of pleasure. Our game event was characterized by a rippling of control, affordance, and being-acted-on across the human and nonhuman agents. We will return to this point with a longer example, but just to make the point clearly, we will look at this in relation to game "death." The pleasure-in-mastery assumptions of conventional game criticism cannot account for the humor and pleasure attendant on the well-managed death in video games. We do not have the space here to explore (nor the psychic explanations for) the degree to which temporary, but frequent and repetitive, failure within games might be argued to be a key, perverse element of video games, though, given the degree to which this constitutes a central element of nearly all games, we must assume this significance and salience.

Lego Star Wars is an uncharacteristic game in that there are generally few game implications for avatar death. There is no limit on "lives" and avatars respawn immediately. Repeated death or failure in some tasks and puzzles remains as frustrating as in other games, the difference here is one of degree, not kind. This said, the peculiarities of this game do foster a notable exploratory approach to game-death:

Helen/Chewie follows Seth/Yoda onto a circular platform. S/he fires a couple of
laser blasts at Yoda.
S & H: (laughter)
      There follows a (largely ineffectual) attempt by each player / avatar to destroy
      the other, attended by laughter and imitations of the noise of Yoda's light saber.
  S: We can't figure out why we're not hitting each other
      Finally Yoda's light saber hits home and Chewie explodes in a shower of Lego
      bricks.
  H: (laughing) Ohhh! You broke me into tiny pieces!
      Chewie respawns and exploration of the platform continues
  S: (attempting to jump Yoda over the barriers at the edge of the platform) can you
      actually jump off the edge?
      After a few fruitless seconds of this attempted suicide...
  H: (Chewie shooting at Yoda) If it's death you're after!
  H: stand still!

In this example, as with some of the others already discussed, it is evident
that gameplay is constituted by the playful negotiation or exploration of the
borders between player and nonplayer agency as well as any impulse toward
mastery. "Death/Life" is not a structural opposition in all games' mobiliza-
tion of agency. Rather, "death" in *Lego Star Wars* is one end of a spectrum of
agency negotiation. At the other end might be the tactic of a player in a two-
player *Lego Star Wars* game of temporarily "dropping out" in a particularly
tricky situation until the obstacle is overcome by the other player. Here the
game suggests the player temporarily hand back his or her (limited) agency
to the game itself. But it is a spectrum and players' relationship to the avatar
and the world is responsive / possessive, containing complex elements of both
a passive responsive "being acted upon" and a sense of possession of that
action — a performative possession: "I am doing," "I am being," as well as "I
am being made to do."

Little Jesuses

In our final example we will attempt to demonstrate something of the
complexity of all these factors — the multiple agents and their pleasures — and
to show that they operate not as discrete phenomena but as imbricated and
overdetermined microevents within, and constituting, the macroevent of the
gameplay itself.
    The players/avatars are faced by a wall. It is clear that the avatars are
being asked to find a way to scale this wall. One player, it isn't clear who,
plays as the young Anakin Skywalker, the other as the multiarmed cyborg
General Grievous. Each wanders around the vertical half-cylindrical structure in the center of the wall. The players are by now familiar enough with

the game's conventions to recognize that this is where ascent will be facilitated once the puzzle is solved. The avatars jump against the wall in an exploratory manner. The avatars are changed — the novelty of cycling through the possible avatars has not yet faded. Seth's avatar settles down as a Jedi. It wanders over to a glowing panel to the right. The game suggests that this might be a step toward progression:

> S: I have to do something with the Force.
>> Helen changes her avatar to a Jedi and moves over to a similar panel on the left. Both press the circle button to apply the Force. Lego blocks emerge from the panels and swing round into the half-cylinder.
> S: Aha! We've got some steps.
>> The steps swing back into their original position.
>> This event is repeated a few times.
> S: why do they keep coming back?
> H: Oh! What?

Eventually the game's demand that the circle button is held down longer — until the steps are firmly in place — is realized. The half-cylinder now has a low step on its left side and a higher one opposite on the right.

> H: (Jedi) After you sir.
> S: (Jedi) Oh, thank you.
> S: (jumps up onto first step)
> H: We are now the same person. (jumps up to second step)
> S: Are we? (jumps up to second step and up to platform above)
> H: Oops (mistimes jump and falls down to ground level).

The virtual camera follows the lead character up to the upper platform making it impossible for Helen to see her avatar.

> S: Tell you what, if I drop out, then er ...
>> (brings up a menu and selects Drop Out)
>> ... you can see what you're doing.

The onscreen character that was Seth's avatar but which is now temporarily controlled by the game jumps down the steps.

> S: Oh — don't jump ... (realizes that rather than getting in the way this temporary NPC is being driven by the game to lead Helen's avatar up the steps)
> S: Oh I see, I've got to show you where to go now ... (although Seth no longer has any agency in the game, the affective link with the onscreen character that is intermittently his avatar persists).

However, the NPC is not as helpful as the game would seem to like:

> S: ... or I could just get in your way!

Helen gets confused over which controls to use and activates her light saber rather than jumping.

S: You don't need your light saber!
H: I know, but how do I put it away. (she inadvertently changes into a droid soldier)

Laughter. The droid soldier falls off the step...

H: This guy can't jump! Great. (Helen reselects a Jedi, an avatar with the ability to jump).
H: why won't my light saber go away? (presses square) Ah!
S: Jar Jar Binks is good at jumping.
H: Is he?

There follows thirty seconds or so of ineffectual jumping.

H: (laughing) do you want to just jump me up there? (hands controller to Seth)
S: I won't be able to do it now...

The NPC once controlled by Seth now jumps alongside Helen's avatar now controlled by Seth, getting in the way.

S: Oh piss off!
   (laughter)
S: they're like little Jesuses jumping around.

Conclusion

The video game engineers a constant imbrication of different operations of human and nonhuman agency. At the very least we can argue that "mastery" is only one pleasure among many, that activity and passivity are not opposites in videogame play but fluctuations in the circuit, and thus that a new conceptual language is needed to attend to both the operations of nonhuman agency and the human pleasures of lack of agency, of being controlled, of being *acted upon*.

What are the implications then of a cybernetic — or cyborgian — aesthetic event in which the player is acted on as well as an actor? How can we conceptualize this heterogeneous engineering of bodies, minds, algorithms, avatars, and actions? We would suggest that concepts of gameplay might be situated between the feedback loops of cybernetic systems, on the one hand, and the earliest version of the modern concept of the aesthetic, on the other. This notion of aesthetics is more closely linked to its early eighteenth-century etymology: *aisthesis*— sense experience, experiences that are both cognitive and evaluative *and* bodily, sensual, somatic.

> That territory is nothing less than the whole of our sensate life together — the business of affections and aversions, of how the world strikes the body on its sensate surfaces, of that which takes root in the gaze and the guts and all that arises from our most banal, biological insertion into the world [Eagleton 13].

Gameplay, we suggest, is characterized by a recombinatory *aesthesis*. The cybernetic processes allow moments for amplification of affect and effect within the game — generating extraordinary moments of visual and kinaesthetic pleasure. We have not attempted to fully theorize either embodiment or pleasure here. However, our small study suggests that ripples of pleasure run through gameplay events, triggered by and interfering with the imbricated agencies we begin to identify above. Perhaps the most evident characteristic of the video records of this gameplay event is the players' persistent laughter. Persistent laugher is the audio track to the game event: it is a corporeal yet automatic index of, and witness to, this *aesthesis*.

Works Cited

Aarseth, Espen. "Genre Trouble: Narrativism and the Art of Simulation." In *First Person: New Media as Story, Performance and Game,* edited by Noah Wardrip-Fruin and Pat Harrigan, 45–47. Cambridge: Massachusetts Institute of Technology Press, 2004.

Aarseth, Espen, Solveig Smedstad, and Lise Sunnana. "A Multi-dimensional Typology of Games." Paper presented at *Level Up: Digital Games Research Conference,* Utrecht University, 2003.

Alloway, Nola, and Pam Gilbert. "Video Game Culture: Playing with Masculinity, Violence and Pleasure." In *Wired-Up: Young People and the Electronic Media*, edited by Sue Howard, 95–114. London: UCL, 1998.

Banks, John. "Controlling Gameplay." *M/C Journal: A Journal of Media Culture* 1.5 (1998). 20 September 2005. http://journal.media-culture.org.au/9812/game.php.

Carr, Diane. "Playing with Lara." In *Screenplay: Cinema/Videogames/Interfaces*, edited by Geoff King and Tanya Krzywinska, 171–180. London: Wallflower, 2002.

Eagleton, Terry. *The Ideology of the Aesthetic.* Oxford: Blackwell, 1990.

Friedman, Ted. "Making Sense of Software." (1995). 11 November 2000. http://www.duke.edu/~tlove/simcity.htm.

Gee, James Paul. *What Video Games Have to Teach Us about Learning and Literacy.* New York: MacMillan Palgrave, 2004.

Giddings, Seth, and Helen W. Kennedy. "Digital Games as New Media." In *Understanding Digital Games*, edited by Jason Rutter and Jo Bryce, 129–147. London: Sage, 2006.

Haraway, Donna. *The Companion Species Manifesto: Dogs, People, and Significant Otherness.* Chicago: Prickly Paradigm, 2003.

_____. *Modest Witness@Second_Millennium.FemaleManMeets_OncoMouse: Feminism and Technoscience.* London: Routledge, 1997.

_____. *Primate Visions: Gender, Race and Nature in the World of Modern Science.* London: Verso, 1989.

_____. *Simians, Cyborgs, and Women: The Reinvention of Nature.* London: Routledge, 1991.

Ito, Mizuko. "Inhabiting Multiple Worlds: Making Sense of *SimCity 2000*(tm) in the Fifth Dimension." In *Cyborg Babies: From Techno-sex to Techno-tots,* edited by Robbie Davis-Floyd and Joseph Dumit, 301–316. London: Routledge, 1998.

Juul, Jesper. "A Dictionary of Video Game Theory." (2005). 17 May 2006. http://www.half-real.net/dictionary/.

_____. "Games Telling Stories? A Brief Note on Games and Narratives." *Game Studies* 1.1 (2001). 19 October 2005. http://www.gamestudies.org/0101/juulgts/.

Kushner, David. *Masters of Doom: How Two Guys Created an Empire and Transformed Pop Culture.* London: Piatkus, 2003.

Lahti, Martti. "As We Become Machines: Corporealized Pleasures in Video Games." In *The Video Game Theory Reader,* edited by Mark J. P. Wolf and Bernard Perron, 157–170. New York: Routledge, 2003.

Latour Bruno. *Pandora's Hope: Essays on the Reality of Science Studies.* Cambridge, MA: Harvard University Press, 1999.

_____. *We Have Never Been Modern.* Cambridge, MA: Harvard University Press, 1993.

_____. "Where Are the Missing Masses? The Sociology of a Few Mundane Artifacts." In *Shaping Technology/Building Society: Studies in Sociotechnical Change,* edited by Wiebe E. Bijker and John Law, 225–258. Cambridge: Massachusetts Institute of Technology Press, 1992.

Lister Martin, Dovey Jonathan, Giddings Seth, Grant Iain, and Kelly Kieran. *New Media: A Critical Introduction.* London: Routledge, 2003.

Manovich, Lev. *The Language of New Media.* Cambridge: Massachusetts Institute of Technology Press, 2001.

McNamee, Sara. "Youth, Gender and Video Games: Power and Control in the Home." In *Cool Places: Geographies of Youth Cultures,* edited by Tracey Skelton and Gill Valentine, 195–206. London: Routledge, 1998.

Morris, Sue, "First-Person Shooters: A Game Apparatus." In *ScreenPlay: Cinema/Video games/Interfaces,* edited by Geoff King and Tanya Krzywinska, 81–97. London: Wallflower, 2002.

Newman, James. "The Myth of the Ergodic Videogame." *GameStudies.* 1.2 (2002). 4 June 2006. www.gamestudies.org/0102/newman/.

Provenzo, Eugene F., Jr. *Video Kids: Making Sense of Nintendo.* Cambridge, MA: Harvard University Press, 1991.

Salen, Katie, and Eric Zimmerman. *Rules of Play.* Cambridge: Massachusetts Institute of Technology Press, 2003.

Sudnow, David. *Pilgrim in the Microworld: Eye, Mind and the Essence of Video Skill.* London: Heinemann, 1983.

Turkle, Sherry. *The Second Self: Computers and the Human Spirit.* New York: Simon and Schuster, 1984.

Wells, Paul. *Understanding Animation.* London: Routledge, 1998.

Wiener, Norbert. *Cybernetics: Or Control and Communication in the Animal and the Machine,* 2nd ed. New York: Massachusetts Institute of Technology Press, 1961.

Wright, Talmadge, Eric Boria, and Paul Breidenbach. "Creative Player Actions in FPS Online Video Games: Playing *Counter-Strike.*" *GameStudies* 2.2 (2002). 4 June 2006. http://www.gamestudies.org/0202/wright/.

Gameography

Halo: Combat evolved, Bungie, Microsoft 2002.
Half-Life II, Valve, Electronic Arts, 2004.
The Legend of Zelda: the Wind Waker, Nintendo, Nintendo 2003.
Lego Star Wars, Travelers' Tales & Giant Entertainment, Eidos & Lucas Arts 2005.
Tomb Raider, Core, Eidos 1996.
WipEout, Psygnosis, 1995.

2

Gaming/Gambling: Addiction and the Videogame Experience

Joyce Goggin

To say that video games are addictive is, to my mind, a truism of the lamest sort. Game developers, in fact, measure the success and failure of their products by their capacity to hook gamers. Television videogame review programs rate games as they hit the market precisely for their power to addict, as though that were a good thing.[1] At the same time, of course, everyone, from parents to high school teachers to government researchers, loudly laments video games' insidious capacity to draw and hold players. In what follows I investigate the videogame addiction issue by first recalling the history of addiction in the West, including how addiction became part of everyday life, and how it continues to construct, direct, and ultimately define gamers and consumers. Following from this, I discuss various features of addiction and addictiveness in light of the contemporary gameplay experience, in order to show how video games occupy a special place in the current paradigm of aesthetic and cultural addictions. In so doing, I will explain why and how the issue of addiction and video games is far more complex than instructors, disciplinarians, authority figures, and gamers themselves may suspect.

Gaming

That video games do something infinitely more complex and interesting with players than I had heretofore imagined, first occurred to me during a job interview. One of the members on the hiring committee asked if my research on play and games included "gaming," which I immediately took to mean "gambling" given that this is the traditional and preferred definition of the word. Many months after the interview — in which I explained the history of the word gambling and why people make no distinction between it and gaming in common parlance — I realized, somewhat to my dismay, that the person had actually meant "to play video games."[2] I now believe that this seemingly superficial semantic shift holds the crux of the addiction issue and raises a number of fundamental questions concerning the construction of subjectivity through gameplay, not to mention the relation of play — and more specifically gameplay — to work.[3]

More recently, the notion that the relationship between video games and addiction is perhaps more interesting than commonly thought, was brought to my attention by students in a course that I now regularly teach on games. To my great surprise, many students reported that they used to play videogames "a lot," but then "sort of grew out of them." To my mind, the concept of "growing out of" something that is purportedly an addiction seems quite remarkable, as it would to anyone who has ever tried to quit smoking. If asked, most smokers would probably recognize smoking as an addiction one grows *into*, developing the requisite wrinkles and "cool" behaviors, moving from the delicate menthol cigarette for neophytes to the full-on, French roast or shag tobaccos for the truly nicotine dependent.

More importantly, for most smokers, serious nicotine addiction is related to a whole spectrum of other vital activities, so that giving up smoking would necessitate remodeling one's entire mode of being. Jean-Paul Sartre's writing, for example, was famously fuelled by the pleasure of tobacco addiction, and some biographers claim to remember how ashtrays filled in direct proportion to the notebooks in which he scribbled down *Being and Nothingness* (Klein 25). So necessary was this evil to the French philosopher that he began smoking again after a brief hiatus taken on the advice of a doctor, who warned him that if he didn't quit "his toes would have to be cut off, then his feet, and then his legs." As Simone de Beauvoir recalled, "[Sartre] said he wanted to think it over" (39). As it turned out, Sartre's addiction did indeed prove fatal, but the French philosopher preferred the narcotic high of nicotine to a life without his closest friend — *ceci est bien une cigarette*. In other words for Sartre, as for just about everyone else, addictions like smoking are *not* something out of which one simply "grows."

A Brief History of Addiction and Gambling

The West has long been wary of, yet inexorably drawn to, addictive behaviors. Early on in the history of addiction, a great deal of the attraction to addictive practices was a consequence of their close relationship with chance, as in gambling where the outcome of any wager depends on chance, barring the possibility of cheating. The surrender of control to chance is, however, associated with a fatalistic world view, which is classically understood as being germane to a premodern disposition and, therefore, antithetical to the drive to modernity. Hence, while the ancient Greeks might have been content to think that their lot in life was determined by Zeus, who casually tossed good fates along with bad to hapless mortals, the Western process of modernization supposedly drove people to demand answers, control and Reason.

The moment of changeover to a more modern worldview is marked by St. Augustine as he hovered on the brink of conversion to Christianity. In his *Confessions* (A.D. 397), St. Augustine repeatedly protests that he has not yet sufficiently enjoyed the delights of paganism and is, therefore, not yet ready to appreciate the modernizing force of monotheism. Hence, before heeding his mother's entreaties to convert to Christianity, the young Augustine argues that he must become more intimately acquainted with the pleasures of multiple sexual partners, stealing, cheating, and, importantly, gambling on games of chance and sport. Given his enjoyment of gambling, then, it is not surprising that his famous moment of conversion — *tole lege* — finally arrives when he opens the Bible *at random* to a passage where it is poised, significantly, on a gaming table.[4] In other words, even St. Augustine's moment of conversion from polytheism to monotheism and his renunciation of a fatalistic worldview is intimately associated with the workings of chance and the trappings of gaming.

In the intervening centuries, both chance and its most direct expression, gambling, would be subject to a number of vicissitudes before coming to us in their present digitized and highly commercialized forms. One important moment in this history was the publication of Cardano's *Book on Games of Chance* in 1520, which is often cited as the first work to attempt anything like a theory of probability. The author, a serious gambler himself, outlines the probabilities of simple draws in medieval dice and card games, such as Prime, in an attempt to help gamblers make their own luck. A little more than a century later, and quite without knowledge of Cardano, the Pascal-Fermat correspondence of 1654 made further advances in charting and, they hoped, predicting and controlling chance. Prompted by a question concerning the divvying up of winnings based on odds, directed to them by a gambler named Chevalier De Mere, Pascal and Fermat were able to work out mathematically that the chance of throwing at least one six in four rolls of a single die is one, minus the chance of throwing no sixes in four rolls.

It was also in the seventeenth century that the West learned to smoke tobacco and drink coffee, both indulgences which proved to be excellent accompaniments to the simple and highly aleatory card games on which people gambled inveterately.[5] And while individuals gambled fiercely and compulsively on just about everything including the infamous tulip bulb (on which fortunes were squandered in speculative trade from 1634 to 1636), institutions were involved in all kinds of gambling, sometimes known as banking. This period of frenzied experimentation with instruments of credit reached a crescendo in the South Sea Bubble, and slowed down briefly when the bubble burst in 1720.[6]

At roughly the same time, however, during a period of supposed economic rationalism known as the Enlightenment, people like Jeremy Collier were beginning to sober up and really smell the coffee. In his "Essay on Gaming" (1713), Collier admonishes readers against the woes of gambling addiction. In it, he coins the term "deep play" which continues to have currency today with scholars working on gambling, gaming and other immersive behaviors:[7]

> Deep play sets the spirits on float, strikes the mind strongly into the face [sic], and discovers a man's weakness very remarkably. You may see the passions come up with the dice, and ebb and flow with the fortune of the game. The sentence for execution is not received with more concern than the unlucky appearance of a cast or a card. [...] Why resign repose of mind and credit of temper to the mercy of chance? When misfortune strikes home, the temper generally goes with the money, according to the proverb, "Qui perd le sien, perd le sens." When your bubbles are going down the hill, you lend them a push, though their bones are broken at the bottom [32–33].

As an antidote to the wild swings of deep play, chance, gaming, and institutionalized speculation, which itself resembled large-scale organized gambling, some Enlightenment thinkers prided themselves on rationalism and scientific regulation. Mathematicians such as Laplace and Poisson busily worked out systems for controlling chance and predicting the outcome of gambles, picking up where Cardano and Pascal had left off. Laplace's theory of large numbers, for example, intended to provide shelter from the mercurial movements of chance. This was to be accomplished by studying a large enough sample of events or gambles in which Pascal hoped it would be possible to perceive a pattern. Such theories held out the vague promise of predictability and they gained yet greater currency in the centuries to follow.[8]

By the nineteenth century, mathematical systems for calculating probability had spawned utilitarianism, an economic system that strived to achieve closure and regulation through the careful maintenance of double-ledger, zero-balance accountancy. Paradoxically, given the rather bleak accounts of this assiduous form of economic management proffered in novels such as

Dickens's *Hard Times*, the basic tenet of utilitarianism was actually the avoidance of pain and the pursuit of pleasure for the greatest possible number. The idea was to carefully balance in-put and out-put, while keeping at bay the kind of economic catastrophes that had plagued the seventeenth and eighteenth centuries. This was to be accomplished, according to economist Jeremy Bentham, by eliminating all forms of nonutilitarian expenditure — "money given for evanescent services" — such as singing, dancing, prostitution, and particularly gambling.[9] While these activities arguably provide certain individuals with momentary pleasures, utilitarians weigh such fleeting pleasures against the projected pains of a population addicted to dissipatory expenditure.[10]

Chance, Addiction, and the Twentieth Century

Thus far I have traced developing trends in thinking about gaming and chance from the ancient Greeks through the nineteenth century. I have also implicitly been arguing that the control of chance and the seeming will to minimize addiction parallels the development of economic modernity, including the hopeful distinction of speculation from gambling. This history can be succinctly illustrated through an historical survey of gambling games played with cards, their relationship to addiction and the regulation or prevention thereof. For example, early card games such as Basset or Faro were simple matching games and involved betting on the turn of a card, matching suits and rank, or gambling on a particular order in which cards would appear. In such games, turnover is rapid and downtime between each new bet is held to a minimum. Early card games were, therefore, highly addictive because turnover was hot and heavy with a minimal cooling off period between new bets.[11] Such games induced players to give themselves up to what Collier called deep play, or what is now sometimes referred to as immersive play. This is the kind of play that casino owners hope to induce in their patrons by ensuring that there are no clocks on the premises, as immersed gamblers notoriously forget what time it is and even neglect bodily functions rather than tearing themselves away from the game.

As both Dummett and Reith have argued, throughout history there has been a trend to increasing complexity in card games, a sometimes conscious development meant to increase downtime before turnover, thereby giving gamblers a longer cooling down period between rounds in which to consider their losses.[12] In other words, the idea is that increased complexity should reduce the capacity of games to addict, thereby minimizing player losses and increasing fiscal responsibility. Fittingly enough then, it was in the nineteenth century — the age of utilitarianism — that the St. George's Club and the New York Whist Club began developing a hybrid card game by crossing Whist and possibly the Russian game Vingt, with the idea of encouraging more cerebral and less aleatory card playing. The game was bridge — an elaborate system of bidding and accounting — and the result was yet more gambling and the founding of clubs devoted to those who play the game with all the fervor of addiction.[13]

As the case of bridge suggests, attempting to curb addiction by complexifying the rule-based structure of games, or governmental scheming to curtail feverish speculation and mass frenzy through the application of probability theories, doesn't really work. What the history of such strategies appears to have taught us by the twenty-first century is that people will find ways to gamble with even the most complicated games and that probability theory cannot reason away the chance occurrence of, say, a Nick Leeson, as the Barings Bank learned in 1995. Hence, as Gerda Reith has pointed out, after the mass chaos of the first half of the twentieth century, the West seems to have adopted an attitude of "if you can't beat 'em join 'em." The current approach to chance and gambling, therefore, involves containing it in centers such as Reno, Las Vegas, reservations, and riverboats, to be commodified and marketed.[14] At the same time, there is an increasing trend in Western countries to fund such "public goods" as health care, education, and old-age pensions through state-run lotteries and casinos.[15]

That gambling, and the potential for addiction that accompanies it, would present itself as an appropriate means of generating public funds is, I believe, an outgrowth of one particular aspect of modernity. The modernization of the West came into full swing with the industrial revolution and brought with it a very specific, *serialized mind-set*. This applies to modes of production — repetitive, shared, nonartisan labor culminating in Taylorism and Fordism — just as it applies to modes of consumption, particularly in the areas of entertainment and leisure. This is to say that the assembly line was more than merely a means of production and had a serious and permanent impact not only on the minds of workers who had to learn to keep up with the ceaseless flow of the conveyor belt, but also on the minds of consumers who were groomed to buy in step with production.

The novel, a truly modern, popular literary form, is a revealing yet perhaps less obvious example of the link between the industrialization of the production and consumption of culture, and addiction in the twentieth century. The rise of the novel coincides with the industrial revolution in the English tradition, and the novel's appearance in the eighteenth century was predicated on the mass production of text, which became possible with increasingly sophisticated print technology, along with modern logistics and transportation, which were needed to distribute text to an increasingly literate and leisured audience. Authors responded to this new technology and leisured reader consciousness by writing expansive texts, which they published serially.[16] Moreover, the division of novels into chapters makes them per se serial and repetitive in nature, catering to readers who consume narrative fiction in discrete, chapter-length segments with a distinctive and satisfying stasis / conflict / resolution structure. The idea is to draw readers into a mesmerizing pattern of episodes, which can be consumed in single sittings or, better yet, in one very long sitting for the ideal reader who loses track of time and "just can't put down" a page turner once s/he is stuck in.

What I am arguing then is that industrial modernity brought with it a new, serialized form of consciousness and leisure that has come to inform almost ever aspect of human experience from labor to consumption and virtually everything in between, including slot machine play, TV viewing and, of course, video games.[17] Importantly, seriality is also highly addictive and produces captive-audience consumers and markets based on repetitive need.

Video Games, Addiction, and Pleasure

Perhaps the most important essay ever written on seriality, repetition, and modern consciousness is Freud's *Beyond the Pleasure Principle*. Freud begins his essay by introducing "an economic point of view" of the human psyche, thereby establishing the link I have been making between modern economics (production and consumption), consciousness, and the serialization of experience. In this essay, Freud's psychoanalytic model is, significantly, indebted to Bentham's model of utilitarian expenditure (mentioned earlier), based on the avoidance of pain and the production of pleasure for the greatest number. In Freud's essay, the human psyche is regulated by the pleasure principle, which strives to reduce "unpleasurable tension," which is accomplished through the "avoidance of unpleasure or the production of pleasure" (1).

From this postulate, Freud goes on to explain psychic responses to the frequent failure of pleasure to dominate experience. His theory is based on an examination of "the method of working employed by the mental apparatus in one of the earliest *normal* activities, [namely ...] children's play" (8). The subject of Freud's reflections is a little boy, whom he observed repeatedly throwing a toy under his crib and reproducing it by pulling on a string, while exclaiming '*fort*' (gone) and '*da*' (there). Because the boy played this game only during his mother's absences, Freud concluded that this repetitive activity was the infant's way of responding to the unpleasure of her absence. In other words, throwing away a surrogate version of his mother (*fort*) in the form of a toy, the child mimicked his mother's departure and absence, while pulling the toy back and causing it to reappear (*da*), produced a sort of satisfaction in the child, based on an artificial sense of mastery over his situation. Freud concludes that in this simple child's game, we may isolate not only the pleasure principle and all of the economic regulatory principles connected with it, but also "the compulsion to repeat which over-rides the pleasure principle," while at the same time driving it (16).

Following Freud, I argue that the drive to repeat based on the pleasure principle to some extent informs, or is informed by, the serialization of modern industrial consciousness.[18] But when does the mundane, normalized repetitiveness of contemporary culture in which we mark the passage of time by serialized TV dramas and movie sequels, spill over into the realm of addiction? And more importantly, what, if anything, makes video games more addictive than say *The Gilmore Girls* or, to pull up an historical and perhaps less immediately apparent example, *Little Dorrit*? Is gaming, in fact, the same thing as gambling?

First, it is important to proceed with caution on the score of video games and addiction as many adamantly deny, in spite of what might seem convincing evidence to the contrary, that video games are in fact addictive. For example, there is "currently no category for videogame addiction in the Diagnostic and Statistical Manual of Mental Disorders" and participants in a recent blog on the topic consistently used scare quotes to frame the word addiction (Schlimme). Yet even though these bloggers hesitate to use the word, they all report symptoms of what researchers on addiction refer to as primary disorders (manic episodes, obsessive compulsive behavior, neurochemical adaptation to the increased flow of adrenaline) and comorbidity (withdrawal from social contact and professional responsibility, indifference to personal hygiene, guilt).[19] For example, one participant reported that her "addicted" boyfriend forgets "to brush his teeth on a daily basis," even though he has few responsibilities "outside of personal hygiene." Another reports that her son has "few social skills, few friends and is now in withdrawal 'literally,'" and one gamer claims that the feeling he gets "when [he plays] video games versus when [he has] done drugs is EXACTLY the same" (Schlimme).

One of the earliest attempts to tackle the specific question of video games and addiction was Loftus and Loftus's *Mind at Play* in which the authors attribute video games' drawing power to three basic aspects of the experience: partial reinforcement, cognitive dissonance, and regret. By partial reinforcement, the authors refer to reward systems based on points and collectables, writing that "any behavior that is followed by reinforcement will increase in frequency" (14). Partial reinforcement is a powerful incentive since it keeps the player striving after the ultimate reinforcement without ever attaining it, such as a perfect score.

Cognitive dissonance theory assumes that people will "act so as to reduce conflict" or to rectify a situation gone wrong, and that, therefore, players of video games are motivated by limited rewards that are not easily obtained (29). This keeps the player eager to rectify losses by repeating games in an endeavor to do better with each subsequent trial. But while people are attracted to difficulty and penalties that keep them yearning to correct imbalance, the amount of difficulty must not be excessive or players will disengage. This is related to what the authors call "regret," a factor that also plays a decisive role as it pushes players to take every "opportunity to make an alternate world a reality," by passing from one level to another or by achieving a particular score (Loftus 31). According to Loftus and Loftus, by 1983 game developers had learned to program a schedule of reinforcements into games like *Pac Man* that was continuous and difficult, but not too difficult or constant enough to be predictable, either of which would cause players to lose interest and to disengage. The combined ways in which video games stimulate and challenge these basic drives is, according to the authors, what gives video games their potential to addict.

In his book entitled simply *Videogames* (2004), James Newman has concurred with the Loftuses, at least regarding the question of difficulty.[20] He cites the *Edge Online* discussion board in which players complain of disengagement factors such as an "oversimplification of controls," "a ramping down of overall difficulty levels," and "shorter games that require less commitment to play, completion and mastery" (51). At the same time, Newman cites "the way in which the content is delivered" as contributing to games' addictive nature, making them "substantially different to [sic] watching film or television or listening to the radio" (58). What he is referring to is the leveling-up structure of games, which compels players to stay involved, while the levels "force and control the pace of experience," something that is particularly evident in horizontally scrolling games like *Super Mario World*, where the pace is dictated by the game.

In *Massively Multiplayer Online Role-Playing Games*, R.V. Kelly 2 puts forward an opposing view, namely, that games provide a "failsafe" where players can take risks without consequences. According to Kelly 2, players become addicted to pleasure rather than to difficulty and regret, as Loftus and Loftus suggested. Among the pleasures afforded the addicted MMORPG player in Kelly 2's view are: getting ahead by accumulating virtual merchandise and points; accomplishing something; being part of something bigger, such as an epic romance; escaping reality; helping others; solving problems and making money; leading a heroic life by overcoming obstacles; interacting without consequences; and living in a world that makes sense (66). While I take some of Kelly 2's more altruistic and grandiose game values such as "helping others" and "being part of an epic romance" with a healthy grain of salt, there are two aspects of his argument that I believe bear further investigation. The first involves his claim that MMORPGs often attract and addict "people who [have] no history of obsessive behavior," while the second is linked to his notion that players become addicted to "the furtherance of the plot" and the idea of writing themselves into a book (67, 69). These claims are important to my argument because I suspect that "addiction" to video games (if indeed they are technically addictive) comes with its own contextual and historical specificity, which must not be ignored, and which at the same time sets it apart from previous modes of addiction.

The Drone of (Post)Modernity

As a means of approaching the specificity of video games in contemporary culture, I would like to turn to Foucault's 1966 essay on Maurice Blanchot's philosophical and fictional writings. Although *The Thought from Outside* [*La pensée du dehors*] predates even *Pong*, Foucault saw in Blanchot's fictional and philosophical worlds the roadmap of what was ahead, namely, the intensification of the modern serialization of human experience in postmodernity. Interestingly, he described this future in ways that are highly reminiscent of the videogame experience. For example, the thought world of Blanchot's writings is distinguished by his use of language, which defines a postmodern notion of experience that closely resembles the repetition and seriality of gameplay. According to Foucault, Blanchot speaks a language at the edge of a "void ... a silence ... where words endlessly unravel," into an "infinite void that opens beneath the feet of the person it attracts" (22, 28). In this sense, Blanchot's discursive worlds, like gameplay, are the result of an ongoing oscillation between the self and the void, or the world that William Gibson conceptualized as receding ceaselessly beyond the computer screen.[21] This dialectical movement into infinitely eroding exteriority is "not a contradiction but a contestation that effaces; not reconciliation but a droning on and on; not mind in laborious conquest of its unity, but the endless erosion of the outside [...] the streaming and distress of a language that has always already begun" (22).

This constant projecting of the self into the drone of postmodernity, and into the streaming and distress of language, recalls the experience of dedicated gamers who speak of *World of Warcraft* as being infinite and infinitely compelling. Both the space of Blanchot's writing and game worlds are spaces outside of the self. The experience of this space outside the self has been described by one gamer in terms of images and patterns that get "burned into" his brain, which then come to supplant sleeping and waking dream images. According to him "the addiction is based on trying to complete a pattern *that has no end*" (Schlimme, my italics). This is a kind of thinking outside of the self that takes the participation in speech into the void, allowing oneself to be drawn into the rhythmic and endless drone of technologized play. In the fictional world of the game, players are drawn into the pulsating, receding surfaces of the gamescape where they are held by the mechanical drone of a potentially infinite series of rapidly recurring moments of pleasurable expenditure of the self in which, as Foucault wrote, one is exposed "to the naked experience of the outside" (27).[22]

Equally applicable to the videogame experience is Foucault's notion of "being attracted and negligent." Here he refers to the addictive attraction of "emptiness and destitution ... where one is irremediably outside the outside," which "tirelessly carries the attracted person forward" (27, 29). The gamer is drawn on and into a cyberself with the negligence necessary to "infinitely fold outside" into a "mute, unjustified, obstinate diligence in surrendering oneself, against all odds, to being attracted by attraction, or more precisely [...] to being, in the void, in the aimless movement without a moving body of attraction itself" (29). The attraction to the endless drone of serialized patterns makes the gaming experience reminiscent of what Foucault called a rehearsal of death, that brings the subject "in contact with death [...] in the flash of infinite oscillation," where "death opens interminably onto the repetition of the beginning" (57).[23] The gamer, like the subjects of Blanchot's work, is drawn on with a zeal that forms the flip side of negligence, through a silence and repetition "too ambiguous to be deciphered and definitely interpreted," as s/he dizzily and stubbornly "forget[s] an entire life" (29). What I am suggesting then, is that this is the kind of forgetfulness that distinguishes gamers who reportedly withdraw from friends and family, ignore personal hygiene, and collapse in exhaustion or even death after marathon sessions.

As I see it, cyber game worlds are a space of deep, immersive play and what Foucault calls exteriority. Their designers, in fact, tally success by how effectively they manage to eradicate any hint of an inside/outside barrier that would distract the gamer, and work hard at smoothing out the rough edges of the player's transition into the experience of exteriority, that is, into the game world.[24] To this end, digital game designers have always tried to "erase the boundary separating the player from the game world [by playing] up tactile involvement," immersing corporeality in technology, and "envelop[ing] the player in the environment of game space," or in Foucauldian terms, the environment of the exterior (Lahti 519). In first-person digital games like

Halo, the landscape is designed to disperse persistently outward while the gamer is drawn on to serialized expanses of the same, dropping off and beyond the player's first-person eye. Game worlds, as Foucault writes, "unfold a place-less place" where figures unravel infinitely, "gleaming and sparkling" in the moment of their disappearance (52).

There is a further striking similarity between Blanchot's fictional and philosophical worlds and the code of digital game worlds, defined by the near-ness of virtual reality and the irremediable absence of the environment in which one is playing, where one is "continually [confronted] by doors open and [yet] prohibited by the great wheel [of fortune] handing out ... undeci-pherable fates, by the overhang of an upper storey ... from which anonymous orders fall" (35–36). The projection of the self into just such an endless pas-sage through a chance-based environment is what game developers refer to as "[t]he boundary experience of simultaneously being and not being there," or what the people at PS2 referred to as the third place (Lahti 164). Gamers, like characters in Blanchot's narratives, move ceaselessly through,

> placeless places, beckoning thresholds, closed forbidden spaces [...] hallways fanned by doors that open rooms for unbearable encounters and create gulfs between them [...] corridors leading to more corridors [...] filled with those who *ceaselessly cease living*; a long narrow room, like a tunnel, in which approach and distance — the approach of forgetting, the distance of the wait — draw near to one another and unendingly move apart [my italics] [24].

Importantly, the exteriorizing and receding language and the reader's experience thereof that marks Blanchot's writing is part of a trend that began, according to Foucault, in the nineteenth century with experiments like Mal-larmé's *Coup de dés*, or "the aleatory and autonomous theatricality of the *Book* — as the movement of the speaker's disappearance" (18). His writing relies on a constant foregrounding of chance as the force that generated it, and it fits, not surprisingly, into the chronology of chance that I outlined above. The heightened acceptance of chance in twentieth-century fiction has been theorized as a self-conscious awareness of the link of writing to play and games.[25] This, in turn, has been trumped by interactive videogame narratives. Game stories are necessarily dialectical, yet they open endlessly onto infinitely receding spaces with multiple, random points of entry, surpassing traditional mimesis and referring ceaselessly to themselves, to their own autonomous fic-tional worlds. And indeed it is chance that animates the permanent oscilla-tion between 0 and 1 from which digital worlds are built, and informs the random variation of virtual worlds. The possible worlds of the gamescape, therefore, belong to the realm of chance and are structured by a dialectical, aleatory oscillation between poles such as winning and losing or comprehen-sion and confusion that give form to them.

Modern serialized consciousness and the subjective embrace of chance meet in gameplay, making it perhaps the ultimate expression of postmodern being. The account of addiction I am presenting here broadens the notion of addiction beyond its usual location in the addicted subject, to also take into account the greater historical paradigm. While a Foucauldian reading of gaming and addiction addresses the loss of agency that takes place when one surrenders one's self to immersive activities and the drone of endless repetition, it also enlarges the field of inquiry to include the notion of mechanized existence and the perception that existence is informed by chance and its commodification. While this approach might seem more diffuse than the more usual moral and ethical emphasis that is directed toward players and producers, the current approach is useful in identifying these other neglected, yet pervasive sociohistorical forces. From such a perspective, then, it is little wonder that people who have never exhibited symptoms of addiction become "addicted" to video games. Indeed, videogame "addiction" is seen as part of contemporary living like any other of the countless "addictions" that we drift into and out of again.

While addiction is clearly a fraught concept, until recently carrying all kinds of moralizing baggage, I argue that it is worth retaining and that it actually tells us a great deal about appropriate responses to contemporary consumer culture. This is a culture that spawns novels like *Bridget Jones' Diary*— which provide us with extensive shopping lists — and one in which the novels of Sophie Kinsella's *Shopaholic* series become best-sellers.[26] Indeed, seen from an historical perspective as the acceptance of chance that developed out of a compulsion to control random events, coupled with industrialization and heightened consumerism, addictive behaviors present themselves as just about the only game in town. Roger Lockard makes a similar point in "'Self-Will Run Riot': The Earth as an Alcoholic," when he writes that "addiction and its resolution hinge on transformations of the experience of self [so that] questions of selfhood and identity once considered philosophical recreations have become urgently pragmatic" (1). Gamers have been molded by the same transformation in the experience of self that we have all been compelled to make in order to become the kind of subjects that digital capitalism requires.

Conclusions

In this chapter I have surveyed the background to such issues as chance, modernity, subjectivity, industrialization, and seriality in an attempt to answer some questions surrounding the complex and pressing issue of video games' addictive dimension. In the process I have had occasion to direct my discussion to the increasing serialization and intensification of experience, which are intimately linked to industrialized economic modernity and heightened through postmodernity. The view of addiction and its history that I have sketched out here helps to account for the projection and relinquishing of the self into simulacra such as game worlds, as well as the subjective high that accompanies it. This is what the postmodern subject is said to have in common with its premodern homologue, namely, a subjective outline fluid enough to permit merging with imaginary worlds, the capacity to meld with a group as in oral cultures, and the desire to relinquish the self to the swoon of chance and loss.[27] It may also be possible to draw an arc from the postmodern un-individual, content to spend the majority of his or her waking hours in a MMORPG, to the loss of faith that comes with the secularization of culture which began early in the seventeenth century and has been progressively intensified by capitalism and industrialization in the West ever since. In this regard, we are all possibly "Lookin' for to fill that GOD shaped hole," doing so with a plurality of discourses rather than monotheistic logic.[28] According to Derrida, under such circumstances "the sky of transcendence comes to be emptied, and not just of Gods, but of any Other, a fatal rhetoric fills the void, and this is the fetishism of [...] addiction" (29). The contemporary subject therefore dreams "of emancipation and of the restoration of an 'I,' of a self or of the self's own body [...] of the restoration of a subject once and for all taken back to the forces of alienation [...] and to the law which speaks in religion, metaphysics, politics, the family, etc." (30). The dream of subjective restoration is relinquished as we learn to look for its alternative in addiction.

Perhaps the release of the self into the kind of exteriority Foucault described, or into the enchanted landscape of digitalized premodern worlds where one's body is replaced with an enhanced avatar body, is a response to the world in which we live as well as an instinctual attempt to regain a metaphysical worldview. Derrida goes on to caution, however, that such remedies, such addictions, "can always invent new orifices, in addition to and beyond those, for example the mouth, which we think we naturally possess" (33). This immediately calls to mind the characters in David Cronenberg's *eXistenZ*, and the surgical operation they gladly undergo in order to have an extra orifice created as a spinal tap through which they can jack into the game to which they are apparently addicted. To me, the coincidence of the videogame experience with so many of the economic, historical, and metaphysical issues of modernity suggests that gameplay may well be more aligned with, rather than disruptive of, the contemporary life world. This is what makes it possible for people to play with varying degrees of obsession over the course of a lifetime; hence, my students' assertion that they "grew out" of their supposed addiction to games.

Notes

1. For instance, the local Dutch television program *Gammo.* The announcer for this weekly review program, who sounds like a cross between Chuck Barris and the Grim Reaper, volubly proclaims that the really good games are "*echt* verslavend" [*really* addictive].

2. The interviewer who drew my attention to this was Professor José van Dijck and I am grateful to her for it.

3. I refer here to a cluster of important problems surrounding the practice of "grinding," that is, the production of virtual items, often in sweatshops in developing nations, on sale for "off-screen dollars." That grinding is the motor behind what is now known as the "secondary gold market" should alert us to the fact that this is no minor feature of the current economy. For more on this see Goggin, "Fantasy and Finance: What Money does in Play Worlds," forthcoming. See also Castronova 2001 and 2003, as well as Dibbell and Krotoski.

4. This scene occurs in Book VIII of *The Confessions* and the scripture that he comes upon by chance is Romans 13:12–14, which admonishes him to give up debauchery such as gaming.

5. On the relation of tobacco and seventeenth-century trade and speculation see Weber 100–101. On gambling, speculation and tobacco in The Netherlands in the seventeenth century, see Schama, particularly "Money unconfined: I invest, he speculates, they gamble" (343–373) and "Stygain fires and aqua fortis" (188–220).

Richard Klein places the beginnings of Europe's interest in substance abuse somewhat earlier: "The introduction of tobacco into Europe in the sixteenth century corresponded with the arrival of the Age of Anxiety, the beginning of modern consciousness [...] the development of rational, scientific methods, and the concurrent loss of medieval theological assurances" (27). Derrida's anonymous interviewer in "The Rhetoric of Drugs," however, equates "the concept of drug addiction [...] in the modern sense," with the publication of De Quincey's *Confessions of an English Opium-Eater* (1821).

What I would like to stress here is that all of these authors associate addiction with modernity. I will have the opportunity to go into this point in greater detail below.

6. In Deborah Moggach's novel *Tulip Fever,* she follows historians Zumthor and Schama in describing the Dutch in the seventeenth century as a people who gambled on everything from the sex of a child to the time of day. As one character muses, "underneath we are all gamblers. We are a people possessed" (143).

The South Sea Bubble burst in 1720 and its ramifications were felt most in England and France. This ended a period of virtually uncontrolled, mass speculation, based on fly-by-night companies (one named "For carrying on an undertaking of great advantage; but nobody to know what it is") much like those that grew up during the dot.com craze of the 1990s (Mackay 60). For more on gambling, economy and this period in financial history see Mackay (46–88), Kavanagh (29–107), Goggin (1998: 100–108), Galbraith (28–58) and de Goede (21–46). On the dot.com craze see Thrift.

7. See for example Geertz (432) and McMahan(69).

8. Cf. Gigerenzer et al., 3–40.

9. See Bentham's *An Introduction to the Principles of Morals and Legislation* and particularly, "Value of a Lot of Pleasure or Pain, How to be Measured." It is worth noting that Bentham was also the master mind behind the Panopticon, which he proposed as the architectural model for prisons and other institutions that regulate and educate individuals. As Foucault has explained at length in *Discipline and Punish,* the Panopticon was all about economics as it maximized surveillance while minimizing expenditure on regulatory

force. As such, it provides a good example of the kind of thinking that informs utilitarianism. See "Panoptism" (197–229).

10. By "dissipatory," I mean expenditure that is not compensated with material returns, such as money gambled away or spent on non-procreative sex as in prostitution or on public spectacle. Another good example of non-utilitarian expenditure would be hours whiled away at *Tetris* or *WoW*. On this topic see Bataille's *La part maudite* (28–31) and Goggin (1998 114–120).

11. The speed at which gamblers may make new bets is known as the rate of play (Reith 95–97).

12. For more on this point see Reith (75–76). Dummett writes that "the development of [games of chance] strives constantly toward reducing the role of chance to a minimum" [*Die Entwicklung des [reine Glücksspiel] ging stets dahin, die Rolle des Zufalls auf ein Minimum zu reduzieren*] my translation, 63.

13. See Parlett, "From Whist to Bridge" in *A History of Card Games*, 214–37. See also the chapter on the social development of the game of whist in Chatto, 47–60. Further, on the Bridge craze in the USA Irving Crespi reports that in 1950 alone over 80 million decks of cards were sold and that cards, including bridge, were played on a regular basis in 87 percent of American homes. Judging by the numbers then, it does not appear that increasing complexity serves as a deterrent to addiction. Crespi, 717–721.

14. See Reith 33–44.

15. This last consideration is of a piece with the trend toward accepting and commodifying risk that really took hold with the expansion of the insurance industry in the second half of the nineteenth century. For more on this topic, see Beck 19–51.

16. Although the serial publication of novels is most frequently associated with Dickens, novels generally came out in serialized form in magazines like *Schribner's* beginning in the eighteenth century. Novels that were initially serialized and intended for mass, popular consumption include even the works of more high-brow and notoriously difficult writers such as Henry James and Edith Wharton. Fittingly enough, given my argument here concerning addiction, seriality and modern consciousness, De Quincy's *Confessions of an English Opium Eater* was also published serially in the *London Magazine* in September and October of 1821.

17. As I mentioned above (n.3), grinders who earn their living playing videogames, games constitute both leisure and labor, consumption and production.

18. Freud is certainly not the only theoretician who has reach this conclusion, however, in the present context I give his theory particular emphasis as it is a self-declared theory of the human psyche as well as of play, pleasure and economy. Cf. Dyer, particularly 78–81.

19. See for example Peele 211 and Schaffer 182–183. For more on guilt in particular as an impetus to gambling, see Freud's famous essay "Dostoyevsky and Parricide."

20. One should keep in mind that the addictive potential of difficulty, especially in games, is what Caillois referred to long ago as *ludus* in his watershed book, *Man, Play and Games*.

21. I refer to William Gibson's oft-quoted remark that his inspiration for *Neuromancer* came from a glance into a video arcade on Vancouver's Granville Street where "rapt kids [...] believed in the space games project [...] some kind of *actual space* behind the screen, someplace you can't see but you know is there" (cited in Cavallaro 63).

22. As I have remarked elsewhere, this is how casino space worked in Las Vegas, where gamblers are drawn in by impressive light displays and held there by the constant drone of slot machines (Goggin 1997).

23. In this connection, I have always found it intriguing that MMORPG is pronounced "morgue," as though gamers understand that entering such a game world implies leaving one's off-screen subjectivity behind.

24. EA Games developer Alex Hutchinson recently commented that designers now want to eliminate the obvious breaks of leveling up, including cut scenes, as such breaks interrupt immersive flow. Private correspondence with author.

25. This is one of the central theses in Reith's *The Age of Chance*. See particularly 24–39. See also "Play and Games" in Taylor (43–53) and part two in Kavanagh, "Chance and the Novel" (107–123).

26. The impressive number of books and products in the *Shopaholic* series attest to the addictiveness of seriality and, of course, the novels and products they have spawned are just one more thing that consumers currently claim to be addicted to.

27. On premodern subjectivity and its relationship with the postmodern construct of subjectivity see Godzich and Comay.

28. This is a line from a U2 song. Cf. Moser on this topic (33).

Works Cited

Bataille, Georges. *La Part maudite*. Paris: Éditions de minuit, 1967.

Beck, Ulrich. *Risk Society: Towards a New Modernity*. Trans. Mark Ritter. London: SAGE Publications, 1992.

Caillois, Roger. *Les Jeux et les Hommes*. Paris: Gallimard, 1958.

Cardano. *The Book on Games of Chance* [Ludo alea]. Trans. Sydney Henry Gould. Princeton, NJ: Princeton University Press, 1953.

Cavallaro, Dani. *Cyberpunk and Cyberculture*. London: Athlone Press, 2000.

"Cavendish." *Card Essays, Clay's Decisions, and Card-Table Talk*. London: Thos. de la Rue & Co., 1879. (Author Henry Jones).

Castranova, Edward. "On Virtual Economies." *Game Studies* 3:2 (2003). 14 March 2007. http://www.gamestudies.org/0302/castronova/.

_____. "Virtual Worlds: A First-Hand Account of Market and Society on the Cyberian Frontier," *CESifo Working Paper No. 616* (2001). 14 March 2007 <http://papers.ssrn.com/abstract=294828>.

Chatto, William Andrew. *Facts and Speculations on the Origin and History of Playing Cards*. London: John Russell Smith, 1858.

Comay, Rebecca. "Gifts without Presents: Economics of 'Experience' in Bataille and Heidegger." *Yale French Studies* 78 (1990).

Crespi, Irving. "The Social Significance of Card Playing as a Leisure Time Activity." *American Sociological Review* 21 (1956): 717–721.

Derrida, Jacques. "The Rhetoric of Drugs." In *High Culture: Reflections on Addiction and Modernity* edited by Anna Alexander and Mark S. Roberts, 1–43. New York: SUNY Press, 2003.

Dibbell, Julian. "Surfing the Web: Black Snow Interactive and the World's First Virtual Sweat Shop" (2003). 14 March 2007. http://www.juliandibbell.com/texts/blacksnow.html.

Dryer, Jennifer. *Traveling Concepts: Meaning, Frame, Metaphor*. Eds. Joyce Goggin and Michel Burke, 77–92. Amsterdam: ASCA, 2002.

Dummett, Michael. "Kartenspiele des 15. Jahrhunderts und das Hofämterspiel."
Hofämterspiel, 62–79. Vienna: E.R. Ragg, 1976.

Foucault, Michel. *Maurice Blanchot: The Thought from Outside*. Trans. Jeffrey Mehlman and Brian Massumi. Cambridge: Massachusetts Institute of Technology Press, 1987.

_____. *Surveiller et Punir*. Paris: Éditions Gallimard, 1975.

Freud, Sigmund. *Beyond the Pleasure Principle*. Trans. James Strachey. New York: Norton & Company, 1961.

_____. "Dostoevsky and Parricide." *The Standard Edition of the Complete Psychological Works of Sigmund Freud* XXI. Trans. and Ed. James Strachey, 175–196. London: Hogarth, 1961.

Galbraith, Kenneth. *Money, Whence It Came, Where It Went.* London: Deutsch, 1975.

Geertz, Clifford. "Deep Play: Notes on the Balinese Cockfight." *The Interpretation of Cultures.* New York: Basic Books, 1999.

Gigerenzer, Gerd, et al. *The Empire of Chance: How Probability Changed Science and Everyday Life.* Cambridge: Cambridge University Press, 1989.

Godzich, Vlad. "Subjects without Society." Forward to Doris-Louise Haineault and Jean-Yves Roy. *Unconscious for Sale: Advertising, Psychoanalysis, and the Public,* ix–xix. Minneapolis: University of Minnesota Press, 1990.

Goede, Marieke. *Virtue, Faith and Finance: A Genealogy of Finance.* Minneapolis: University of Minnesota Press, 2005.

Goggin, Joyce. "The Big Deal: Card Games in 20th-century Fiction." Unpublished Ph.D. diss. Université de Montréal, 1998.

_____. "Cuttin' Loose in Vegas, or Sensuality in the Themed Environment." Amsterdam: ASCA Press, 1997.

_____. "Fantasy and Finance: What Money Does in Play Worlds." *The Computer Culture Reader.* Cambridge: Cambridge Scholars Press, forthcoming.

Kavanagh, Thomas M. *Enlightenment and the Shadows of Chance: The Novel and the Culture of Gambling in Eighteenth-Century France.* Baltimore: Johns Hopkins University Press, 1993.

Kelly, R.V. *Massively Multiplayer Online Role-Playing Games.* Jefferson, NC: McFarland, 2004.

Klein, Richard. *Cigarettes Are Sublime.* Durham, NC: Duke University Press, 1993.

Krotoksi, Aleks. "Real Profits from Play Money." *Guardian Unlimited* (April 15, 2004). 14 March 2207. http://www.guardian.co.uk/online/story0,,1191678,00.html.

Lahti, Martti. "As We Become Machines: Corporealized Pleasures in Video Games." In *The Video Game Theory Reader,* edited by Mark J. P. Wolf and Bernard Perron, 157–171. New York: Routledge, 2003.

Lockard, Roger. "'Self-Will Run Riot': The Earth as an Alcoholic." *Janus Head* 6.2 (2003): 190–207.

Loftus, Geoffrey R., and Elizabeth F. Loftus. *Mind at Play: The Psychology of Video Games.* New York: Basic Books, 1983.

Mackay, Charles. *Extraordinary Popular Delusions and the Madness of Crowds.* New York: Barnes & Noble, 1993 [1841].

McMahan, Alison. "Immersion, Engagement, and Presence: A Method for Analyzing 3-D Video Games." In *The Video Game Theory Reader,* edited by Mark J. P. Wolf and Bernard Perron. New York: Routledge, 2003.

Moggach, Deborah. *Tulip Fever.* London: Vintage, 1999.

Moser, Walter. "Dieu et ses mutants discursifs." *Théologiques* 6.2 (1998): 33–49.

Newman, James. *Videogames.* London: Routledge, 2004.

Parlett, David. *A History of Card Games.* Oxford: Oxford University Press, 1991.

Peele, Stanton. "Is Gambling an Addiction like Drug and Alcohol Addiction?: Developing Realistic and Useful Conceptions of Conceptions of Compulsive Gambling." In *Gambling: Who Wins? Who Loses,* edited by Gerda Reith, 208–218. New York: Prometheus, 2003.

Reith, Gerda. *The Age of Chance: Gambling in Western Culture.* London: Routledge, 1999.

Schama, Simon. *The Embarrassment of Riches: An Interpretation of Dutch Culture in the Golden Age.* London: Fontana Press, 1991.

Schlimme, Mary "Video Game Addiction: Do We Need a Video Gamers Anonymous?"

(2002). 14 March 2007. http://serendip.brynmawr.edu/bb/neuro/neuro02/web2/mschlimme.html.

Shaffer, Howard J. "A Critical View of Pathological Gambling and Addiction: Comorbidity Makes for Syndromes and Other Strange Bedfellows." In *Gambling: Who Wins? Who Loses,* edited by Gerda Reith, 175–191. New York: Prometheus, 2003.

Taylor, Mark C. *Confidence Games: Money and Markets in a World without Redemption.* Chicago: University of Chicago Press, 2004.

Thrift, Nigel. "It's the Romance, not the Finance, That Makes the Business Worth Pursuing." *Economy and Society* 30.4 (2001): 412–432.

Weber, Max. *The Protestant Ethic and the Spirit of Capitalism.* Trans. Talcott Parsons. London: Unwin University Books, 1974.

Zumthor, Paul. *Daily Life in Rembrandt's Holland.* Stanford, CA: Stanford University Press, 1994.

Gameography

Halo: Combat Evolved, Bungie, Microsoft, 2001.
Pong, Atari, 1972.
Super Mario World, Nintendo, 1990.
Tetris, Nintendo, 1989.
World of Warcraft, Blizzard, 2004.

3

Forbidden Pleasures:
Cheating in Computer Games

Julian Kücklich

Cheating as an Aesthetic Phenomenon[1]

Cheating is an aspect of computer games that has thus far received scant attention from the discipline of game studies. The reasons for this oversight are not entirely clear, since it is immediately obvious that cheats are an important part of gaming culture. There is hardly a gaming magazine or website that does not offer cheats, and special publications in electronic or book form complement this already abundant supply. Furthermore, there is hardly a game that does not come with either built-in cheat modes or design loopholes that can be exploited by cunning gamers. In other words: whenever we play digital games, cheats are an option. Whether we actively employ cheats or not, the experience of playing a game is always influenced by the possibility of "illegal" manipulation.

Building on the work of Torben Grodal, Rune Klevjer has pointed out that "the gaming experience, even though the 'passive' competencies required by film are also involved, characteristically is an aesthetics of control." An aesthetics of digital games must therefore take into account the "illegal" modes of enhancing or diminishing the player's control. Similar to the way video recorders have changed the experience of watching films, both at home and in the theater, by giving the viewer more control over the viewing process, cheats change the perception of games, by transferring the power over the order, duration, and frequency of their sequences to the player.

Additionally, cheat codes carry cultural significance beyond the games

Cheats are an important part of game culture (rights to the Xbox Cheat Guide belong to Future US, Inc; used with permission).

they stem from. In an article entitled "Up, Up, Down, Down" Jon Katz quotes a cheat combination for several games on the Nintendo Entertainment System (NES). He goes on to say that if you "[r]ecite this combination to millions of younger Americans, [...] it's like a secret handshake" (1). Therefore, cheat codes can be regarded as a sort of symbolic currency within gaming communities. In a similar vein, Keri Facer argues that "games [...] function as a means by which young men are 'allowed' to speak to each other. The exchange of cheats, games and computer expertise [...] functions as a currency by which friendship is constructed" (209).

In multiplayer games, however, cheats change not only the experience of the cheater, but also the experience of the other players. In a game like *Counterstrike*, players equipped with automatic aiming algorithms, or "aimbots," are so vastly superior to other players that their avatars are virtually invulnerable. In many cases, the real challenge for "professional" cheaters quickly shifts from competing with other players to trying to outwit the cheat detection systems of the game servers. At this point, cheating turns into an "illegal" activity, whose pleasure presumably derives from the fact that it is in some form transgressive of social norms.

What Are Cheats?

But before we discuss these issues in detail, we should try to clarify what exactly we are talking about when we speak of cheats. To define cheating proves a difficult task, however, since the phenomenon of cheating is inevitably tied to the phenomenon of games — and games are notorious for defying an all-encompassing definition. Indeed, cheats are almost as diverse as the games to which they pertain, and they resemble each other only superficially. While it is certainly true of most cheats that they give the player an advantage that the rules of the game do not allow for, this is not always the case. Some cheats simply change the way things look. For example, in Germany, graphic depiction of violence is usually removed from games prior to their publication in order to appease the rating board, but the gore can be restored by changing the game's locale settings.

Employing these so-called blood-cheats does not constitute a breach of the game's rules, but it often requires a direct manipulation of the game files ("patching"). Usually, players are expected to manipulate these files only indirectly, that is, through their interaction with the game. Therefore, accessing and altering them directly must be regarded as a practice that goes beyond the game's intended use. Can we define cheats as *using a game in a way that is not intended by its designers*, then? I don't believe so. First of all, it is not always possible to determine the "intended use" of a game. A mod like *Counterstrike* can be seen as a way of playing *Half-Life* that was not intended by its designers, but it is not a cheat.

But in order to cheat players do not have to use the game in such a fashion. Walkthroughs, that is, detailed instructions on how to get through a game, are a common cheating strategy in adventure games such as *Tomb Raider* that require a lot of puzzle-solving. Clearly, the designers intended these puzzles to be solved, so the criterion of "counterintentional use" does not apply here. Still, this practice gives players an advantage they would not possess otherwise, and it can be likened to cheating strategies such as peeking at other players' cards in a game of Poker.

In fact, cheats seem to have only one thing in common: they change the way players experience the game. They do so either by literally changing the look and feel of the game environment and the objects therein (by accessing a game's physics engine, players can often tweak factors such as gravity or friction, thereby changing the experience of the game dramatically), by rendering the obstacles put up by the game's designers instantly surmountable, or by increasing the strength and abilities of the players' avatars to such a degree as to make them vastly superior to all the other players.

A working definition of cheats should therefore be based on their ability to change a player's perception of the game world, rather than their manipulative or even destructive qualities. Such a definition serves not only as a safeguard for a value-neutral assessment of the subject at hand but also enables us to distinguish different types of cheats by the ways in which they change the players' experience of the game. In the analysis of the role cheats play in the context of games and gaming culture a precise classification of cheats should prove an indispensable tool.

Toward a Typology of Cheats

Cheats can be classified into a whole range of categories, the broadest of which are platform, game mode, and game genre. By the category *platform*, I refer to the differences between PC, console, and arcade games, which pertain mostly to the ways in which cheats are entered into the machine. While PC games usually allow direct access to the game files, which can be altered using a hexidecimal editor,[2] console and arcade games do not offer this possibility. In many cases, this means the range of possible manipulations is much larger in PC games, since players can use the bin hex editor to search for individual values (such as number of lives, hit points, or amount of game currency), and change them directly.

The term *game mode* is used here to differentiate single-player games, "closed" multiplayer games (usually played over a LAN or privately owned servers) and "open" multi-player games (usually played over the Internet on public servers). While cheating in single-player games affects only the person playing the game (and is essentially of no consequence to others), cheating in multiplayer games is often a source of conflict. Closed multiplayer games do not offer the anonymity of the Internet, therefore cheating is usually not much of a problem, and if it becomes a problem, it can usually be resolved face to face. In open multi-player games, however, cheating can destabilize whole game worlds, and therefore, the industry spends much time on anti-cheating measures. Quoting game designer Ralph Koster, Katie Salen and Eric Zimmerman estimate that "tracking down cheaters and hackers can occupy approximately half of all the resources spent on maintaining and improving an online game" (280).

Game genre is another useful category in classifying different kinds of cheats. As I have pointed out elsewhere (53), computer game genres can be mapped onto a triangular matrix, according to their specific levels of narrativity, interactivity, and openness. In this model, the term *interactivity* refers to the frequency of the players' physical interaction with the game, while *openness* refers to the range of actions the players can choose from. Thus, a fast-paced action game like *Space Invaders* scores high on interactivity, but it has a comparatively low level of openness. This model can serve here as an auxiliary theoretical construction, which enables us to discuss game genres in rather simple terms.

In adventure games such as *Monkey Island*, the level of narrativity is significantly higher than in other types of games, while the levels of interactivity and openness are comparatively low (in "translating" the textual interface of early adventure games into the point-and-click interface of their graphical successors, the limitations of the parsers' vocabularies become painfully apparent). Therefore, most adventure game cheats serve to remove "narrative obstacles," either by "foretelling" the game's story (walkthroughs), or by offering instant access to higher levels. Interestingly, "novelizations" of adventure games such as Chris Ratcliff's *Sam and Max Hit the Road* can serve as cheating devices, but they have aesthetic value independent of the games themselves.

Fast-paced action games, including arcade games, first-person shooters, beat-'em-ups, and sports simulation games typically have a high level of interactivity, but they score rather low on narrativity and openness. Action adventures such as the games of the *Tomb Raider* series usually oscillate between fast-paced action sequences, exploration, and noninteractive cut-scenes responsible for narrative progression. Typical cheats for action games increase the games' interactivity by making the players' avatars invulnerable, supplying them with an infinite amount of ammunition, or giving them access to all the weapons available. Since action games typically require the players to perform rather repetitive interaction patterns, much effort is spent on designing attractive settings (arenas, dungeons, racing courses, etc.) for the actual gameplay. Often, these settings must be "unlocked" by winning a predetermined number of matches or performing a similar feat. Cheats offer a convenient way to circumvent these arbitrary restrictions.

A high level of openness is usually found in simulation games such as *SimCity*. Classic simulation games have no narrative progression to speak of, and since the game's pace depends on the player, the level of interactivity is also low. Lack of funds and arbitrary restrictions (such as the types of buildings that can be built at a certain developmental level) limit the level of openness, and therefore it should come as no surprise that many cheats address these limitations. In competitive simulation games such as *Civilization*, cheats also include strategic hints that give the player an advantage over the other players. In *Civilization II*, the internal rules of the game governing the behavior of the computer-controlled players are stored in an ASCII-file that can be opened and manipulated using a text editor. *Civilization: Call to Power* features cheats as a regular option in the game's menu. This is consistent with the prevalent philosophy in simulation gaming, which emphasizes explorative play as the feature that sets simulation games apart from other types of games. Therefore, cheats are often an integral part of simulations, rather than an added feature.

Adventure games, action games, and simulation games can be regarded as genre prototypes, as they are "pure" manifestations of one of the three interactive modes (narrativity, interactivity, and openness). In comparison to those, strategy games and role-playing games must be regarded as hybrid forms, since they typically incorporate two different interactive modes. Role-playing games combine a comparatively high level of openness with narrative progression, while strategy games can be seen as a compromise between interactivity and openness. Therefore, the types of cheats that can be found in these game genres are often a mixture of the cheats found in genre prototypes. Role-playing game cheats, for example, often give the players access to magical items, or allow them to increase their characters' stats, which is equivalent to generic simulation game cheats. But since role-playing games also contain narrative elements in the form of "missions" or "quests," walkthroughs and maps are also in high demand.

Strategy games, especially real-time strategy games such as *Command & Conquer*, or *Age of Empires*, challenge players to make quick tactical decisions, without letting the momentary action lure them into forgetting the strategic context within which the action takes place. Strategy game cheats address this dilemma by either giving players access to superior weaponry (tactical cheats) or by allowing them to change the rules of the game. Several titles of the *Command & Conquer* series come with a rule set file that can be altered at will by changing numerical values such as the price of certain buildings, and so on.

While this general overview of genre-specific cheats is necessarily an oversimplification, and does not take into account differences within genres, it draws attention to the fact that each genre has a set of prototypical cheats that are to some degree expected by the game community. In other words, far from contributing to the "corruption" of games, cheats are part of the definition of game genres. This holds especially true for highly formalized genres such as the first-person shooter, in which a game can be regarded as incomplete if it does not feature a certain set of generic cheats such as those for invulnerability or teleportation. As game producer Gordon Walton points out in regard to *The Sims Online*: "If you leave a cheat long enough, it becomes part of the culture of the game" (quoted in Wayner).

But how does this classification of cheats pertain to the way in which they change the player's perception of the game? And how can we make this classification independent of the rather crude genre distinction it is based on? In order to answer these questions we should review the kind of cheats that are characteristic of individual game genres. There are, according to my brief overview, basically three kinds of cheats:

(1) cheats that speed up narrative progression,
(2) cheats that increase the player's frequency of interaction, and
(3) cheats that enhance the range of the player's options.

As Fuller and Jenkins, as well as Lev Manovich point out, narration becomes "spatialized" in adventure games, that is, narrative progression is mapped onto the three-dimensional space of the game world. From this point of view, speeding up narrative progression can be regarded as an implosion, compression, or condensation of space. Therefore, the first type of cheats can be understood as effecting a change in the way players perceive game space, while the second type of cheats changes the players' perception of game time. Indeed, the continuous interaction (without the avatar's intermittent death and rebirth) made possible by the "god mode" of many first-person shooters is bound to change the perception of time radically — from striated time to smooth time, to borrow a spatial metaphor.

Since time is such a crucial factor in most action games, the cheats found in this genre are essentially time-savers: inventory cheats in first-person shooters can be regarded as shortcuts from the player's current position to the desired object (weapons, ammunition, power-ups, etc.), which effectively limit the time spent gathering these objects to an absolute minimum. Cheats that unlock the different areas in which the game's action takes place have a similar effect of reducing the time that would otherwise be spent playing toward this goal.

The third kind of cheats is of an entirely different order. Cheats that increase the range of options available can be said to change players' perceptions of the relation between subject and object, or, in less dramatic terms, their feeling of agency. As Donald Winnicott has pointed out, children learn to differentiate between their selves and the outside world through transitional objects such as toys. In digital games, players have the unique opportunity to reset the parameters of that rather stable sense of agency that has been developed by the end of childhood, and cheats that allow them to change the level of openness enhance these possibilities of experimentation even further. It should not come as a surprise, then, that it is the genre of "god games" in which these kinds of cheats are most commonly found.

In theory, it should be possible to further differentiate the cheats in each category by creating subcategories such as depth, perspective, and resolution in the category of space; frequency, order, and duration in the category of time; and levels of agency ranging from the fulfillment of everyday tasks to the working of miracles. But this is a task for future inquiries, and the descriptive typology developed so far should supply a solid basis for the following theoretical approaches to the subject of cheats.

Theoretical Approaches to Cheats

So far, computer game theorists have by and large shunned the subject of cheats, possibly because of its rather elusive nature. If the phenomenon of cheats is mentioned at all, it is usually treated as a trivial aspect of games that requires no further inquiry. Fuller and Jenkins's treatment of the matter is a typical example:

> A related feature of the games are warp zones — secret passages that, like De Certeau's bridges, accelerate one's movement through the narrative geography and bring two or more worlds together. Knowledge about warp zones, passwords, and other game secrets are key items of social exchange between game players. More to the point, they have become important aspects of the economic exchange between game companies and players [67].

Although the authors' focus is different than mine, the economic aspect seems tantamount to the fact that cheats warp the space of games, considering the fact that Fuller and Jenkins describe games as a form of spatial narrative, or travelogue.

But Fuller and Jenkins must be given credit for broaching the subject of cheats at all. The widespread negligence of this phenomenon seems to indicate a wariness of the subversive potential of cheats, which might, after all, destabilize carefully balanced theories. If, for example, one regards digital games as ergodic texts, as many theorists do, it becomes immediately obvious that cheats offer a convenient way of decreasing the effort it takes to traverse the text, thus diminishing their ergodicity.

Clearly, the problem of cheats cannot be addressed by using theoretical models that emphasize the aesthetic autonomy of games; instead, a theoretical approach to cheating must take the context of games into account. Games should be regarded not only as *texts* in which cheats can be used to skip certain passages, but also as *media* that foster new forms of symbolic interaction between individuals, and as cybernetic *systems*, in which cheating performs a sort of "reentry" of the environment into the system itself. In the following sections on single-player games, multi-player games, and MMORPGs, I employ, respectively, concepts from literary studies, media studies, and systems theory, which should allow for new insights into this largely neglected part of gaming culture.

Single-player Games

The first context I want to focus on is the single-player adventure game. This setting can be regarded as a "controlled environment," as it were, in which cheats can be observed without addressing the problem of destructive potential. Furthermore, adventure games are in many ways similar to literary texts, and they can be studied with the tools of textual analysis. While literary studies' claim to the field of computer games is debatable in many cases, this is one area in which the advantages of such an approach clearly outweigh the danger of "theoretical imperialism." Thus, the way in which cheats distort the narrative space of a game can be likened to similar strategies in literature. The section following this one will focus on fathoming the extent to which these findings can be integrated into the larger context of multi-player games.

While the generic adventure game seems to have expired at some point in the early 1990s, games such as *Ico* still bear a structural resemblance to this genre. In *Ico*, players still engage in the same activities as they did in *Zork* — gathering items, fighting against adversaries, and exploring a mazelike environment. As *Ico* is a highly linear game with some minor action elements, the number of cheats from the second and third category is rather small. Most of the "cheats" published fall in the category of "Easter eggs" rather than being actual cheats. But if players get stuck in the game and cannot figure how to solve a puzzle, they can seek advice from one of the many "walkthroughs" available on websites such as gamefaqs.com.

In many cases, these documents will supply players with detailed instructions on how to solve the puzzle in question. Therefore, consulting a "strategy guide" is usually the last resort for players. In an article on adventurecollective.com, Jeremiah Kauffman describes this predicament as follows:

> I am sure you have all experienced the feeling of being stuck. Not only can you not figure out the solution and move on, but the illusion forms that there is no solution, which is, of course, a ludicrous thought, but when you have spent hours wandering around and trying items on randomly it begins to seem reasonable.

This description of "being stuck"—another spatial metaphor—draws attention to the fact that it is perceived as a constriction of narrative space, which can be overcome only by referring to a "hint book" or a similar document.

In adventure games, the players' pleasure derives from a careful balance between the puzzles they are confronted with and the resources the game supplies them with in order to solve these puzzles. In some cases, there are one or several alternative solutions to that which looks, from the players' perspective, like the most obvious way to overcome the narrative obstacle, and this might make it easier for them to find a solution. In any case, the players' pleasure depends on their having the sense that there *is* a solution. If it can be found at first try, this is usually experienced as anticlimactic, but if it cannot be found at all, this quickly becomes a source of frustration. Therefore, the "pleasure of the game," which is lost through a puzzle that is too hard, can be regained only by taking recourse to resources outside of the game.

How can we analyze this mode of reading that simply skips over some of the narrative obstacles in the reader's way? In reference to hypertext, Espen Aarseth speaks of "topological constraints laid down by the author" (78) that limit the reader's freedom to read in a "tmesic" manner. In other words, hypertexts guide the reading process by allowing the reader access to some of its parts, while others remain inaccessible until certain criteria have been met. Aarseth's allusion to Roland Barthes's concept of *tmesis*, "the reader's unconstrained skipping and skimming of passages" (ibid.), seems to offer a convenient model to approach the phenomenon of cheating theoretically, were it not for the fact that *tmesis* in literary texts does not require the reader to leave the fictional world of the text. Therefore, the use of the term should remain limited to the area of literature.

Nevertheless, it makes sense to consider cheats in terms of means that can be used to overcome the topological constraints of the game. After all, the pleasure of any game depends on a balance between its rules and the freedom these rules leave the player for unconstrained interaction. From the player's perspective, playing can be regarded as a dynamic process that oscillates between a maximum and a minimum level of constraint. Once the game process goes beyond either one of these thresholds, it deteriorates into a state of overcodification or a state of contingency, both of which leave the player at a loss for what to do. "Being stuck" in an adventure game can be regarded as an instance of overcodification, since there are more conditions for narrative progression than the player is able to meet. Cheats can solve this dilemma by decreasing the perceived level of constraint in the game, thus setting the playing process in motion again.

Multi-player Games

Textual analysis might seem well suited for single-player adventure games, but it cannot be applied in the analysis of multi-player games. As I indicated above, multi-player games must be regarded as media that foster new forms of interaction between players. As Jacques Ehrmann points out, "any theory of communication (or of information) implies a theory of play ... and a game theory. And vice versa" (56). This statement involves several relevant points in reference to our subject. First of all, this means that we can regard games, especially multi-player games, as media that enable the players to communicate in a certain manner. Furthermore, Ehrmann seems to imply that communication is an inherently playful activity, that is, a process whose rules themselves are subject to playful interaction.

The kind of communication that takes place within the medium of the game is therefore a form of meta-communication about the process of playing. This is also recognized as a fundamental quality of play in Gregory Bateson's article "A Theory of Play and Fantasy," in which he relates his observations of playing monkeys in a zoo: "I saw two monkeys *playing*, i.e., engaged in an interactive sequence of which the unit actions or signals were similar to but not the same as those of combat. It was evident, even to the human observer, that the sequence as a whole was not combat, and evident to the human observer that to the participant monkeys this was 'not combat'" (315). From this, Bateson concludes that "play [...] could only occur if the participant organisms were capable of some degree of meta-communication, i.e., of exchanging signals which would carry the message 'this is play'" (ibid.).

Quite obviously, humans are capable of a greater degree of meta-communication than monkeys. While the monkey's game still depends on the rules of combat, games between humans can be defined entirely by abstract rules, or the rules themselves can become the subject of play. This practice of playing *with* the rules, rather than *by* the rules is as widespread and multifaceted as the practice of playing itself, and ranges from changing individual rules of a game to changing the whole rule-set, or changing the rules that apply to each individual player: "Breaking the rules seems to be part of playing games" (Salen and Zimmerman 268). The common denominator of these practices is their social nature: a change in the rules needs to be agreed to by all the players involved. In contrast, cheating can be regarded as an attempt to make one player exempt from the rules agreed upon by the other players, thus creating an individual rule-set for the cheater.

This seems to apply to computer games as well. "In playing a computer or video game players must decide what constitutes proper game behavior, navigating the space of possible rule violations" (Salen and Zimmerman 281). While computer gaming is every bit as much a social phenomenon as board or card games are, the conditions under which these activities take place can differ widely. Multi-player games played on a console or over a LAN can be compared rather well to traditional games, because attempts at cheating can be easily detected and appropriate steps taken. On the Internet, however, players often don't know each other personally, and cheaters are protected by the anonymity of the game space. Salen and Zimmerman point out that face-to-face interaction is important because "[a] game is a sort of social contract. The presence of the other players is important to maintaining the authority of the magic circle, because if a group of players are all obeying the rules, they implicitly police and enforce proper play" (269).

To differentiate the various forms of cheats found in multi-player games, it makes sense to introduce the distinction between cheats and so-called exploits often found in the popular discourse about games. Exploits are usually defined as bugs or loopholes in the game design that players can use to their advantage. Wright et al. describe one such exploit in the game *Counterstrike* that allows "dead" team members to communicate with the living: "[A] fellow CT [counter-terrorist] member who is 'dead' [...] uses the vote command to place the following vote, 'vote Tom Tunnel.' The server issues an automatic response, 'Sorry, DeadEar, Tom Tunnel was not found on this server'" (9). In this example, "Tom Tunnel" is a coded message by which a remaining team member is advised about the way to approach the adversary team.

It is often difficult to distinguish between cheating and playing very well, as players who have undeservedly been accused of cheating can testify. In her discussion of "power gamers," TL Taylor writes:

> Power gamers often push systems to their limit by trying to "break" them or find points at which the game architecture is internally contradictory or malleable. In many ways it is these kinds of behaviors that get seen by the broader game community (and quite often by the administrators) as looking far too similar to cheating. But power gamers generally see these kinds of explorations into the dynamics

of the game as simply smart moves — that only by understanding the constraints of the system will you be able to most effectively play. How do mobs [monsters] path through a zone and what is the most efficient route to take when fighting them? [...] As power gamers work and rework these questions their knowledge of the game can almost at times appear *too* good. They seem to understand how things work at a level the average player does not quite grasp. Given the gap in understanding how power gamers actually play this kind of knowledge sometimes gets labeled negatively, as cheating or trying to exploit the system [304].

These practices are within the bounds of the game's rules, but it might well be construed as cheating, especially by the players against which this tactic is used. Nevertheless, Wright et al. subsume the behavior described above under the heading of "creative player actions" along with game features such as game talk, map creation, and "sprays." In this respect, exploits can be compared to "emergent gameplay," that is, a way to interact with the game world unforeseen by the designers. Quoting Harvey Smith, Salen and Zimmerman describe the famous example of proximity-mine climbing in *Deus Ex*:

[T]he proximity mine is an explosive device that can be "stuck" onto walls in the game space. After the game's release, players realized something that the game's developers did not anticipate. Exploiting the game's physics and interactivity, players learned to climb up on proximity mines, and using (or misusing) a series of these objects like a ladder, they could ascend the game's vertical surfaces, ruining many of the carefully designed levels [280].

While this comparison is clearly justified in respect to the comparatively harmless example given above, the distinction between creative and abusive is blurred as soon as one takes into account more severe exploits such as those that make use of time lag in the player's connection to the server. In his article "How to Hurt the Hackers," Matt Pritchard describes the effect of extreme lag in games such as *Age of Empires*:

When this happened, the game engines stopped advancing to the next game turn while they waited for communications to resume. [...] While the game was in this state, a player could issue a command to cancel construction of a building, returning its resources to the player's inventory — only the player would issue the command over and over as many times as possible. [...] The result was the command executed multiple times during one game update.

The difference between these examples cannot be determined in reference to the rules of the respective games, since they are all actions that require no active manipulation of the game's rules on the part of the player. It is to be found rather in the social dimension of these games, that is, in the way in which these exploits change the interaction between the players. If single-player adventure games can be said to create a narrative space for the player to explore, multi-player games create an ad hoc social space which is constituted as much by the player's consensus as by the game architecture. Whether a player is perceived as a "power gamer" or a cheater is therefore more often decided by the context than by objective criteria.

This is necessarily a process of inclusion and exclusion, and one of the means to achieve this delimitation of a social space is to use specialized rule-sets. As in every form of symbolic interaction, these rules often stem from an aberration that has been taken over by other interactors over time, and which is thus conventionalized. It might seem a sign of deterioration if *Diablo* players have to take recourse to cheating in order to survive in the game world (cf. Kuo), but, from a cultural point of view, it can be considered an indicator of evolution, albeit not the sort of evolution intended by the manufacturers of the game.

Within gaming cultures, wallhacks, aimbots, and other "illegal" manipulations are defining cultural activities that are as much a part of the culture of a particular game as clans or mods. While some of these activities are welcomed by publishers for their potential economic value (one of the most prominent examples being the phenomenal success of the *Half-Life* mod *Counterstrike*), others are frowned upon by the industry due to the disruption they create for mainstream players. This schizophrenic attitude toward the uncontrollable creativity of the player community indicates that the social space created by games is far from uncontested territory. In fact, the vehemence of the industry's anticheating measures is a very real manifestation of a less author-centric cultural paradigm that has begun to replace the traditional model of media production, distribution, and reception.

Sue Morris foregrounds this aspect of cheating in her article on multiplayer games as co-creative media:

> Issues of cheating are mostly played out at the community level. While developers try to make games as cheat-proof as possible, the innovative and creative ethos of the community means that game hackers are always looking for new challenges, and players have developed cheat programs that, for example, automate aiming and firing of weapons, make walls invisible, or extend player models, so they can be seen from any location in the game. The development of cheats is done much in the same spirit of other hacking and cracking activities — for the challenge and the kudos. Anti-cheating programs are developed in the same way, leading to an ongoing battle of wits at a code-writing level. Major anti-cheating inventions such as PunkBuster have been developed by amateur programmers in the game community, and later incorporated into official game updates [e.g., in Quake III: Arena 1.32].

From an aesthetic point of view, this is an interesting development, since it seems to constitute an excess of games' inherent possibilities, a playfulness on the part of the players that goes beyond the game itself and transforms an object of consumption into a creative medium. This is not to say that all cheaters are artists, but the sum total of the creative energy that they invest into a game is bound to change its public perception, thus endowing the game with a "social aesthetic," that is to say, an aesthetic that depends on the participation of a large number of recipients to achieve its effect. While this effect is not necessarily the effect intended by the "authors" of the game, it is an effect to be reckoned with if one takes into account gaming cultures' history of using games against their original purpose, from cross-dressing in *Quake* to Jodi.org's "deconstructivist" mod of *Castle Wolfenstein*.

Massively Multi-Player Online Role-Playing Games

This social aesthetic is probably most pronounced in massively multiplayer online role-playing games (MMORPGs), such as *Ultima Online*. It is also here that the problem of cheating is felt most acutely, by players and providers alike. While cheating in single-player games might create an internal conflict for the individual player, and cheating in multi-player games is likely to create tensions within the players' social dynamic, the implications of cheating in MMORPGs are far more widely felt. This large potential for disruption exists because online role-playing games strive to create a persistent world that is influenced and shaped by all its inhabitants.

The showcase example of the damage cheaters can do to an online role-playing game is Blizzard's *Diablo*. Released in 1997, it predates persistent-world games such as *Everquest* and *Asheron's Call*, and for this reason its developers were unprepared for the invasion of cheaters that followed its release. In a *Games Domain* interview with a Blizzard spokesperson the company admits to having been surprised at the level of cheating in *Diablo* and to being "outnumbered" by cheaters (Greenhill 1997). What happened then is described by Andy Kuo in his article "A (Very) Brief History of Cheating":

> Then the cheaters came. As a social construct, despite being virtual, the online world of *Diablo* was just as susceptible to cheaters as the real world. Imagine yourself as a player, having spent countless hours laboriously developing your character to a very high level, possessing powerful equipment. Then one day, you encounter a ridiculously high level character, possessing unimaginably powerful equipment, asking questions like "How do I attack a monster?" Such obviously new players had found ways of illegitimately altering their characters. Using a technique called "duping," they could duplicate any item they owned, or even fabricate them out of thin air.

In *Diablo*, the nightmare of any capitalist society came true: the means of production (in the form of "compilers, dissemblers, debuggers and utilities" [Pritchard]) were handed over to the masses, and the masses used them recklessly, thus destabilizing the carefully balanced economy of the game world. In economic terms, there is hardly a difference between a character's possessions and his or her stats, so the cheaters' ability to "raise their character's statistics to impossibly high numbers" has the same result: a good whose value is dependent on its scarcity is thrown on the "market" in vast amounts, which results in a sort of deflation of the game's economy: "[W]hatever the reason, it's indisputable that every item or weapon created from thin air, will lend a hand to completely depreciating the value of it" (Greenhill).

It should be noted at this point that the "damage" done by cheaters is mainly in the domain of the illusions other players might harbor about the game world. While it is certainly painful to see a character that has been developed over the course of several months destroyed by a "ridiculously high level character" created, as it were, out of thin air, there is no actual physical or emotional damage. After all, the possibility of the character's "death" is always a distinct possibility in games — whether it is Parcheesi or *Diablo*. It could even be argued that such a form of cheating engenders a critique of other modes of playing (e.g., power gaming) that try to transfer the work ethic of the real world into the game.

Other cheats, most notably the infamous "townkill" and "autokill" commands, damaged the social fabric of *Diablo* rather than its economic model. In the original game, it was not possible to kill another player within an urban space, so new and inexperienced players could take refuge there. Once the "townkill" cheat was introduced to the game, new players were slain with such frequency that their only choice was to resort to cheating as well. This rationale is used even in the "advertising" of *Diablo* cheats: "Tired of getting town-killed? Punish the curs before they get you. Tired of players you can't kill? Become godly yourself (hey Jesus did it).... Bottom line, if cheating on Battle.net has ruined the game for you, then ruin it for some other poor non-llama!!!" (quoted in Kuo).

Player-killing should not be condemned outright. As Elizabeth Reid points out in regard to multiuser dungeons (MUDs):

> On some adventure MUDs users' characters are able to kill one another. [...] For some users, the possibility of player killing adds depth and spice to the virtual world. The addition of greater threat and greater danger to the virtual universe enables users to identify more strongly with their virtual persona. The thrill which users describe as a part of such battles, the sheer excitement of adding an unprogrammed human element to the game universe, makes that universe all the more real. Death and danger make the imagined life all the more worth living, and lift the game beyond the confines of the predictable. It is a fear of losing control inherent in a game style that stresses a fight for greater control that makes the game emotionally compelling [123].

MMORPGs are perhaps best regarded as complex cybernetic systems, in which a change in one of its constituent parts affects all other parts to some degree. The economical model of the game world and different social systems (such as classes, guilds, etc.) can be seen as subsystems of the game system, which is, of course, a sub system of the real-world social system that encompasses us all. Borrowing a term from systems theory, cheating is a form of "reentry," a figure that reintroduces into the system the basic distinction by which the system is differentiated from its environment. In the case of games, this distinction is marked by the difference between playing *by* the rules and playing *with* the rules.

In real life, we are constantly required to adjust the rules of social interaction with others, depending on various contexts, which causes a rather high level of contingency in nonstandard interactions. In contrast, games set up a frame for rule-based interaction that leaves not much room for contingency, thus constituting a "safe" social space: "[T]here is a special kind of lucidity and intelligibility about games. 'Real life' is full of ambiguities and partially known information [...] In ordinary life it is rare to inhabit a context with such a high degree of artificial clarity" (Salen and Zimmerman 123).

By reintroducing the possibility to play *with* the rules into the game, cheaters simultaneously reintroduce the contingency of real life, which explains the noncheating player's outrage at the cheaters. In the light of this conceptualization it seems rather ironic that in the above quote cheats are advertised as endowing players with "godly" powers. After all, a world ruled by willful gods is a very fitting metaphor for a contingent universe, a universe in which anything can happen at any time.

Cheats in MMORPGs fall into the category of cheats that influence the players' perception of their agency. While this type of cheat is associated with simulation games in the classification I have developed above, it can be employed in the analysis of online role-playing games as well, since they simulate a persistent world. Cheats shed a dubious light on the persistence of the game worlds, however. The hacking of the *Diablo Realms* servers in December 2000 is a case in point: although Blizzard was quick to assure players that the killed characters would be restored and the stolen items returned, the players' confidence in the persistence of online game worlds was shaken. Thus, one player's increase in agency is another player's loss of immersion. Cheats introduce a nagging doubt about the consistency of the game world the players inhabit, subjecting them, in effect, to the same doubts and fears they might experience offline.

Conclusion

In the real world, activities that prompt us to question the validity of our assumptions about the world we inhabit are often regarded as works of art. In game worlds, such activities are mostly regarded as vandalism, unless they are nondisruptive, such as Eddo Stern's *Summons to Surrender*, a collection of MMORPG characters programmed to perform the same action over and over. From an aesthetic point of view, it is hard to differentiate these "subversive" activities, since they differ only in the magnitude of their effect. While artistic projects in the real world are unlikely to unhinge economic systems or result in the loss of lives or possessions, these dangers are very "real" in virtual worlds.

While the loss of virtual items or characters might mean a real financial loss for the person owning them, now that these items sell for real money, the actual danger lies in the disillusionment of the players. Cheating in game worlds is a signal to the players that these worlds are not exempt from the rules of the real world. Rather, games are subject to the same power relations as the social systems we inhabit in everyday life. This does not necessarily make cheating a noble activity, but it serves as a reminder that the playing field extends far beyond the boundaries of these game worlds, and what is at stake is our perception of games as cultural objects.

In summary, we can say that cheats are deserving of more critical attention than they have received so far, as they contribute to our understanding of the perception of digital games. Cheating has its own pleasures and gratifications and will remain an integral part of gaming culture. Therefore, the study of cheats foregrounds the fact that games are embedded into a larger social and cultural context with undeniable links to the world we inhabit. The phenomenon of cheats is of special interest in multi-player role-playing games, as these are novel participatory media forms that are infused with cultural codes from the real world such as the flow of currency and commodities. Insofar as the characters themselves become a commodity in MMORPGs, cheats that address this commodification can be said to possess critical potential. Whether or not this critique is intentional is beside the point. As in the case of games themselves, authorial intention plays second fiddle to creative use of the objects created. If for nothing else, cheats deserve credit for making us aware of this "social aesthetic" of the games we play.

Notes

1. I would like to thank René Meyer (mogelpower.de) for supplying me with material about cheating techniques and Ren Reynolds for his valuable comments and setting up the cheaters mailing list.

2. A hexadecimal editor (also called a hex editor) is a software tool that enables the user to view and alter game files in a hexadecimal format. An example is the following cheat for *Command and Conquesr: Generals:* "Open 'INI.big' in the generals program folder. Using a Hex editor, find "InitialStartingCash." Normally you start with 10000 but you can change that to anything up to 99999." (codetycoon.com)

Works Cited

Aarseth, Espen. *Cybertext. Perspectives on Ergodic Literature.* Baltimore: The Johns Hopkins University Press, 1997.

Atkins, Barry. *More Than a Game. The Computer Game as Fictional Form.* Manchester, England: Manchester University Press, 2003.

Bateson, Gregory. "A Theory of Play and Fantasy." In *Play, Games and Sports in Cultural Contexts,* edited by Janet C. Harris and Roberta J. Park. Champaign, IL: Human Kinetics, 1983.

Ehrmann, Jacques. "*Homo Ludens* Revisited." In *Game, Play, Literature. Yale French Studies,* no. 41, edited by Jacques Ehrmann. New Haven, CT: Yale University, 1968.

Facer, Keri. "What's the Point of Using Computers? The Development of Young People's Computer Expertise in the Home." *New Media & Society* 3.2 (2001): 199–219.

Fuller, Mary, and Henry Jenkins. "Nintendo® and New World Travel Writing: A Dialogue." In *Cybersociety: Computer Mediated Communication and Community,* edited by Steven G. Jones. London: Sage Publications, 1995.

Greenhill, Richard. "Diablo, and Multiplayer Games' Future." *Games Domain* (May 1997). 1 February 2004. http://www.cs.auc.dk/~njo/Diablo.htm.

Grodal, Torben. "Filmfortælling og computerspil." In *Multimedier, Hypermedier, Interaktive Medier,* edited by Jens F. Jensen. Aalborg, Denmark: Aalborg Universitetsforlag, 1998.

Katz, Jon: "Up, Up, Down, Down." *Slashdot.org* (November 30, 2000). 1 February 2004. http://slashdot.org/features/00/11/27/1648231.shtml.

Kaufman, Jeremiah. "Cheating: For the Love of God, Don't Do It." *Adventure Collective* (September 17, 2000). 1 February 2004. http://www.adventurecollective.com/features/feature-cheating.htm.

Klevjer, Rune. "Computer Game Aesthetics and Media Studies." Paper presented at the 15th Nordic Conference on Media and Communication Research. Reykjavik, Iceland (11–13 August 2001). 1 February 2004. http://uib.no/people/smkrk/docs/klevjerpaper_2001.htm.

Kücklich, Julian. "Literary Theory and Computer Games." *Cosign 2001 Proceedings,* 51–58. Amsterdam: CWI, 2001.

Kuo, Andy. "A Very Brief History of Cheating." *How They Got Game Archive* (March 2001). 14 March 2007. http://shl.stanford.edu/Game_archive/StudentPapers/BySubject/A-I/C/Cheating/Kuo_Andy.pdf.

Manovich, Lev. *The Language of New Media.* Cambridge: Massachusetts Institute of Technology Press, 2001.

Morris, Sue: "Co-Creative Media: Online Multiplayer Computer Game Culture." *Scan* 1.1 (2004). 14 March 2007. http://scan.net.au/scan/journal/display_synopsis.php?j_id=1.

Pritchard, Matt. "How to Hurt the Hackers: The Scoop on Internet Cheating and How You Can Combat It." *Gamasutra* (July 24, 2000). 14 March 2007. http://www.gamasutra.com/features/20000724/pritchard_pfv.htm.

Reid, Elizabeth. "Hierarchy and Power: Social Control in Cyberspace." *Communities in Cyberspace,* edited by Marc A. Smith and Peter Kollock, 107–133. London: Routledge, 1999.

Salen, Katie, and Eric Zimmerman. *Rules of Play: Game Design Fundamentals.* Cambridge: Massachusetts Institute of Technology Press, 2003.

Taylor, T. L. "Power Gamers Just Want to Have Fun?: Instrumental Play in a MMOG." In *Level Up. Digital Games Research Conference,* edited by Marinka Copier and Joost Raessens, 300–311. Utrecht: Faculty of Arts, Utrecht University.

Wayner, Peter. "Do Cheaters Ever Prosper? Just Ask Them." *New York Times*, 27 March 2003.

Winnicott, Donald. *The Family and Individual Development*. London: Tavistock Publications, 1965.

Wright, Talmadge, Eric Boria, and Paul Breidenbach. "Creative Player Actions in FPS Online Video Games. Playing Counter-Strike." *Game Studies* 2.2, December 2002. 14 March 2007. http://www.gamestudies.org/0202/wright/.

Gameography

Age of Empires, Ensemble, Microsoft, 2003.
Asheron's Call, Turbine, Microsoft, 1999.
Civilization, Microprose, 1991.
Civilization II, Microprose, 1997.
Civilization: Call to Power, Activision, 1999.
Command and Conquer, Westwood Studios, Virgin Interactive, 1995.
Counterstrike, Valve, 2000.
Deux Ex, Ion Storm Inc., Eidos, 2000.
Diablo, Blizzard, 1997.
Everquest, Sony Online Entertainment, Verant Interactive, 1999.
Half-Life, Valve, Sierra, 1988.
Ico, Sony Computer Entertainment, 2001.
Quake III: Arena, id Software, Activision, 1999.
Sam and Max Hit the Road, LucasArts, 1993.
The Secret of Monkey Island, Lucasfilm, Softgold, 1990.
Sim City, Maxis, 1989.
The Sims Online, Maxis, Electronic Arts, 2002.
Space Invaders, Taito, 1978.
Tomb Raider, Core, Eidos 1996.
Ultima Online, Origin, Electronic Arts, 1997.
Zork, Infocom, 1980.

4

Movement and Kinaesthetic Responsiveness: A Neglected Pleasure

Melanie Swalwell

Setting the Scene

It was my first LAN. I was there to find out from players about their aesthetic experiences playing computer games. Initially, I had thought I would be able to talk with players away from all the noise and activity of the LAN. I realized quickly this wasn't going to happen. Everyone was busy, including the admins I had initially made contact with. Not really knowing anyone, I walked around looking over players' shoulders at the games they were playing. While I felt a bit out of place, I was aware that I had stumbled upon something important, an entirely different scene. After all, it's not everyday that you see more than 100 PCs networked in the same space. Beyond that, the fast and (to me) disorienting visual perspectives were also making an impression. I talked a bit with Martin, a self-described "hard core" gamer with whom I had exchanged a few e-mails. He introduced me to other players in his clan, before I left them to it. Then I met John and Matt, two gamers who were friends and seemed happy to talk with me *while* they played. I found a chair so I could sit with them and after a while, with their assent, started my tape recorder. I wasn't sure what I was going to record, as this was hardly an interview; instead, John and Matt took me through several of the games they played, including *Quake II*, a Shane Warne cricket simulator, a multi-player racing game with a luge track (whose title I missed), and *Thief,* among others.

At the start of *Grand Prix Legends*, John insisted I put his headphones on. Featuring classic vehicles from 1967, the sound of twelve Ferrari engines warming up (actually *screaming* is more accurate) on the grid was exhilarating and intensely visceral.[1] I thought that I was beginning to appreciate some of the aesthetic pleasures of gaming. Then the race began and I found my body starting to move involuntarily in response to the fuel-rich sounds of 'my' car's engine, anticipating and responding to its gear changes. This was a surprise to me; I hadn't *meant* to do anything.

Fast forward to 2004: I am at a LAN in Wellington, watching one of the admins delighting in the simplicity of the 2D Flash game, *N* (though referred to simply as "that jumpy-jumpy game"). *N*'s animated stick figure–like avatar must shimmy up walls and leap from point to point, collecting gold on ever more difficult levels. This admin's enthusiasm for the game was at least partly ironic — he was, after all, playing a single-player Flash game in the presence of several hundred thousand dollars worth of networking equipment and state-of-the-art gaming PCs — something that the other lanners teased him about. But while he may just have been playing *N* for a change, to relieve the monotony, watching him play I became aware of a tension in myself, a kind of holding-on feeling, willing the avatar to make the next (unlikely looking) leap — which it usually did — and an anticipation of this in my body.[2]

Sprite sheet from *N* showing the range of movements of the surprisingly agile ninja avatar (images from *N* by Metanet Software, used with permission).

Motivated by such experiences and inspired by the stories gamers have told me, in this chapter I ask why *N* and *Grand Prix Legends* elicited such bodily responses from me? I aim to think through some of the ways in which digital games *move* their players, across different materiality and reality statuses (Morse 200, 208). I do this through examining a suite of movement-related issues: from the initially disorienting perspective of the mobile camera, and the skill required to maneuver an avatar well within a game to the more puzzling moments of kinaesthetic responsiveness when players report themselves *moving with* an avatar. Considering gameplay as an aesthetic engagement with computing technology — where aesthetics is understood etymologically (*aesthesis, aisthitikos*) as referring to the sensory experience of perception — I set out to understand and unpack these diverse movement scenarios, situating them within longer arcs of writing on audience responsiveness to media.[3] In doing this, I refer to writing from a range of traditions, including scholarship theorizing human relations with technology and nonhuman others, play, embodiment and spectatorship of nongames moving image media, and digital game studies.

Since my initial surprise at my response to *Grand Prix Legends*, I have discovered that moving with a game is far from uncommon. Many gamers joke about it, for instance, recounting the way they lean when cornering in a driving simulation. Games researchers have also observed such kinaesthetic activity (e.g. Morris 86–87). A student of mine who is an avid gamer speculated that people's reactions to games had increased with their familiarity ("as more people have grown up used to using games"), but accounts of early game play suggest that players' visceral reactions are not just a by-product of greater realism. In the late 1980s, Umberto Eco's claim that "You don't play pinball with just your hands, you play it with the groin too" articulated the underlying (erotic?) dimension whereby the machine must be coaxed and at times physically cajoled into compliance by the player (222). Earlier still, Karen Van Rooyen-McLeay reported some dramatic instances of physical excitation during her fieldwork in Wellington's arcades:

> This player's actions clearly represented what I had seen so many times before. His hands furiously beat the buttons on the machine and his legs uncontrollably "danced" beneath him, as he attempted to come to grips with the excitement of the game [6].

Significantly, she observed this not only in players but also in onlookers: "occasionally, an onlooker would let out a wail, or his or her legs would twitch with excitement" (6). Grahame Weinbren has described kids "twisting and grinding as they manipulate the control pad of a video game" (405). Clearly, playing a digital game — or watching someone else play — is far from a static activity; yet, while these public displays and at home antics are accepted as the signs of intense embodied experience, players of PC-based games can seem more static and less affected, and are perhaps thought by some to be less responsive (I suspect partly because of their seated position combined with the computer still being primarily considered a productivity tool), and so, asensual. Conducting research with players, I have found that many have an intuitive understanding of the phenomenon. In this chapter I gather anecdotal accounts and observations, combining these with theoretical insights, in an attempt to unpack what player responsiveness reveals about digital game play and player subjectivity. I discuss several different types of movement in this chapter, but will begin with the way in which the mobile camera mobilizes the player. I use this to foreground the complex constellations of habit, mastery, and experiential novelty that are involved in learning to play a game.

The Mobile Gaze and Perceptual Adaptation

While pinball and early arcade games serve as a nice foil for contemporary 3D games, these early games clearly differ in important respects from the mobilizing potentials of the first person shooter, for instance. One of the specific ways in which games in this genre mobilize their players is through the use of the mobile camera; the resultant mobile (visual) perception is demanding because of its kineticism. When I watched gamers playing *Quake* at that first LAN, I found the fast paced twisting and turning through (what seemed to be) mazelike architecture extremely disconcerting. I was unaccustomed to having my vision guided by a mobile camera. It felt as if my body could not keep up with my vision. After watching it for a while, the twisting mobile perspective began to colonize my vision so that I would see it in places where it wasn't present (the carpet began to swirl).

Ross Harley discusses the history of mobile visuality in his video-essays and writings. While Harley's main concern is with "panoramic perception," he usefully introduces the principle of perceptual adaptation by referring to the work of Wolfgang Schivelbusch. In his classic text *The Railway Journey*, Schivelbusch discusses the way that during the course of the nineteenth century, train passengers' perceptual abilities underwent significant change:

> The train passenger of the later nineteenth century who sat reading his book ... had a thicker layer of ... skin than the earlier traveler, who could not even think about reading because the journey still was, for him, a space-time adventure that engaged his entire sensorium [165].

Harley suggests that the effect of many contemporary immersive entertainments on audiences is analogous to the nineteenth-century train passenger, with the effect being like that of "a 'perceptual vortex': it [is] as if the rider disappeared into an uncharted geographic space." His blending of insights from the history of technology with film represents a shift in focus from the moving image per se, to the ways in which viewers (or players) are moved. It also serves to underline the historicity of perception: the fact that human sensory and perceptual capabilities change; these are not "just natural," but learnt, enculturated, and affected by shifts in technology.[4] Like the early nineteenth-century train passenger, the contemporary newcomer to games must also grow a "thicker skin," developing and adjusting their perceptual abilities and responses so that they do not become lost or dizzy or disoriented by the fast-paced moving camera.

Harley's concern with mobile perception goes some way to understanding the feelings that movement through games space generates for nongamers (though it is important to note that this is something that most players report they quickly become accustomed to, with the architecture being all too predictable for some). Much of the time — particularly when he mentions disappearing into a vortex — I understand Harley to be referring to the mobile camera. It is the camera's mobility in an IMAX film, for instance, with its swoops and dives over the edges of cliffs, buildings, or the (slightly different) motion over waves that (may) bring on feelings of nausea. Alternatively, think of the use of "Vertigo" shots — looking down over the edge of a building as Scottie does in the opening scene of Hitchcock's eponymous classic (or as Bigelow's "Strange Days" does in homage), or the utterly sick-making shots from the top of the Empire State building in Peter Jackson's recent remake of *King Kong*,[5] or the first-person perspective used when a vehicle rolls and there is a desire to make the audience feel as if they are in it. The mobile camera is not used solely in this way, of course: think of *Russian Ark*, Sokurov's feature shot in the Hermitage Museum in one take, in which the mobile camera appears to float or levitate at times. In all of these examples, the camera's motion mobilizes the viewer's gaze to an extent, and may result in the viewer having sensations of movement in their body.

If panoramic perception refers to a sense of movement relative to one's surroundings as a subject travels through space, then game theorists need a set of similar concepts for describing movement through virtual game space. While games clearly present some different dimensions of movement to film, I am arguing that there are also some clear relations in terms of mobile visuality, which would benefit from further inquiry. Lev Manovich has noted that while there are many theories on the representation of space, a poetics of navigation through space has yet to be developed (259). Digital games are surely well positioned to contribute to such a poetics, but it is also true that there is a significant degree of interchange, borrowing, and repurposing of conventions

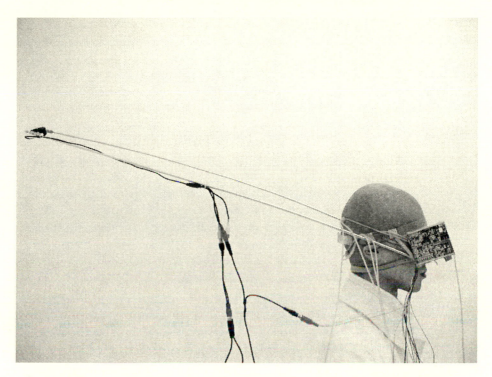

Takehito Etani and his "Third Eye" headgear, 2002 (image courtesy of the artist).

between different visual media (television, film, digital games, etc.), meaning that there are similarities in the movement through space experienced across different media. While I have focused only on first person perceptual conventions here (in film and games), I am heartened by work such as Takehito Etani's "Third Eye Project," a performance in which Etani borrows the third-person perspective of digital games and substitutes this for his own vision via an elaborately mounted camera, which sits above and behind his own head.

Skillful Maneuvers

In a first-person shooter like *Quake*, not only must one adapt to the camera's mobile perspective, but also the speed of game play and everything else that is happening at the same time. Lulls in the action are few and far between, and information comes from multiple sources at once: players must monitor their "health," weaponry, and ammunition statuses; keep track of where they are within the map; shoot other players, and dodge ammunition fired at them. Then there are options to set and scrolling commentary and weapons statuses to follow, and often at a LAN, conversations in addition to text chat, with teammates or other lanners, suggesting that a degree of poly-attentiveness must be developed. While my interrupting presence no doubt added to John and Matt's attentive requirements, my "method" of convers-ing with Matt and John while they were playing not only helped me to bet-ter understand what they were saying — their commentaries were extremely rich, and they could demonstrate any difficult to articulate points — it also allowed me to reflect with them on the process of adapting to the game's rhythms, speed, and requirements. Matt talked about the speed of the game, and the demanding nature of keeping pace with it all while doing the moves, saying (with characteristic understatement) "you don't really get much time in this ... when there's ten players on the level. Every corner you turn there's someone there waiting for you." He continued, "It's a long day because games like this are very taxing on your mind ... especially *Quake*: with that many people playing on one level, you're running on adrenalin all the time because there's people all around you and it comes down to reaction time." I remarked to John on the skill and requisite finger agility that seemed to be required. He provided a different (possibly more experienced) perspective, noting that "it takes you a couple of hours but once you get used to it, you think about doing something and it just happens." He was referring to the way that after a while the interface comes to feel natural, and that moving one's avatar ceases to require conscious thought. The finger movements become intuitive, as they do for a touch-typist who does not need to think consciously about where the keys are. Conscious directing of the body ceases, such that it might be difficult to explain how you actually executed a move, as the knowledge is not in your head. It is kinaesthetic knowledge. This is something that Mor-ris has remarked upon, comparing the way that "The skilled player's hand movements ... become unconscious to a degree [similar to] a trained dancer [who] performs a pirouette from 'muscle memory'" (87).

Just where this perceptual adaptation and acquired skill moves into the terrain of habituation remains an open question. A certain degree of fluency with the interface is required before it's possible to react without conscious effort. In the Frankfurt school tradition, such automaticity, formed from repetitive practice, has been viewed as alienating, impoverishing experience and deadening an ability to respond. While the same games do not seem to address players' bodies in such a direct way over time (a player might need to purchase another game in order to be affected in the way that they were by an old favorite), any simplistic equation of automaticity in game play with alienation is not convincing. Julian Stallabrass is one who has argued this, writing about the automatic reflexes computer gaming requires and drawing an analogy to the figure of the gambler in Walter Benjamin's writing (which recalls his work on shock and unskilled labor in the factory system), where gesture is reduced to reflex (1939: 173–75). The playing of computer games, for Stallabrass, is characterized by,

> Just this combination of automatic action and affective engagement.... Especially with arcade games, the computer produces in the player a simulacra of industrial work: the autonomy of each action, its repetition, precise timing and rare completion are all reminiscent of Benjamin's analysis of the gambler's actions.... As in work, the effect of this endless iteration is dulling [100].

What Stallabrass's analysis fails to address is the skill that maneuvering one's avatar in many games requires. This is a point that Weinbren has made, noting that the pleasures of connoisseurship and skill are largely ignored in the design of much interactive work, owing to software companies' concerns with immediate usability. By contrast, he notes, computer games represent a model of interactivity where "acquired expertise [is a] cardinal ingredient of the ... experience" (403).[6] Movement — and particularly moving well — emerged as one of the major pleasures of playing games for my informants. Movement was a theme that John and I returned to often in our conversation. He acknowledged that maneuvering his avatar well was a source of satisfaction for him: "I'm pretty disappointed sometimes, yeh, but it's just a game." Of *Grand Prix Legends* he admitted that "Just trying to get through the race without crashing..." was a significant challenge: "With this game, they say, it's really hard to take the corners in this game, [see,] the computer car just took off and you're supposed to be able to race like that, but ... [it's really hard]." Crucially, this skill distinguishes computer gaming from the game of chance that concerned Benjamin, in which each action is separate, not affected by the last. The gamer's devotion and the time they invest in learning a particular game results in certain personal satisfactions, suggesting that discounting players' pleasure and skill as necessarily just the result of alienation is not that helpful. Furthermore, the players I have spoken with have retained an ability to respond; that is what concerns me here; while their game play may provide a pleasurable distraction from other realities of their lives, their gestures are not merely reactions, reflex actions committed without any awareness.

Thus far, I have touched on several different figures and sources of movement in games: the disorientation of the mobile camera and the perceptual adaptation that this requires; the development of a degree of automaticity, so that players only need to think about moving their avatar and it happens; and the pleasure that players derive from maneuvering well, with a degree of elegance. These are underdiscussed aspects of movement in games that are helpful for understanding gamer's relations with digital games as contemporary technical media. I want now to return to the movement scenarios with which

I began: kinaesthetic responsiveness to sound and movement. How and why was I so "moved" as to begin involuntarily manifesting the appropriate movements in response to the engine sounds I heard in *Grand Prix Legends* when I wasn't even playing the game? And how to understand my internal holding and willing of the *N* avatar to make it up a wall and onto the next platform? While there has been little written on this subject, reviewing the work of film theorists Aaron Anderson and Anne Rutherford on audience responses to on-screen movement is helpful.

A Cinema of Embodied Affect

Addressing martial arts films, Anderson notes that current scholarship "usually understates bodily movement's effect on audience response," with many scholars denying the primacy of motion in action cinema. Given the lack of suitable concepts to describe movement from within film studies, Anderson turns to dance analysis, analyzing martial arts films in terms of metakinesis and muscular sympathy. He argues that certain martial arts throws — where bodies fly head over heels through the air in "high, graceful yet painful looking arc[s]" — function "as a kinaesthetic cinema of attractions," "inevitably evok[ing] in the viewer some form of physical, emotional sympathy or response" (1998: 1, 9). Anderson's description helps me to make sense of other moments of media spectatorship when I've felt some sympathy in my muscles: apart from viewing *N* and dance, I have absorbed flying lessons when watching Aussie rules football and the ski jumping (once more than 120 meters!), as well as empathizing with the birds winging their migratory way north in "Traveling Birds." Watching Olympics coverage of the horses in show jumping and dressage events, I feel something similar — and it's not just pity at how contrived their movements are; there is also the exhilaration of making it over the jumps. Fish and other marine life have also activated this feeling within me, both in mediated and immediate contexts. The footage of hundreds of jellyfish pulsing separately yet together in Dorothy Cuss's film *Come into the Garden Maude*— shot from below toward the surface — is irresistible to me. More immediately, underwater encounters constitute some of my most cherished memories. I grew up loving being beneath the water, where the look and feel of things and the light are so different to dry land. Snorkeling with my marine studies class one sunny spring day, it felt like I had gone off into a different dimension: the tails of scores of little fish caught the light as they darted and changed direction, with me in their midst. I was swimming *among* them, I was swimming *with* them, I *was* one of them, so agile and weightless did I feel in the water.

Theorizing what she terms a "cinema of embodied affect," Anne Rutherford argues for a move beyond film theory's traditional "concern with sensation or with emotion understood as sentiment organized along the axis of narrative identification, to an understanding of embodied affect, in its theorization of spectatorship." She pays particular attention to spectators' bodily responsiveness to movement in cinema, writing:

> ...in *Microcosmos* you may be down there in the mud with the copulating ladybirds — it doesn't mean that this is identification... — it may be red-and-black-spottedness, or jiggleness that attracts you, just as in watching an aquarium you may not have an anthropomorphic identification with a fish, but a recognition of floatingness or bubbleness — it may contact some place in your self that knows weightless suspension and set up a sympathetic vibration with it. Similarly you may find rollingness in the image of [a] giant wave, spinningness with a windmill, or bristliness with the spiny protuberances on a prickly pear (*2003*).[8]

Rutherford is spot on: I never wanted to be a fish or thought I was one, but loved swimming with them as if I were one. I will have cause to return to the animality of these examples below.

You Don't So Much See as Feel Yourself Being Moved

To these theoretical and anecdotal references to audience and player responsiveness discussed thus far, I want to add one more gaming story. Again referencing *Quake*, Martin told me about the way that, after a particularly long or intense session of playing, he used to have trouble getting to sleep, reliving scenes from the game, tossing and turning in bed, and even feeling like he was moving "robotically" in his sleep (my word, for what he demonstrated to me). That is, as he was lying asleep in bed, he would periodically become aware of the fact that his movements were *similar* to those of avatars in the game he had spent so long playing. Reflecting on this experience, he accounted for it intuitively in terms of the constant and demanding sensory engagement involved in playing; being so affected was understandable — if a bit funny — for him in terms of the particular kind of game that *Quake* is. Martin is not the only one to have experienced this type of response to digital games. Leon Hunt, for instance, writes: "After playing for a lengthy period, I sometimes find myself dreaming in 'PlayStation Vision'..." (201), and neuropsychological research conducted by Stickgold et al. reported on subjects who see the shapes of the game *Tetris* in their dreams after playing it (including some amnesiacs with brain injuries who can't remember playing the game). What particularly interests me is that Martin didn't report seeing the image, but feeling the movement, and feeling like he was making those movements.

What was going on here? I will use this case as my "jumping off" point for the rest of this chapter.

For some, the temptation to read Martin's dream as evidence of his identification with his avatar will be strong, so influential is the logic (and fear) of players imitating and reenacting virtual acts from games outside the game. Some at the Australian Office of Film and Literature Classification (the censor) would probably interpret Martin's story this way. In 2001, the office proposed "imitability" as a criterion for a revised set of guidelines for classifying digital games (21), thus perpetuating this common belief that to play at being an avatar in a digital game means that the player will take on and imitate aspects of an avatar's "character" and their behavior. It didn't make it into the guidelines thankfully, but the fact it was proposed shows how little understanding there still is about what it is to "enter" a game. As I have argued elsewhere, such assumptions render what are complex negotiations between the different materiality and reality statuses in a painfully simple fashion.[9] Furthermore, such assumptions are built on a conception of audience that is not only not well suited to participatory media, but also, in its conjuring of inescapable impact upon the gamer, repeats the failure of classic Frankfurt School analyses to appreciate that audiences are more than hapless, helpless, in need of (our) benevolent protection.

Rather than taking Martin's bodily responsiveness as evidence of players being *taken in by* the power of the technologized spectacle, it is, I argue, more useful to consider the way that one's senses can be *taken by* a game. To be "taken by" something: it is an archaic expression, but a useful one, I think. If sentience takes us outside ourselves, as Benjamin suggests, then this term can serve to describe the stirring of the senses, analogous to the experience of the art lover on whose experience he reflects in the following passage from "One Way Street":

> ... the paid reviewer, manipulating paintings in the dealer's exhibition room, knows more important if not better things about them than the art lover viewing them in the gallery window. The warmth of the subject is communicated to him, stirs sentient springs. What, in the end, makes advertisements so superior to criticism? Not what the moving red neon sign says — but the fiery pool reflecting it in the asphalt [89–90].

Taken by paintings viewed in the gallery window and a neon advertisement reflected in a wet footpath, the gazes of the art lover and philosopher respectively are drawn by the object of their perception.[10] In the act of looking, both become less cut off and self-contained; there is an element of surrender to the object by which they are taken, a dissolution of the boundaries of self. It is an example of the mimetic faculty at work.

Becoming Indistinct

"Mimetic activity includes thought, behavior, language and even unconscious processes such as telepathy" (Rabinbach, 64, n.16). According to Anson Rabinbach, for Benjamin the mimetic faculty was a "pre-rationalistic world" in which things are not fully closed off from the subject. An off-shoot of mimesis often forgotten in the priority accorded representation and verisimilitude in Western philosophy, the concept, which speaks to perception, spatiality, and interface, is very useful for understanding digitally mediated experiences such as game play. In addition to Benjamin's scattered writings, there exists a rich line of scholarship on mimeticism, from writers such as Roger Caillois, Eric Auerbach, Michael Taussig, Douglas Kahn, and Laura Marks. Unlike Platonic notions of mimesis, which tend to be concerned with the *faithfulness* of a likeness or copy, Benjamin's conception (on which I will focus) is premised on the notion of *similarity*. While he speculated on the possible mimetic foundations of astrology, graphology, and language (among other things), play was a privileged mode of access to the mimetic. Children's play and the way that children read or engage with picture books are accorded a special importance. In his early writing on the subject, he speculated that, in apprehending pictures, "The objects do not come to meet the picturing child from the pages of the book; instead, the gazing child enters into those pages, becoming suffused, like a cloud, with the riotous colors of the world of pictures" (1926: 435). The mimetic here is participatory: overcoming the illusory barrier of the book's surface, the child is drawn out of themselves in order to join in the play. The concept crops up not just in picture books, but also in children's theater, in which improvisation unleashes powerful energies, with the result that "New forces, new innervations appear — ones that the director had no inkling of while working on the project. He learns about them only in the course of this wild liberation of the child's imagination" (1929: 204–05). Of children's play generally, Benjamin claimed, "[It] is everywhere permeated by mimetic modes of behavior, and its realm is by no means limited to what one person can imitate in another. The child plays at being not only a shopkeeper or teacher but also a windmill and a train" (1933b: 160).

Benjamin recognized that mimetic forces and objects change over time ("The gift which we possess of seeing similarity is nothing but a weak rudiment of the formerly powerful compulsion to become similar and also to behave mimetically" [1933a: 69]) and that adults are more likely to have brought this "compulsion" under control than children. But as we can "unlearn" the mimetic, so, as Rutherford argues, can it be reschooled, stimulated, and awakened (2005). And, while the perception of similarity may sometimes become conscious, Benjamin argued that much of it must remain unconscious:

> ... the cases in which people consciously perceive similarities in everyday life are a minute segment of those countless cases unconsciously determined by similarity. The similarities which one perceives consciously, for instance in faces, are, when compared to the countless similarities perceived unconsciously or not at all, like the enormous underwater mass of an iceberg in comparison to the small tip which one sees projecting above the waves [1933a: 65].

Like the philosopher's gaze taken by a red neon reflection, and the child's projection into the picture book, Martin's hypnagogic dream state is, I argue, an instance of mimetic responsiveness. It is not about mimicry, at least not in an identificatory sense (in this case, it is not about identity, understood as the logic of the Same, but about difference). As a fully perceiving subject, he is *taken by* the avatar, partially projecting himself into the games space and responding to its movements, moving with it. Thinking of players' responsiveness to avatars as a form of mimeticism, it is useful to recall Benjamin's example: a child who plays at becoming a windmill or a train imitates these things by becoming similar *in some respect* (we assume gesturally), perhaps just moving their arms around like blades in the wind. Similarity is here a kinaesthetic similarity, not a psychic identification, nor a mistaking of the other or thing for the self. Benjamin's examples clearly show that imitation as a function of the mimetic faculty should not be confused with identification; nor is becoming similar limited to becoming similar to some*one* (as the windmill and car examples ably demonstrate). The child becoming like a windmill is not concerned with whether they *exactly* meet the specifications for the role they have envisaged for themselves. Rather, play is about approximating some aspects of a role or object; it is a *partial* becoming.

Becoming

Becomings are in-between states. Probyn compares becomings to the hyphen, to the trapeze artist at the moment when they are between rings, arguing that there is a precariousness to becoming (42–43). I think of Donna Haraway's cyborg, the boundary status of which is important to the political potential envisaged for the figure (1985). In a state of becoming robotic, Martin is in some sense in-between the familiarity of the body he knows and what it can do, including how he can move, and the body that he is in the process of becoming empathetically. Gamers are peripatetic subjects, in tension between where and what they have been and where they are going / what they are becoming. As a practice, gaming sustains a tension between different kinds of bodies, and the spaces through which these move. By bodies, I'm talking about material *and* virtual bodies *and* the negotiations between these different sorts of bodies. Such negotiations can produce new ways of being, new spatial negotiations, new orientations, different affects.

Thinking of gamers' responsiveness to avatars' movements in mimetic terms is consistent with the move counseled by Anderson and Rutherford, to consider the way that audiences are moved along a kinaesthetic "axis." James Newman seems to be heading in a similar direction when he argues that the notion of "character" is inappropriate for "the controlling player during game-play sequences." For him,

> the "character" is better considered as a suite of characteristics or equipment utilized and embodied by the controlling player. The primary-player-character relationship is one of vehicular embodiment. In suggesting this model, I seek to challenge the notion of identification and empathy in the primary-player-character relationship and, consequently, the privileging of the visual and of representation-oriented approaches.

Newman later quotes one of his player informants who offers "when I play *Tetris*, I am a tetraminoe," before arguing that this type of player-avatar relation "demands a totally new framework within which to understand the relationship between player and gameworld." This is a useful contribution, with the *Tetris* example showing, yet again, that a response to movement is not confined to the much lauded (and feared) graphical realism of 3D games (cf. also *N*). The idea that avatars provide not character for the player but rather "vehicular embodiment"—a set of capabilities that players embody in the game world—is a concept that scholars have found useful, and it seems compatible with my thinking about the potential for negotiating the differences between gamers' material and virtual bodies. In what follows, I want to continue thinking through the finer points and subjective significance of what must be a partial vehicular embodiment. My argument is one about difference, about what it is to imaginatively project oneself inside other bodies, to experiment with what it is possible to do, be, and think. Ultimately I am asking whether this might not be innervating of subjectivity.

I was reminded of Martin recently, sitting in front of the gas fire with my dog Bella while she was napping, several weeks after she had been hit by a car. One of her hind feet was bandaged from the accident, yet her front feet would periodically twitch, as if she was dreaming she was running, her usual mode of transport (her nose was also going madly). One of the most interesting things about Martin's dream for me is that—unlike Bella—he was dreaming of a way of moving, which is not how he ordinarily gets around: though it *is* how he moves within the virtual game world, it is not how he moves in the material world. Flying across a space with the aid of a grappling hook, for instance, or jumping off a high ledge are ways of moving (or for Newman, "capabilities" of the particular vehicular embodiment offered by an avatar) that are not possible in the material world. Games are often described as freeing because they offer possibilities to move and do things that are ordinarily impossible. Perhaps this is one of the reasons why the figure of the superhero crops up so often in relation to games: because impossible feats become possible. John linked the discrepancy between what the game would let you do and real life, to the idea of super heroic status, saying "This is something [I'd] see on TV when I was smaller, and I'd think great ... now I'm doing it." In his account of vehicular embodiment, Newman stresses that players choose an avatar based on their capabilities; by contrast, my concern is with the opportunities avatars provide for improvisation, for a kind of "experiential research into the relationship between the moving/sensing body and its environment" (Dantas, Davida, de Spain).

"No Imagination without Innervation"

In thinking about a mimetic responsiveness to a game avatar's movements and the significance of this, Miriam Hansen's excavation of Benjamin's work on aesthetics and technology is useful, and so I will briefly introduce this before returning to my main argument. In her article, "Benjamin and Cinema: Not a One Way Street," Hansen focuses on Benjamin's use of the term "innervation," which she says is his term for conceiving an alternate relation to technology, for reversing technology's failed reception. As she writes:

> If there is a key term in Benjamin's efforts to imagine an alternative conception of technology, it is the concept of innervation ... [which] refers, broadly, to a neurophysiological process that mediates between internal and external, psychic and motoric, human and mechanical registers [313].

To briefly outline her reading of this aspect of Benjamin's work, Hansen describes the intent of her essay as being "...to reactivate a trajectory ... between the alienation of the senses that preoccupied the later Benjamin and the possibility of undoing this alienation that he began to theorize as early as "One Way Street," particularly through the concept of innervation" (309). While her argument is complex, involving detailed readings ranging across much of Benjamin's oeuvre, Hansen argues convincingly that rather than understanding "innervation" as the supply of nerve force to organs and muscles (as in the discourse of physiology), or as simply a unidirectional conversion of psychic excitation into "*something somatic*" (as in Freud's early work on hysteria), Benjamin understood innervation as a *two-way* process, so that the opposite — "the possibility of reconverting, and recovering, split-off psychic energy through motoric stimulation" (317) — was also possible. Innervation, then, stands for the possibility of reinvigoration, for the reactivation of "the abilities of the body as a medium in the service of imagining new forms of subjectivity," as she so nicely puts it (321). Or, more concretely, Hansen writes "what seems important to me regarding Benjamin's concept of innervation and its implications for film theory is the notion of a physiologically 'contagious' or 'infectious' movement that would trigger emotional effects in the viewer" (318).

Innervation is linked to the mimetic faculty, with movement and the kinaesthetic sense having a significant role to play. Indeed, while other bodily aesthetic experiences might also conceivably innervate the psyche, the conversion of somatic, motoric stimulation into new forms of imagination is the primary example Benjamin considers. In line with this thinking, my argument is that the kinaesthetic responsiveness of players to digital games is consistent with a reawakened mimetic faculty, from which an innervation of subjectivity is possible. Being brought into close relation with avatars during the course of gameplay can foster a relation of intersubjectivity between player and avatar, rather than the oft-presumed distanced relation of mastery. Allowing oneself to be *taken by* an avatar's movements creates opportunities for improvisation (as one becomes similar to it). The player-avatar relation represents a (potentially destabilizing) encounter with otherness, which can open up new and imaginative subjective possibilities (as Hansen points out in relation to Benjamin's two-way concept of innervation). I would go so far as to say that gaming might even be a better example than those Hansen cites from Hong Kong cinema, though she would probably not agree (Hansen specifically excludes the possibility that computer games might in any way "allow for new forms of innervation," on the grounds that they "naturaliz[e] violence, destruction and oppression."[12])

So What If We Dream of Electric Sheep?

Avatars have entered our imaginings. While some might not like it, some of us *are* starting to experience ourselves moving in nonfluid, nonhuman ways, if not quite like machines (Schwartz 108). As theorists of technology, we are obliged to inquire into the significance of relations with these new "significant others" (Haraway 2003; Little). How exactly is becoming similar to an avatar's movements experimental? Avatars' "capabilities" (Newman) create opportunities for improvisation in kinaesthetic terms. Players can move in a variety of ways that are ordinarily impossible, because movements through games space are not subject to the same conventions, restrictions, or determinations as those that we normally inhabit. Territory can be explored and apprehended in a different way. Through the electronic intermediary of an avatar, players can make the most of the pleasure of orienting themselves in space, enjoying the kinæs-thetic pleasure of exploring a space neither hampered by convention nor weighed down by bags, able just to feel movement through that space. Bodily gestures are not restricted to learned or planned ways of moving, or even possible move-ments, for impossible acts are possible in this arena, feats that the laws of physics and mechanics do not permit. Moreover, avatars constitute a new and signifi-cant kind of other, one that happens to be nonhuman. Indeed, their provision of improvisational opportunities stems from their otherness. Donna Haraway's notion of an "unfamiliar unconscious" is suggestive for thinking through the significance of such *encounters* between players and avatars. She argues that because oedipal constructions have monopolized our awareness of relationality, it is important to develop accounts both of other types of relations with humans and of relations with nonhumans. The alliances that Haraway speaks of with nonhuman others — crossing both sentient and species barriers — are *unfamil-iar* in two important senses of the word, being both strange and nonfamilial, no longer speaking just to the family. She argues that "It is time to theorize an 'unfamiliar' unconscious, a different primal scene, where everything does not stem from the dramas of identity and reproduction" (2000: 123). Haraway's arguments about relationality and an unfamiliar unconscious build on her ear-lier cyborg work (particularly her insistence on the cyborg's partiality), recog-nizing that human relations are not the only ones that matter.

Conclusion

As a practice, digital gaming facilitates experimental encounters between players and avatars. I will flag two main points of significance. I have argued that mimetic interrelations with avatars offer gamers improvisational oppor-tunities. These are most immediately evident in terms of the movements that avatars can make in and through games space. It is particularly avatars' dif-ference from human players and already familiar human-machine movements that generate possibilities for player becomings. Where movements are already familiar, player might kinæsthetically *recognize* (Rutherford) these, but "kinaesthetic *responsiveness*" also takes in possibilities beyond the known (though it might be that one usually responds to that which is known, my argument also seeks to draw attention to responses to that which is unfamil-iar). This is a point of difference between Martin's becoming robotic and my becoming Grand Prix vehicle. Though (sadly) I don't usually get around in a vintage Porsche, I do know the sound and feeling of gear changes and the way that one is thrown around within a car by hard driving; these are all too familiar to me, having grown up with a father who liked to hot up engines and drive hard through the gears. While my physical response to the sound of *Grand Prix Legends* was a surprise, the game was not introducing me to anything new, any movements I didn't already know, whereas it would appear that Martin, through his early encounters with *Quake*, was being exposed to ways of moving that were not known to him, ways that were strange and different.[13]

Beyond experiencing oneself moving differently, player-avatar improvisations also offer players the chance to experiment with new, potentially interesting kinds of relations with unfamiliar avatar-others, as well as with technology itself, moving beyond overly familiar relations with technology, which so often revolve around humanist fears and desires. My preferred definition of humanism is voiced, appropriately enough, by a dog, in Kafka's "Investigations of a Dog":

> ... all that I cared for was the race of dogs, that and nothing else. For what is there actually except our own species? To whom else can one appeal in the wide and empty world? All knowledge, the totality of all questions and all answers, is contained in the dog [536].

A dog caring only for the race of dogs parodies the humanist subject enamored only with its own kind, fearful of technology (and difference) and armored fascistically against otherness (Foster). Rather than such a subject, what players' kinaesthetic responsiveness to avatars highlights is a more multidimensional conception of subjectivity, and a subject who is testing such boundaries and potentially reconceiving relations with self, others, things, space, and so on. Non-human others do not make the relation "dehumanizing"; distinctions must be drawn between barbaric dehumanization and that which is nonhuman because it exceeds or moves beyond the limits of a humanist worldview, or relations considered consistent with such a worldview (Benjamin 1933c). Such a subject, which moves beyond humanism's limitations, is posthumanist.

Notes

1. F1gamers.com write of this game: "With fast and unstable cars and perilous tracks devoid of safety measures, "Grand Prix Legends" offers the most extreme and realistic racing experience ever for the PC."

2. The description of *N* is as follows: "You are a ninja ... with an unquenchable thirst for gold, a natural propensity for exploring rooms infested by increasingly lethal ninja-killing robots, and a devout belief in N ... 'the way of the ninja' ... [which] emphasizes pacifism, humility, and the need to traverse a series of five rooms before the end of your lifetime; a feat known only as 'beating an episode'" (*N*, www.harveycartel.org/metanet)

The game artist Chad Chatterton, has since cited this game independently as one of his favorite examples of kinaesthetic responsiveness: "the movement sensations are really engrossing" (private communication).

3. It can be difficult to know exactly how to describe the sensory aspects of gaming. As sentient, embodied subjects, players' experience of playing a computer game is aesthetic; gaming involves what Marks terms "the complex perception of the body as a whole" (145). Gamers enjoy an almost constant sensory-aesthetic engagement with the computer. By this, I do not mean to suggest that the senses function as some kind of organic whole, but rather, to problematize any suggestion that gaming is simply an audio-visual activity. As Vivian Sobchack writes with regard to the cinema, "such received knowledge is reductive and does not accurately describe our actual sensory experience at the movies." In attempting to account for the distinctive kinæsthetic and proprioceptive sensations described, we might say (paraphrasing Marks again) that gamers "invest" all their senses in the act of gameplay; or, that they play not just with their hands, but with their entire body (cf. Eco, below).

4. Walter Benjamin provides another example of such adaptation, in writing of the perceptual challenges facing urban dwellers: "Whereas [Edgar Allan] Poe's passers-by cast glances in all directions which still appeared to be aimless, today's pedestrians are obliged to do so in order to keep abreast of traffic signals. Thus technology has subjected the human sensorium to a complex kind of training" (1939: 171).

5. These are essentially vertigo shots, both in the Hitchcockian sense as well as in Caillois' typology, where they correspond to "illynx," causing a disturbance of spatial perception.

6. Eleven years after Weinbren's call, the expertise of gamers is still frequently neglected. I was recently asked to comment on the Radio New Zealand consumer show "This Way Up" on a large Auckland event known as XLAN, a preparation round for the World Cyber Games, the "Olympics" of digital gaming. Despite conducting some interesting vox pop at the event, the journalist who had prepared the report couldn't help asking if these gamers weren't "freaks." "This Way Up," 22 July 2006, National Radio.

7. I believe "empathy" is the right term here, because of the projection that is involved. The *OED* definitions and examples all emphasize projection, with some pointing to the feeling involved as being a muscle, rather than an emotional, state.

8. In a more recent article, Rutherford argues for a spectatorial engagement that is simultaneously embodied, intellectual, emotional, and corporeal (2005). This combination of aesthetics, cognition and emotion reminds me of Cam Shea's comment, cited in the documentary "Just a Game": "With something like *Quake 3*, for me it's not about shooting people. It's about elegance and the skill of manipulating your player in the environment. It's about using the physics of the game engine to your advantage. And that's what I'm thinking about when I'm playing the game. I'm not thinking about killing people. I'm thinking about outwitting them."

9. Morse's approach to thinking about the overlaps and discontinuities between different materiality and reality statuses (with respect to Virtual Reality) is useful for thinking about the condition of being in between material and virtual spaces and bodies. As I have argued, these inform and punctuate each other. I also follow Morse and Haraway's emphasis on the partiality of the games cyborg; the material body and its demands do not go away. See Swalwell (2003) for a more extended discussion of these issues.

10. The neon advertisement, that phantasmagoric form par excellence, provides a sensory attraction that is not for Benjamin simply reducible to its attempt to entice the consumer to buy; like the artwork, it too provides aesthetic interest. Where other commentators are fixed by the phantasmagoria's potential to *take in* the unsuspecting passerby, "duping" them, this possibility is accompanied by a mediation on what it is that makes advertisements superior to criticism, in which their ability to captivate the senses

is an important factor. Benjamin does not dismiss phantasmagoric forms on the grounds that they are merely spectacular or manipulative, glittering with promise and failing to deliver on this; or that the phantasmagoria just covers over the "real" situation.

11. The integrating of rhythm, physical posture and mental processes in yoga is one example Benjamin gives of this.

12. Going into Hansen's argument in detail would take me too far from the focus of this chapter; briefly, it returns to reflect on the debate between Adorno and Benjamin on Disney characters and "the usability of the Disney method for fascism," implying a parallel between Disney and computer gaming (1993). I read more ambivalence in Benjamin's position than Hansen does here.

13. Leon Hunt raises an issue that is relevant here when he invokes Alison Landsberg's notion of "prosthetic memory" to explain how it is possible to "[know] kung fu" through media reception, rather than practice of the martial art. Prosthetic memory designates "memories which do not come from a person's lived experience" (200). Kung fu is perhaps a limit case in terms of the argument I have been making here. Depending on the production technique, a martial arts game might well feature maneuvers that have been performed by human bodies, albeit virtuosic and highly trained bodies, through the use of motion capture. The human or nonhuman status of such an avatar's movements becomes a more complex matter.

Works Cited

Anderson, Aaron. "Action in Motion: Kinesthesia in Martial Arts Films." *Jump Cut* 42 (1998): 1–11, 83.

_____. "Violent Dances in Martial Arts Films." *Jump Cut* 44 (2001). 14 March 2007. http://www.ejumpcut.org/archive/jc44.2001/aarona/aaron1.html

Benjamin, Walter. "One Way Street." Trans. Edmund Jephcott and Kingsley Shorter. *One Way Street and Other Writings*, 45–104. London: Verso, 1997 [1925–26].

_____. "A Glimpse into the World of Children's Books." Trans. Rodney Livingstone. In *Walter Benjamin: Selected Writings, 1913–1926*, vol. 1, edited by Marcus Bullock and Michael W. Jennings, 435–443. Cambridge, MA: Belknap; Harvard, 1996 [1926].

_____. "Program for a Proletarian Children's Theater." Trans. Rodney Livingstone. In *Walter Benjamin: Selected Writings, 1927–1934*, vol. 2, edited by Michael W. Jennings, Howard Eiland, and Gary Smith, 201–206. Cambridge, MA: Belknap; Harvard, 1999 [1929].

_____. "Doctrine of the Similar." Trans. Knur Tarnowsky. *New German Critique* 17 (1979 [1933a]): 65–69.

_____. "On the Mimetic Faculty." Trans. Edmund Jephcott, Kingsley Shorter. *One Way Street and Other Writings*, 160–163. London: Verso, 1997 (1933b).

_____. "Experience and Poverty." Trans. Rodney Livingstone. *Walter Benjamin: Selected Writings, 1927–1934*, vol. 2, edited by Michael W. Jennings, Howard Eiland and Gary Smith, 731–736. Cambridge, MA: Belknap; Harvard, 1999 [1933c].

_____. "On Some Motifs in Baudelaire." Trans. Harry Zohn. In *Illuminations*, edited by Hannah Arendt, 152–196. London: Fontana, 1992 [1939].

Caillois, Roger. "Mimicry and Legendary Psychasthenia." Trans. John Shepley. *October* 31 (1984 [1935]): 17–32.

Chatterton, Chad. Private communication with author. 28 November 2005.

Dantas M., D. Davida, and K. de Spain. "The Kinaesthetic Sense: Touching from the Inside." Paper given at "Uncommon Senses: The Senses in Art and Culture," Concordia University, Montreal (27–29 April 2000).

Eco, Umberto. *Foucault's Pendulum*. Trans. William Weaver. San Diego: Harcourt Brace Jovanovitch, 1989 [1988].

Etani, Takehito. "Third Eye Project." (2002). 9 August 2006. http://www.takehitoetani.com/3rdeye.html.

Flgamers.com "Grand Prix Legends." (n.d.) 4 July 2006. http://www.flgamers.com/fl/games/gameinfo.php?game=gpl.

Foster, Hal. "Postmodernism in Parallax." *October* 63 (1993): 3–20.

Hansen, Miriam. "Of Mice and Ducks: Benjamin and Adorno on Disney." *South Atlantic Quarterly* 92.1 (1993): 27–61.

Hansen, Miriam Bratu. "Benjamin and Cinema: Not a One way Street." *Critical Inquiry* 25.2 (1999): 306–343.

Haraway, Donna J. *The Companion Species Manifesto: Dogs, People, and Significant Otherness*. Chicago: Prickly Paradigm Press, 2003.

_____. "A Manifesto for Cyborgs: Science, Technology, and Socialist Feminism in the 1980s." In *Feminism/Postmodernism*, edited by Linda J. Nicholson, 190–233. New York: Routledge, 1990 [1985].

Haraway, Donna J., and Thyrza Nichols Goodeve. *How Like a Leaf*. New York: Routledge, 2000.

Harley, Ross. "Motion Landscapes: A Video-Essay on Panoramic Perception." Unpublished DCA thesis, University of Technology, Sydney, 1999.

Hunt, Leon. "'I Know Kung Fu!': The Martial Arts in the Age of Digital Reproduction." In *ScreenPlay: Cinema/Videogames/Interfaces*, edited by Geoff King and Tanya Krzywinska, 194–205. London: Wallflower, 2002.

Kafka, Franz. "Investigations of a Dog." Trans. Willa and Edwin Muir, 527–551. *Franz Kafka*, London: Secker & Warburg, 1976 [1931]).

Kahn, Douglas. *Noise, Water, Meat: A History of Sound in the Arts*. Cambridge: Massachusetts Institute of Technology Press, 1999.

Little, Gregory. "A Manifesto for Avatars." *Intertexts* 3.2 (1999): 192(21).

Manovich, Lev. *The Language of New Media*. Cambridge: Massachusetts Institute of Technology Press, 2001.

Marks, Laura U. *The Skin of the Film: Intercultural Cinema, Embodiment, and the Senses*. Durham, NC: Duke University Press, 2000.

Morris, Sue. "First Person Shooters — A Game Apparatus." *ScreenPlay: Cinema/Videogames/Interfaces*, edited by Geoff King and Tanya Krzywinska, 81–97. London: Wallflower, 2002.

Morse Margaret. "Nature *Morte*: Landscape and Narrative in Virtual Environments." In *Immersed in Technology: Art and Virtual Environments*, edited by Mary Anne Moser and Douglas MacLeod, 195–232. Cambridge: Massachusetts Institute of Technology Press, Banff Canter for the Arts, 1996.

Newman, James. "The Myth of the Ergodic Videogame: Some Thoughts on Player-Character Relationships in Videogames." *Game Studies* 2.1 (2002). 4 July 2006. http://www.gamestudies.org/0102/newman/.

Office of Film and Literature Classification. "Review of the Classification Guidelines for Films and Computer Games: Discussion Paper." Commonwealth of Australia, 2001.

Probyn, Elspeth. "Becoming-Horse: Transports in Desire." *Outside Belongings*, 37–62. New York: Routledge, 1996.

Rabinbach, Anson. "Introduction to Walter Benjamin's 'Doctrine of the Similar.'" *New German Critique* 17 (1979): 60–64.

Rutherford, Anne. "Cinema and Embodied Affect." *Senses of Cinema* 25 (2003). 4 July 2006. www.sensesofcinema.com.

_____. "Precarious Boundaries." *Senses of Cinema* 31 (2004). 4 July 2006. www.sensesofcin
ema.com.

Schivelbusch, Wolfgang. *The Railway Journey: The Industrialization of Time and Space in the 19th Century.* Berkeley: University of California Press, 1986.

Schwartz, Hillel. "Torque: The New Kinaesthetic of the 20th Century." In *Incorporations* 6, edited by S. Kwinter and J. Crary, 70–127. Cambridge: Zone; Massachusetts Institute of Technology Press, 1992.

Sobchack, Vivian. "What My Fingers Knew: The Cinesthetic Subject, or Vision in the Flesh." *Senses of Cinema* 5 (2000). 4 July 2006. www.sensesofcinema.com/contents/00/5/fingers.html.

Stallabrass, Julian. *Gargantua: Manufactured Mass Culture.* London: Verso, 1996.

Stickgold, Robert, et al. "Replaying the Game: Hypnagogic Images in Normals and Amnesics." *Science* 290 (2000): 350–353.

Swalwell, Melanie. "Multi-Player Computer Gaming: 'Better than Playing (PC Games) with Yourself.'" *Reconstruction: An Interdisciplinary Cultural Studies Community* 3.4 (2003). 4 July 2006. http://reconstruction.eserver.org/034/swalwell.htm.

Taussig, Michael. *Mimesis and Alterity: A Particular History of the Senses.* New York: Routledge, 1993.

Van Rooyen-McLeay, Karen. "Adolescent Video-Game Playing." Unpublished MA thesis, Victoria University of Wellington, 1985.

Weinbren, Grahame String. "Computer Games, Intuitive Interfaces, and Interactive Multimedia." *Leonardo* 28.5 (1995): 403–408.

Gameography

Grand Prix Legends, Sierra, 1998.
N, metanet software Inc., 2005.
Quake II, Activision, id software, 1997.
Shane Warne Cricket '99 (Lara 96), Audiogenic software, 1997.
Thief, Eidos Interactive, Looking Glass, 1998.

Filmography

Come Into the Garden Maude, Dorothy Cross, Public Art Development Trust, 2001.
Just a Game, CM Film Productions, Film Finance Corporation, Australia, 2003.
King Kong, Peter Jackson, director, 2005.
Microcosmos, Marie Pérennou and Claude Nuridsany, directors, 1996.
Russian Ark, Aleksandr Sokurov, director, 2002.
Strange Days, Kathryn Bigelow, director, 1995.
The Traveling Birds, Jacques Perrin and Jacques Cluzaud, directors, 2001.
Vertigo, Alfred Hitchcock, director, 1958.

5

"Participation TV": Videogame Archaeology and New Media Art

Jason Wilson

One of the foremost tasks of art has always been the creation of a demand which could be fully satisfied only later. The history of every art form shows critical epochs in which a certain art form aspires to effects which could be fully obtained only with a changed technical standard, that is to say, in a new art form.
—Walter Benjamin, *"The Work of Art in the Age of Mechanical Reproduction," 1936.*

Although the art of the future could take any one of a number of directions, it seems to me that, with the steady evolution of information processing techniques in our society, an increasing amount of thought will be given to the aesthetic relationship between ourselves and our computer environments — whether or not this relationship falls into the scope of the fine arts.... As our involvement with electronic technology increases ... the art experience may undergo a process of internalization where the constant two-way exchange of information becomes a normative goal. We should rightfully consider such a communication shift as an evolutionary step in aesthetic response.
—Jack Burnham, The Aesthetics of Intelligent Systems, *1970.*

The "archaeology" of videogame play and culture is emerging as a productive focus for scholarship. As videogame history moves beyond what Huhtamo calls its "chronicle era," more researchers are trying to "broaden the historical perspectives of digital games from the internal history of computing to the general cultural history of modernity and modern media technologies," to understand the "rules, practices, conditions and functions governing the actual instances of cultural events" (Suominen and Parikka). Huhtamo defines the project of videogame archaeology as "the cultural and historical mapping of electronic gaming. Its basic premise is at least seemingly simple: electronic games did not appear out of nowhere; they have a cultural background that needs to be excavated."

Rather than seeing video games as a self-contained cultural field with only an internal, technological history, videogame archaeology instead connects games with broader contexts and longer histories. Rather than offering linear accounts of the medium's development within the discourse of "upgrade culture" (Dovey and Kennedy), videogame archaeology tries to understand video games as enmeshed in wider cultural, economic, and technological changes.

There has already been significant and valuable work in this area, which has two main thrusts. On the one hand, there is research that places video games within the history of popular culture and popular amusements. Early on in the history of game studies, Fuller and Jenkins connect the "spatial stories" of platform games with popular travel writing. Darley ties video games and other "new media genres" with the history of fairground amusements and attractions. Huhtamo traces the connections between videogame play and the entire modern history of slot-machine amusements, showing that video games emerged into a preexisting matrix of venues, audience behaviors, and even censorious official discourses. And a range of authors — including Juul (2001, 2003) and Frasca — insist on the continuities between video games and pre-digital games. All of these archaeologies connecting games to other forms of popular culture allow comparative studies of video games by drawing out analogies between them and earlier or parallel forms of popular culture.

There is a second broad emphasis on the connections between videogame technologies and the "military-entertainment complex" or the history of human-computer interaction. Lowood and Lenoir show parallels between the emergence of the video games and military simulation industries, and they show too that personnel cross between video games and simulation industries. Crogan reflects on the epistemology and phenomenology of real-time strategy games, and he compares them with the board-based wargames that they superseded. Lowood focuses on connections between *Pong* and the history of computing. This tradition in videogame archaeology reminds its readers of the close links between video games and the technological changes that underwrite both the information economy and new forms of conflict.

This chapter aims to extend the range of videogame archaeology by considering the relationship between the earliest video games and an artistic and creative milieu that pertained throughout the West and beyond in the 1960s and 1970s. The direct comparisons that are made between video games and new media art may run counter to the sense, which can be detected in the work of many artists and theorists, that video games are a problematic, reactionary counterpoint to the critical work of new media artists. Charlotte Davies, designer of important works of virtual art such as *Osmose*, is representative of a tendency to rhetorically position games in opposition to new media art when she writes:

Commercial computer games approach interactivity as a means of empowering the human subject through violence and aggression. These conventional approaches to digital media reflect our culture's Cartesian world-view, with its tendency to reduce the world and its myriad of inhabitants to a "standing-reserve" for human consumption [quoted in Shinkle].

In writing this chapter, I hope to show that because of their deep, mutual involvement at their origins, there is no easy way to separate video games and new media art, and that drawing sharp binary distinctions between early games and new media art is less productive than seeing differences alongside important resemblances. Early games and new media art embody a series of shifting relationships with the technology and institutions of television, which in the 1960s and early 1970s — the focal period of this analysis — were bound in the model of mass broadcasting. This moves beyond Wolf's noting of the countercultural engagement of many early game designers in relation to the abstract visuality of early video games. Apart from the happenstance of "hippie programmers," I hope to show that the earliest examples of new media art and videogame design were produced from similar impulses, which drew on a series of related discourses in 1960s culture.

This chapter first discusses the early 1960s "TV works" of Nam June Paik. It shows how the works were simultaneously a critique of the nexus of television technology and the apparatus of broadcasting and an effort to create "real-time" works that were open to viewer participation. Second, there is a discussion of the context that informed Paik's interventions. Both the artist and these works lie at the crossroads of the Fluxus movement, early new media art, conceptual art, and what Burnham (1978), and later Drucker, calls "postobjective" art. Third, there is a tracing of the evolution of video games as a viable commercial medium over the course of the 1960s and early 1970s, which looks at Ralph Baer's efforts toward the Magnavox Odyssey, and Nolan Bushnell's attempts to market first *Computer Space* and then (successfully) *Pong* as coin-operated (coin-op) arcade technologies. Throughout the account of Baer and Bushnell's work, there are asides that compare it with Paik's and relate it to the context of "postobjective" practice. A concluding section makes the differences and important similarities between all these efforts to make "Participation TV" explicit. While this chapter at no stage suggests any explicit mutual influences, it shows that both early new media artists and early game designers articulated a desire to change broadcast television, created manipulable televisual images, and incorporated "playfulness" in their contributions in these areas.

Nam June Paik and Participation TV

Beginning with his first television exhibition at Rolf Jahrling's Galerie Parnass in Wuppertal-Elberfeld, Germany, in March 1963, Nam June Paik, who had been and was to be so involved in the reconfiguration of institutional art, made his attempt to change the relationship between television technology, images, and the viewer.

In *Zen for TV*, Paik redefined television as a technology of rapt attention, rather than a technology of distraction as it had hitherto, and has even hence, been seen.[1] The work consists of a single, vertical white strip on the blank, dark background of a television monitor, produced by distorting the television's monitor image with a magnet. It is a highly abstract, static image set within the television set, a technology that is here reconceived as the basis for a new kind of sculptural work, or as a new kind of frame for abstract pictorial works. Its visual simplicity is the way the work reveals its own importance, though. It announces that from this moment, as Cynthia Goodman puts it, "For Nam June Paik, television was not simply an iconic presence, but a malleable medium." *Zen for TV* reimagines television as an object for meditation, whose visual output was in this case given transcendent, religious connotations.

The means by which Paik produced *Zen for TV*'s image — a magnet on top of the set — revealed the televisual image as amenable to direct, local action, and defined the screen as a pictorial surface for the artist. In an allusion to the vertical "zips" which appeared in the work of mid-century abstract artist Barnett Newman, from *Onement I* forward, Paik not only playfully mocks the high seriousness of high Modernism, but also takes over some of Newman's purpose — the reorientation of the artwork toward the establishment of a closer relationship with the observer's body, and the relocation of the sublime in the products of human industry.[2]

From the same exhibition is a work that further sculpts the image produced by direct manipulation of the electronic image, *Magnet TV*. Like *Zen for TV*, *Magnet TV* was produced by means of magnetic interference with a television monitor image, however, this time the image produced was a more complex and aestheticized abstraction: a spiraling, greenish nest of vector lines. Though it is only accompanied by ambient sound, Tancin argues that with this work, Paik

> draws our attention to what had become a commonplace object by 1965: the television. By displacing the television set from the living room to the art gallery, Paik forces the public to separate the physical properties of the television from its content and to evaluate the object for what it is: image and sound.

Magnet TV removes television from its customary venue of reception (the home) and estranges it from its usual purpose (the reception of broadcasting).

As well as revealing television's bare audiovisual properties, *Magnet TV* underlines and extends *Zen for TV*'s discovery of television as a surface immanent to the artist's localized practice — and it shows that there are even greater possibilities for manipulating the television image. By contrast with *Zen for TV*'s depthless flat line, *Magnet TV* is far more complex and sculptural.

Perhaps the most striking of Paik's television works from this exhibition in 1963, particularly considered in relation to video games, is *Participation TV*. In this piece, a TV set's visual output is not fixed; by speaking, yelling, or singing into an attached microphone, the viewer is able to produce a variety of abstract shapes on the screen. The technical means for this new mode of image-making are a microphone and a sound frequency amplifier that transforms and feeds the signals directly to the television's cathode ray tube and its steering coils to produce scattergun kinetic images. Its importance lies not so much in these images themselves, however striking, but in the way Paik incorporates them in a playful, participatory "real-time" work. Television had long offered real-time or "live" images, and indeed most early television broadcasting was transmitted live rather than recorded (Barnouw, Jacobs).[3] Few if any visitors to Jahrling's gallery in 1963 would ever have been able to directly manipulate electronic televisual images. For all its innovations, *Participation TV* is a charmingly jury-rigged technology. It answers nicely to the description Lowood would later give to *Pong*: it represents "a modest investment in electronic components, a modified television set, and some ad hoc wiring and parts" (2). But the results are astounding.

Participation TV is permanently unfinished, and rather than a realized pictorial work, it is a playful structure that invites the viewer into certain kinds of physical intimacy with itself, into performing and laboring within it. It divides the gallery audience: there are still spectators separated from the work as subjects from an object, but one by one the visitors who step up to the microphone inhabit a new kind of productive spectatorship. This is a contrast with the various kinds of separation between spectator and object that had pertained in the experience of visual art, but resembles the bifurcated model of videogames spectatorship offered by Newman, in which "the pleasures of videogames are frequently enjoyed by those that commonsense might encourage us to consider as non-players — "onlookers" that exert no direct control via the game controls." Here, the technology of TV is not only defined as something open to local pictorial activity, but also as a space for the cooperative activity of audience and artist, the latter responsible for designing structures of playful interaction. Even though the images produced by Paik's work are of interest, the questions we ask ourselves about them have less to do with the use of color, line, and composition within the space of the frame, less the kinds of questions we ask of a work that is separated from us as object from subject, and more to do with the elegance of the relationship the artist proposes between our bodies and pictorial space, the kinds of actions we can take within this structure, and the quality of our pleasures of co-creation.

Paik put his innovations, and the immersion in the techniques of electrical engineering that led to them, down to his discovery that television "was made of electrons and protons. It made sense to me that I might as well use protons and electrons directly." He looked forward to "the day when the collaboration of the artist and engineer will progress into the unification of the artist and engineer into one person," since the artist's getting things made to order missed the possibility for "precious errors," and "I have found that the by-product is often more valuable than the envisioned aim" (Kearns). This idea of the union of artist and engineer foreshadows Grau's conception of the "media artist" who represents "a new kind of artist, who not only sounds out the aesthetic potential of advanced methods of creating images ... but also specifically researches innovative forms of interaction and interface design" (3), and Popper's "virtual artist" who differs from traditional artists in pursuing "techno-aesthetic creative commitments" (1).

In 1965, talking about the tendencies in his work of the early 1960s, and looking forward to projects like *Video Synthesizer*, Paik said he wanted his own interventions leading to something

> which anyone could use in his own home, using his increased leisure to transform his TV set from a passive pastime to active creation.... Communication means the two-way communications. One-way communication is simply a notification ... like a draft call. TV has been a typical case of this non-communication and [the] mass audience had only one freedom, that is to turn on or off the TV.... My obsession with TV for the past 10 years has been, if I look back and think clearly, a steady progression towards more differentiated participation by viewers [Kearns].

Paik is critical here of the way television experiences had been framed and organized to this point, and in particular the domestic consumption of broadcast television, which was in the early 1960s the hegemonic use of that technology (Spigel 1992). By using television technology for a new purpose, Paik is trying explicitly to critique the nexus between television as a technology and the apparatus and institutions of broadcasting, which assumed and gathered a mass audience, and which, as Spigel's work shows, was so involved with the "suburbanization" of life in America and the capitalist West after the Second World War. Television has been seen as crucial to the "mobile privatization," which allowed the great transformation that was suburbanization (Williams, Spigel 1992, 2001). It resolved the contradiction between the isolating privacy of suburban life and the continuing dependence of suburban households on the cities they had evacuated. By providing a "window on the world" (Spigel 1992) and a small range of simultaneous broadcast experiences for a dispersed population, television helped constitute the "imagined community" that sustained social cohesion in the face of geographical fragmentation. Paik's identification of mass broadcasting with a Vietnam-era "draft call" shows that his desire to vary the uses of television is bound up with a challenge to consensus, authority, and suburban conformism that, he believed, were involved in broadcasting.

Whatever we might think of Paik's position in the light of long-held notions of TV's active audience (starting, perhaps with Fiske and Hartley), or of warnings such as William Boddy's about the tendency to feminize and passivize the television audience in the promotion of new media, his clear intention is to change and vary the uses of television by *fragmenting* the publicity of broadcasting, and to construct systems of interaction within which the audience could take their place as co-creators.

Paik's work in and of itself did not translate into a wholesale transformation of the uses of television, and they never fed directly into any mass-market domestic media technology. Indeed, beyond a few avant-garde television broadcasts, Paik's work, including his television work, was notably confined to the *public* spaces of galleries and theaters. As McCarthy notes, television has always been in part a public medium, and, indeed, continues to function in regulating public space. Nevertheless, it is striking that Paik's ambition to turn television to new uses — even though he envisions his work as an effort to change a domestic medium — requires him to bring television's new possibilities into public view. What Popper calls the "antitelevision stance" (22) of Paik and other video artists had less of a direct effect on mass media consumption patterns than it did on the emergence of new kinds of artistic practices in public galleries and, later, the Internet. But the technological developments, redefinitions of the idea of the artwork, and broader underlying structural changes that informed Paik's work and its production of new possibilities for television, outlined below, resonated beyond the gallery.

Paik's Context: "Post-objective" Art, Fluxus, Art and Technology and "System Aesthetics"

Paik's work with *Participation TV* was elegant and original, but it arose at a specific conjuncture in the history of twentieth-century visual culture in which a broad range of engineers, artists, and a number of people who combined the interests and skills of both were enthusiastically engaging in areas of interactivity, mass culture, and then-emerging digital and electronic technologies. This conjuncture was part of deeper changes, including a broader desire to turn television to new uses, and to make interactive, real-time works. It overlapped with the emergence of the earliest video games.

In particular, Paik's work can be set alongside what Johanna Drucker calls "postformalist" or "antiformalist" tendencies in art from the 1960s and 1970s, particularly the work of his colleagues in the Fluxus movement and theorists of these movements, such as Jack Burnham. Understanding this context for Paik's TV works can help us further our understanding of its relationship with early video games, as well as opening the intriguing possibility that where such movements in avant-garde practice gave way to the hegemony of conceptual art in the galleries (Gere), some of their objectives, enthusiasms, and tendencies persisted in early videogame design.

Movements like Fluxus and "Art and technology" were important formative influences on Paik's work. As Drucker puts it, in the 1960s and 1970s,

> A serious rethinking of the very idea of "art" appeared on the edge of radical transformation.... Experience-based rather than object-based work sprang up in one location after another.... The concepts of interactivity, algorithmic processes and networked conditions were not fully distilled as principles of digital art until recently, but their broad outlines were apparent by the 1970s [40].

Like many other recent historians (Manovich, Grau, Gere), Drucker sees important precursors not only to the new media art of the 1990s and after, but also to the entire landscape of "network culture" and the "network society" (Castells) in the avant-garde work of the 1960s and 1970s. Historians of the "information economy" trace many fundamental structural changes in the capitalist mode of production to the period — the 1960s and 1970s — when postformalist art was taking shape, when the postwar economic system collapsed, and when Western economies became more geared to the production of "immaterial" goods such as services and information.[4] As we shall see, these transformations were not lost on artists or theorists working at the time. Postformalist tendencies were, for a time in the 1960s and 1970s, present in a range of artworks engaged with technology, the possibilities of offering viewers a new, participatory place in the artwork, and the construction of *systems* rather than objects. This idea of the artwork as a set of conditions that lies in wait for the audience's intervention, and which is only determined by way of that intervention, is increasingly familiar in scholarly and critical approaches to new media art, and art more generally.

Art historians credit Paik as a central figure in the Fluxus movement (Popper, Smith, Drucker). As a network, Fluxus was active from the late 1950s, most visible in the 1960s and 1970s, and formally has never ceased to exist. At least rhetorically, the movement is less about its individual members than about certain crucial ideas and methods (Smith). These central ideas include "first, the primacy of the event (or act), with a correlated concern for participation, and second, a centrality of information exchange, modeling and education" (Smith 122). A more specific account of Fluxus's underlying principles is given by Fluxus artist Ken Friedman, who has written an intellectual history of Fluxus, "Forty Years of Fluxus," and edited the *Fluxus Reader*. Friedman sees Fluxus as having been a "laboratory" in which

> The research program ... is characterized by twelve ideas: globalism; the unity of art and life; intermedia; experimentalism; chance; playfulness; simplicity; implicativeness; exemplativism; specificity; presence in time; and musicality [2002].

For Friedman, these principles underlie the whole variety of Fluxus's output, from performances to musical compositions to later experiments with forms such as mail art.

Several of these principles can be usefully considered in relation to Paik's TV works (and, later in this chapter, in relation to video games). The first idea, of the *unity of art and life*, underpins Fluxus's attempt to demystify the art object, the figure of the artist, and the system of art itself. There is a resemblance here between Fluxus and contemporary developments such as Pop Art, which attempt to efface or question the distinctions between art and commercial culture. The boundaries between the auratic art object and the everyday outputs of mass consumer culture are confused by *Zen for TV*'s combination of painterly visual abstraction and a sacred reference, on the one hand, and Paik's playful technique and use of television on the other. With *Participation TV*, there is a deliberate confusion between acts of artistic creation and the participatory acts of the artwork's audience. Moreover, in Paik's practice there is an integration of engineering practice and aesthetic image-making. *Participation TV* fulfils the criterion of *intermedia*, mixing real-time sound, real-time vision, an electronic visual technique, and the "found object" of the television set itself. *Zen for TV* and *Participation TV* alike embrace *simplicity*, for which "Another term ... is elegance. In mathematics or science, an elegant idea is that idea which expresses the fullest possible series of meanings in the most concentrated possible statement" (Friedman 2002). *Zen for TV*'s density of reference (to religion, Modernism, popular culture), its indication of the possibilities for new uses of television, its conceptual daring in staking out a new area of artistic practice, and its beauty are all remarkable in a work produced with such a simple expedient. And though *Participation TV*'s apparent simplicity belies Paik's immersion in electronics prior to making the artwork, it introduces real-time electronic images, electronically mediated interactions, and a simultaneous critique and extension of the uses of television.

The fact that all of this is so clearly legible in these works may be because of their *exemplativism*, the Fluxus antidote to what they saw as the Gnostic complexities of art criticism, "[which] is the quality of a work exemplifying the theory and meaning of its construction" (Friedman 2002). The meanings of these works are not concealed in depth, and require no specialized critical knowledge to understand, but they are revealed clearly in the titles, on the surfaces, and crucially in the use of the works. With *Participation TV*, meaning, as in Wittgenstein's view of language, seems to overlap extensively with use (2001).

Perhaps most important of all the Fluxus principles underlying Paik's TV works is that of *playfulness*. Friedman describes the function of this idea in Fluxus artworks: "Playfulness has been part of Fluxus since the beginning. Part of the concept of playfulness has been represented by terms such as jokes, games, puzzles and gags" (2002). This playfulness was more than just a rejection of the fetishization of art objects and artistic practice that led to the "rigidities of conception, form and style" (Friedman 2002) that the Fluxus artists saw as characteristic of the late Modernist consensus they were reacting against. In positive terms it was seen as a new mode of comprehension within their artworks, which were not just "gags":

> Play comprehends far more than humor. There is the play of ideas, the playfulness of free experimentation, the playfulness of free association and the play of paradigm shifting that are as common to scientific experiment as to pranks (Friedman 2002).

Playfulness, which interacts with the values of simplicity, the unity of art and life, and participation, is visible in the inclusiveness of individual Fluxus works, and of the movement as a whole:

> Of the multitude of directions and ideas that Fluxus has explored, the most significant one is that it models a way of being creative that offers a communal, participatory and open-ended alternative to the traditional forms and functions of art-making.... By rejecting both the romanticized frames of art as visionary and the modernist notions of art as professional and exclusionary practice, Fluxus returns to a simpler engagement open to all.... In this way, art becomes a social act, because of its participatory nature, and transformative as well, because of this very same inclusionary stance. Although this open, often seemingly uncritical and playful aspect of Fluxus is sometimes dismissed as insignificant or lacking a serious motivation, it is of fundamental import for a collective, collaborative and global-based mentality [Smith 123].

The playfulness of the television works can be seen in terms of Paik's own relationship with his materials, and in his willingness to experiment with television. *Participation TV* extends playfulness to the viewing audience — this is a work whose playfulness is explicitly social and inclusive, comprehensible not through initiation into the professional secrets of late Modernism but through experiential play. In terms of the distinction between *paidea* (roughly:

play) and *ludus* (roughly: game), originating in the work of Caillois, and so important to early debates in videogame studies, Paik and Fluxus's versions of play are firmly in the former category. This is not rule-bound, competitive play, but open-ended experimentation on Paik's part, or in the case of *Participation TV*, an invitation to the audience to engage in similarly open playful experiences.

This "rethinking" of the nature and possibilities of the artwork as *experience* was dubbed "postformalism" by a late 1960s artist and theorist, Jack Burnham, and the description is taken up by Drucker when she observes that:

> The critical vocabulary of postformalism is sprinkled with terms and phrases that call attention to this change from object-based to process-oriented work. The earlier-twentieth-century notion of the "languages of art," for instance, was replaced by reference to "systems." "Processes" became more significant than mere "objects." And the vocabulary of "operations" or "procedures" appears in work with and without technological components, as if the linguistic phraseology of a technological mode were the new lingua franca of conception and production. An overall emphasis on dynamic manipulation of knowledge (again, "the idea is a machine that makes art") replaces the long-standing legacy of "resistance in material" as the condition for a work's coming into being in form [48].

Rather than the objective artwork emerging from the artist's heroic struggle with their materials, artists now put in place processes, procedures, and relationships. This informs a range of contemporary art:

> The moment of the work's intended mutability through the user's input represents a paradigm change in artistic production. Artists now provide a certain framework for action and define the esthetic parameters within which the user can operate; the work itself is a variable [Pfaffenbichler 2004].

The object disappears: it is no more than a "variable" and "mutable" element within the framework that determines its parameters and the parameters of users' actions upon it. The artist is no longer a producer of finished objects, but a producer of affordances, constraints, and fields of action.

The notion of systemic artworks, first proposed by art theorist Jack Burnham in 1968 in "System Esthetics," is one that makes room for a flexible discussion of the relationship between players/viewers, technologies, and the audiovisual spaces created in work such as Paik's, and which, further, can inform our discussion of video games. Burnham compared the new orientation toward systems to a Kuhnian paradigm-shift in the sciences. He insisted on its close relationships to the changes he already saw emerging in the West's capitalist economies, where the management of systems and information was increasingly important, and the production of tangible goods was relatively less important. These changes in the artwork were reflective of broad changes in society as a whole: "We are now in transition from an *object-oriented* to a *systems-oriented* culture. Here, change emanates not from *things*, but from the *way things are done*" (Burnham 1978: 160). According to Burnham, systemic practices are focused on the "creation of stable, on-going relationships between organic and nonorganic systems"; he identified these with the military-industrial development of systems analysis, claiming that the aesthetic impulse must, as technology progresses, "identify itself with the means of research and production" (162). He identifies informing trends in twentieth-century art whereby Marcel Duchamp and others showed that "art does not reside in material entities, but in relations between people and the components of their environment" (162). He sees art freed from the production of objects as an art that can take its place in a variety of contexts.

This opens the way for considering the artwork as a system of relationships, and as a process or a set of possibilities rather than as a fixed object. For Charlie Gere, Burnham's work amounts to a reconception of art that provides the basis for an understanding of creative practice as no longer focused on the production of self-sufficient objects, conceptually removed from the stream of time, to a view of art as "software." A similar conception of artistic practice as software — a product of design by the artist that allows the user certain actions and behaviors — recurs in Lev Manovich's recent notion of information design and information behavior as "post-media" aesthetic categories.

The context of a broad postformalism, which saw the aim of artists as the production of processes, procedures, relationships, and mutable fields that registered users' configurative practices of the principles of the Fluxus movement and of theories of "systemic artworks" such as Burnham's, can all be used to frame Paik's TV works. Further, these concepts are also useful in understanding and analyzing the development and aesthetics of the earliest, commercially available video games which, though they appear subsequent to Paik's works, have a history that stretches back beyond Paik's first exhibition, giving further evidence of the breadth of the aesthetic ambition to create systemic works that left a participatory place for the user or viewer.

Ralph Baer, Television and the Third Spot

A decade before Paik's work appeared, an engineer named Ralph Baer began working on his own problem, which bore close resemblances to Paik's and whose ambitions Baer articulated in similar ways, but whose outcomes had important differences. At a time when television, as a channel of broadcasting, was making its most forceful contribution as a vector of "mobile privatization," and operating so centrally in the postwar reconfiguration of the

American (sub)urban landscape (Spigel 2001), Baer, like Paik, was trying to develop a means for fragmenting the publicity and simultaneity embedded in TV's hegemonic uses, its institutional frameworks, and its address. In the early 1950s, Baer worked with Loral, then a small electronics company. His chief engineer put Baer and a colleague to work on designing a home television set, with the instruction to make it "the best TV set in the world" (Baer). Baer immediately suggested building games into the sets. His idea was rejected by his supervisor, and he was only able to devote serious time and resources to it from 1966, when he himself was a chief engineer at military contractor Sanders Associates. In the meantime, though, Baer recalls that:

> I had frequently been thinking about ways to use a TV set for something other than watching standard broadcasts. There were about 40 million TV sets in the USA alone at that time, to say nothing of those many more millions of sets in the rest of the world. They were literally begging to be used for something other than watching commercial television broadcasts!

Here, Baer's intimate knowledge of television electronics and his scientific and creative ambitions caused him to conceive of TV and its domestic presence in a way that is tantalizingly similar to Paik's. For both, television was not so much a fixed medium as it was a ready-made technological infrastructure, which might allow an ecology of varying uses, the insertion of parallel and parasitic technologies, and a plurality of relationships with its screen. Though they have this view of television in common, it is worth noting that Baer's expression of this view is far less critical than Paik's: he wants these games to be an addition or supplement to broadcasting, rather than aiming to replace television for a radical purpose. Varying television's uses is less a political or critical project than an engineering challenge.

For Baer, the transformation is defined primarily as a technical problem, but Oliver Grau's reminder to us is important here: that where the "media artist" is concerned, scientific and aesthetic problems are difficult to unpick, and we need to remind ourselves of Paik's electronics learning curve leading to his early TV works and Baer's struggle with the aesthetics of play, detailed below. However Baer conceived his practice, it was his work rather than Paik's that more directly led to a wholesale variation in the uses of television. His self–conception as more "engineer" than "artist" allowed him to consider the articulation of his work with the institutions and apparatuses of consumer culture — mass production, mass distribution, and retailing — that would deliver it into ordinary households.

From 1966, Baer's notes show him mapping out ideas for a "range of low cost data entry devices which can be used by an operator to communicate with a monochrome or color TV set of a standard, commercial, unmodified type." This is strikingly similar to what Paik achieves in *Participation TV*, but

Baer's ambition has subtle differences in its direction. He considers different possible means of connecting games machines with television: different kinds of games ("Action games ... Board skill games ... Artistic games ... Instructional games ... Board chance games ... Card games ... Sports games..." [Baer]), with different kinds, and different levels, of interaction. Importantly, what is implied in his plans is a retention of television's capacities as a *representational* medium, a consideration to which we will return.

There was a long period in which Baer and engineers under his supervision tinkered with the problems of "TV games." Working initially with valve-state electronics, he worked on devices that would produce manipulable television images. His experiments with controllers and transmission yielded one moveable spot, then two, and his first game, *Fox and Hounds*, which worked on the principle of tag. Ongoing involvement by engineers like Bill Rusch led to the concept of a "third spot":

> [which] was born sometime in October or November [1967]; unlike the two manually controlled spots we had been using so far, this spot was to be machine-controlled. Bill Rusch came up with the idea of making that spot into a "ball" so that we could play some sort of ball game with it. We batted around ideas of how we could implement games such as Ping-Pong, Hockey, Football and other sports games. I am not sure that we recognized that we had crossed a watershed but that's what it amounted to [Baer].

By the end of 1967 Baer had built and tested prototypes, including one for a light gun that could be used in play, and one for the "ping pong" game, and by 1968 had filed patents, which were finally issued in 1971 for a "Television gaming and training apparatus." The "ping-pong" game was developed with engineers at Sanders Associates, demonstrated in 1967 before Baer's patents were filed, and by 1968 was incorporated in a "complete switch-programmable video game unit capable of playing ping-pong, volley-ball, football, gun games and using colored, transparent overlays as backgrounds" (Baer). Baer modified this design further to create the "brown box," which was the "first fully-programmable, multi-player video game unit." This was displayed to American television manufacturers in 1968, picked up and dropped by RCA, and finally accepted for manufacture by Magnavox in 1971 (Baer, Winter). In the prototype, and in the eventual commercial release, player movement, and the range of actions the player's avatar could take in the visual world of the game was produced and limited by a range of controllers — a dial and the light gun. Baer's essential design was to be issued as the Magnavox Odyssey in 1972. It toured trade shows with the "Magnavox profit caravan" in 1972, and this is how Nolan Bushnell came to play it, and sign the firm's guestbook at the Airport Marina Hotel in Burlingame, California (Baer).

Like Paik, Baer's efforts involve an immersion in electronics, an effort to turn the television screen to new purposes, and the desire to create a "post-objective" work using television technology, in the sense that his efforts are directed at the production of a system of interaction rather than pictorial works with a comparable level of sophistication to those of broadcasting. Like the postobjective artworks discussed by Drucker and Gere above, processes, systems, and frameworks for action are the goal of practice. The significance of the "third spot" was not so much in its minimal enrichment of the screen image, but in its bringing about a more satisfactory relationship between the image and the behavior of users in relationship with it. This is not a finished, objective work, like a broadcast television program, that viewers can watch and interpret but not change. This is a new form of "information design," which has as its primary goal a new form of "information behavior" in relation to television (Manovich). In this sense, we can think about Baer's work in relation to the movement toward postobjective creative practice in the 1960s and 1970s.

Baer did not talk about his work in precisely the same way as Paik, but we can see the early Odyssey games as embodying some of the Fluxus principles that explicitly inform Paik's TV works. Baer's games are "intermedia" in the sense that they combine electronic images, transparent overlays, and games themselves in a new kind of cultural product. It offers a "unity of art and life" in the sense that just as Paik and Fluxus look to dismantle the barriers between art and audience, and offer televisual images as something the audience might act upon. Baer clearly expresses a desire to give the technology of television over to local uses, and thus at least implicitly is prepared to complicate the centralized apparatus of broadcasting. (Certainly, the ongoing consequences of Baer's work — including the global videogames industry — have played their part in the formation of what has been called the "post broadcast age" [Wark]). The work is certainly, centrally "playful," but there are important differences with the quality of playfulness we find in *Participation TV*. This can be seen in the way that Baer does not *stop* with *Fox and Hounds*. Baer's goal is not the institution of unstructured *paidea* play, but the construction of a structured *ludus* game, on the dimension of *agon*, or competitive play, and in retrospect Baer identifies the construction of a viable form of agonistic play as the moment of success. A collaboratively produced image is enough for Paik in designing *Participation TV*; Baer considers his team's key achievement to be the organization of a viable form of competition in interaction.

Also, importantly, there are differences in the function of images in Baer's and Paik's work. Paik's images can be enjoyed on several levels — we can appreciate *Zen for TV*'s allusion to high modernism; *Magnet TV*'s beauty and complexity; *Participation TV*'s relationship to the human voice. But none of these images are truly representational, and indeed only exist as the surface evidence of a conceptual transformation of television's possibilities. Though *Zen for TV* alludes to Barnett Newman and religion, the image is there as a bare sign of the manipulability of television by the artist. The variable image in *Participation TV* is no more than a variable that demonstrates the application of the conceptual title: though the abstract images produced have their own pleasures, they do not represent anything except the results of participation. To paraphrase Galloway, the images here are no more than interaction made visible. But in Baer's games, images and play are thought about by analogy with existing games, and part of Baer's satisfaction with the "third spot" is due to the game's approximation of tennis; there is a newfound capacity for *representing* something in the world. This representational ambition informed the journey made by Nolan Bushnell to producing the first commercially successful videogame, *Pong*.

Nolan Bushnell: Computer Space to Pong

Nolan Bushnell's newly formed Atari released *Pong* in 1972. Its often-remarked commercial success followed the failure of Bushnell's attempt to port *Spacewar!*— designed by Steve Russell and others for MIT's PDP-1 mainframe computer from 1961— to a cheaper, more accessible arcade format in the form of *Computer Space*.[5] The port was simplified, for example, there were no gravity effects as in the mainframe version, but was perhaps not straightforward enough to make it the popular success that *Pong* would be. Whereas the later game would simply require players to move their avatar on a single axis of movement in order to meet the oncoming "ball," the description of *Computer Space*'s gameplay on its Killer List of Videogames listing gives some indication as to what the first players were faced with:

> The rocket ship controlled by the player can be maneuvered through space using rotational buttons and a thrust button. The fire button is used to make the rocket ship fire missiles. When the two enemy flying saucers attack, they will fire missiles at the rocket ship. The player must have the rocket ship fire missiles at the flying saucers to destroy them. The object of the game is for the player to have the rocket ship to destroy the flying saucers more times than the flying saucers can destroy the rocket ship, the player must also try to have the rocket ship outscore the flying saucers in order to get extended play in hyperspace. If the player attains hyperspace the playfield will turn from black to white and feature a vision of daylight in outer space. The game will end if the flying saucers outscore the player's rocket ship and time has expired.[6]

In retrospect, Bushnell recalled the problems with *Computer Space*:

> You had to read the instructions before you could play, people didn't want to read instructions. To be successful, I had to come up with a game people already knew how to play; something so simple that any drunk in any bar could play [Winter].

We can put Bushnell's articulation of the problem he faced alongside Paik's or Baer's: he sees using television as the basis of a new form of play as more engineering problem than critical project, but there is also a decidedly entrepreneurial, commercial edge to his ambitions. Nevertheless, he found his way through some aesthetic problems that had to do with visualization and the range of information behaviors required of players. Beyond Bushnell's own retrospective assessment, Lowood remarks that the idea that *Computer Space* was too complex for its players is a consensus judgment in videogame history (11), but that this needs to be qualified by the technical and design achievements that *Computer Space* did embody, and which were carried forward into the later success of *Pong*, and arcade gameplay:

> These assessments of *Computer Space* as a failure miss its significance for the videogame as a technological artifact. It provided more than a learning experience. *Computer Space* established a design philosophy and general technical configuration for arcade consoles and reduced the laboratory-based computer game to the stable format that would launch the videogame as a consumer product. When Bushnell noted years later that his "engineering friends loved" *Computer Space*, even if "the typical guy in the bar" was completely baffled, it is easy to hear echoes of this appreciation in assessments of his *technical* achievement from engineers, designers and operators [Lowood 11–12].

This "technical configuration" included the placement of a television screen at the heart of a commercial coin-op videogame system, within a cabinet, and the grasping of the possible analogies between computer games and older coin-op amusements. Lowood offers an example of the technical achievements in *Computer Space* that would continue to inform subsequent videogame design. Bushnell's technical solution to the problem of overburdening a CPU with refreshing an entire screen every time a single on-screen object moved was to control each individual game element with a dedicated transistor:

> Bushnell's rockets were essentially hardwired bit-maps that could be moved around the screen independently of the background, a crucial innovation that made it possible to produce screen images efficiently.... The design concept would become part of Atari's shared knowledge.... Bushnell's patch solution later became a staple of game machines and home computers in the form of "sprites" [Lowood 1].

Notwithstanding its achievements in arriving at a basic format for arcade play, and in making crucial technical gains that would be taken forward into the design of *Pong*, as a game, *Computer Space* undoubtedly deterred player engagement because of its complexity. At a time when "computer literacy" was the preserve of engineering faculties, it asked players to learn and understand at once a wide range of information and information behavior, including new kinds of images, and a complex way of enacting relationships with images. The problem of how to attract players beyond the engineering community to engage with a new medium was solved only with the much simpler *Pong*.

Perhaps Bushnell's inspiration for the solution to his central problem did come from his visit to Magnavox's "profit caravan" where he saw a demonstration of the Odyssey; Bushnell admits attending the show but claims to have been unimpressed by Baer's efforts. *Pong* was released several months after the Odyssey, but it thoroughly eclipsed what even Baer describes as his machine's "modest" sales. Successful legal action was brought by Magnavox on Atari in 1973 (Winter). By this time, though, Atari had entrenched itself as market leader, and although the Odyssey sold well, it is *Pong* that is remembered as the first computerized tennis game, and the first successful video game to reach a broad market.

As noted by Lowood, *Pong*'s success is usually put down to its relative simplicity by comparison with *Computer Space* (Winter, Herman, and Cohen). The simplicity of the game is not only in its simple imperatives, but also in the instructions and the character of the images and their movement in space. By contrast with *Computer Space, Pong*'s instructions were almost absurdly simple: "Avoid missing ball for high score." Given that there is no "ball," but only a blocky sprite rebounding around the screen, we could see these instructions as being as much a fictional framing device as an outline of imperatives.

The physical interface was equally uncomplicated. A continuous dial controlled movement of the player's block avatar on a single, vertical axis. Unlike *Computer Space*, there were no "expressive acts" (Galloway) such as firing, and the player was only required to engage in movement-actions. A two-player game — with no computer-controlled avatars — the game allowed players to participate in a very straightforward contest in on-screen space, and the adversarial nature of the contest was reflected in the neat, symmetrical composition of the screen. Squire and Jenkins's doctrine of video games as the "art of contested space" is spelled out very clearly by the game to players: the game's written instructions and the visual composition of the game's world allow the "rules" to emerge easily, to the extent that we might see those rules as being realized representationally. The contestual nature of the game is clearly legible, in a way that, using the vocabulary of Fluxus, we might call exemplative. Whereas *Computer Space* "required instructions," *Pong visualized* its rules.

The ease with which players were able to understand the required information behaviors in relation to the game was shown when a prototype was installed in Andy Capp's tavern:

> One of [them] inserted a quarter. There was a beep. The game had begun. They watched dumbfoundedly as the ball appeared alternately on one side of the screen

and then disappeared on the other. Each time it did the score changed. The score was tied at 3–3 when one player tried the knob controlling the paddle at his end of the screen. The score was 5–4, his favor, when his paddle made contact with the ball. There was a beautifully resonant "pong" sound, and the ball bounced back to the other side of the screen. 6–4. At 8–4 the second player figured out how to use his paddle. They had their first brief volley just before the score was 11–5 and the game was over. Seven quarters later they were having extended volleys, and the constant *pong* noise was attracting the curiosity of others at the bar. Before closing, everybody in the bar had played the game [Cohen 29].

Where *Computer Space*'s structure was complex enough to resist the player's entrance with a range of behaviors and instructions that needed to be understood, *Pong* presented a system in which the relationship between the playing body and screen images, mediated by the simple dial interface, was such that players were quickly able to attend to it, and quickly able, too, to derive pleasure from competitive play. And already, in Cohen's description, it is interesting to note that, just as Paik's works implied a bifurcated audience, on *Pong*'s first night the audience is divided between players and spectators, as in Newman's analysis of the complex videogame audience. In this case, viewers are not attracted by the kind of rich technological spectacle that characterizes contemporary games, and the audiovisual style of *Pong* is a long way from the mimetic audiovisuality of television. The spectacle here is a new form of agonistic play, witnessing a new form of technological representation. In this sense, perhaps, *Pong* shares at least one aspect of the "aesthetic of attractions" that Gunning insists underpins early cinema: its attraction lies partly in "its ability to show something" not only new (52), namely, electronically generated images, but also in its ability to show something *as* manipulable and subject to agonistic play.

By comparison with *Computer Space*, it is striking that *Pong* adds very little to the image of *Zen for TV*. *Pong*'s abstraction of tennis is of such rigor as to constitute the zero degree of representation. It seems to confirm Wolf's argument that the abstraction of early video games is a means by which players are "taught" about the nature of the new medium. But it is representation nevertheless, and, taking Järvinen's framework for analyzing audiovisual style in early video games forward, it is less "abstract" than "caricatural"— it is an extremely schematic representational audiovisual environment rather than one, like Paik's (or that of *Qix* or *Tetris*) that eschews representation. Perhaps it is the balance found in *Pong* between representational ambition and the necessity to initiate players into new kinds of information behavior that marks its success as videogames' first "killer app."

Conclusion: Archaeology and Pong as Killer App

The expansion of videogame archaeology can enrich our understandings of gameplay, of the successes and achievements of game designers, and the consequent transformations of media technologies and institutions. That Paik never really achieved his goal of a critical renovation of television, and that Baer and Bushnell were able to initiate a new industry that transformed our relationship with television as a technology, can be understood in terms of an archaeological analysis.

Despite Paik's wonderfully elegant institution of postobjective artworks with television at their heart, he was prevented perhaps by his critical position, and his "anti-television" stance, from offering his works as a mass-market technology. For all of Fluxus's desire to take art into the world, the institutional framework for his TV works remained the art gallery and his methods remained artisanal, so the audience for these works was significantly smaller than television's mass audience.

The "modest success" of the Odyssey beside *Pong* has been explained by Baer in terms of the confusion and incompetence of Magnavox and retailers in marketing the machine, but the positioning of all of these efforts in relation to the technology and institutions of television in the archaeology that this piece has carried out suggests a different possibility. Given that broadcasting was, as Paik, Spigel (1992), and Williams suggest, a crucial component of the postwar social order, any technology that threatened to break the nexus between broadcasting and television could be seen as a change with broad ramifications. Winston, in his history of media technologies, suggests that new technologies are subject to a law of suppression of radical potential: societies tend toward conservatism, and new technologies that threaten elements of the status quo are problematic, and often take time to gain acceptance and to become institutionalized. Given that Williams's social history of gaming shows that, notwithstanding some successful consoles, it was not until the late 1980s that consoles came to reliably outstrip arcades as a source of revenues for the videogames industry, it could be concluded that Baer's machine, and succeeding consoles, represented too disturbing a change to domestic media consumption.

Bushnell, on the other hand, opted initially for the placement of games in public space, where, as Huhtamo shows, a range of venues, established patterns of consumption and reception, and an economic model of sales and distribution were already in place, ahead of the arrival of arcade games. Huhtamo's archaeology demonstrates that for a long period video games and arcade machines could be seen side by side in arcades, bars, and other venues, comfortably coexisting, accepting the same coins, and offering analogous human-machine relationships. Winston claims that media technologies are usually taken up because they fulfill a "social need": in this case, the coin-op industry's hunger for technological novelty. Rather than changing domestic media consumption, at least initially, Bushnell was more concerned to incorporate the technology of television into a new form of coin-op play, which, though inspired by his experiences with advanced computer technologies, was also informed by his understanding of that industry. *Pong's* status as a "killer app" was in part secured by the cultural and economic framework into which it was introduced.

However, all three can be seen as manifestations of a common desire to turn television to new uses, to encourage new kinds of information behavior in relation to screen images; Paik, Baer, and Bushnell alike conceived of television as not merely a receiver of broadcast content, but in terms of its new potentiality as the center of postobjective, systemic works. Though Paik's work is abstract and Baer and Bushnell's representational, and though *Participation TV* offers open-ended play whereas the game designers' works are structured by agonistic competition, all imagine television transformed, in a new relationship with its audience. The framework within which Burnham and subsequent historians understood the changes in the nature of art in the period that overlaps with the videogame designers' work can be fruitful in understanding games *and* art, and a present where real-time interaction has come to "underpin the whole apparatus of communication and data-processing by which our contemporary techno-culture operates" (Gere 1). From this point of view, we can begin to understand the relationship between games and art with frameworks that transcend simple oppositions.

Notes

1. See, for example, Ellis.
2. See Wilson for a fuller account of the relationship between the work of Newman and Paik.
3. Ivan Sutherland's PhD incorporating Sketchpad, the first graphical user interface (GUI) for computers, was published in 1963, and the technology allowed the production of on-screen line drawings of considerable complexity, but these efforts were directed at monitors attached to large, mainframe computers.
4. See, for example, Cohen, and Castells.
5. See, for example, Burnham 2001, Cohen, and Winter.
6. A mastery of a number of rules, various functionalities and behaviors of on-screen objects, and a range of narrative events were all part and parcel of playing this game. The game demanded that the players learn to use different kinds of controllers, both for the "move-acts," which "change the position or orientation of the game environment" and "expressive acts," which "exert an expressive desire outward from the player to objects in the world" (Galloway 22–23). To move in *Computer Space*, the player must understand

the interplay of directional and thrust controllers, and the relationship between their actions and an unfamiliar on-screen object. Expressively, the player must understand the requirement to target and fire at other objects. Added to this was a mise-en-scene which was arguably richer than any other videogame between it and *Space Invaders*, featuring a background of stars and several differently-shaped objects (the rocketship, the flying saucer, the projectiles). A two-player version introduce further complications, with players controlling differently-shaped craft with varying capabilities.

Works Cited

Baer, Ralph. "How the Home Video Games Industry Began" (2004). 27 October 2005. http://ralphbaer.com/how_video_games.htm.

Barnouw, Eric. *Tube of Plenty: The Evolution of American Television*. Oxford: Oxford University Press, 1990.

Boddy, William. "Archeologies of Electronic Vision and the Gendered Spectator." *Screen* 35:2 (1994): 105–122.

Burnham, Jack. "System Esthetics." In *Esthetics Contemporary*, edited by Richard Kostelanetz. Buffalo, NY: Prometheus Books, 1978.

Burnham, Van. *Supercade: A Visual History of the Videogame Age, 1971–1984*. Cambridge: Massachusetts Institute of Technology Press, 2001.

Caillois, Roger. *Man, Play and Games*. New York: Schocken, 1979.

Castells, Manuel. *The Rise of the Network Society*. Oxford: Blackwell, 2000.

Cohen, Scott. *Zap! The Rise and Fall of Atari*. New York: McGraw Hill, 1984.

Crogan, Patrick. "Wargaming and Computer games: Fun with the Future." In *Level Up: Digital Games Research Conference Proceedings*, edited by Marinka Copier and Joost Raessens. Utrecht: DIGRA/University of Utrecht, 2003.

Darley, Andrew. *Visual Digital Culture: Surface Play and Spectacle in New Media Genres*. London: Routledge, 2000.

Dovey, Jon, and Helen Kennedy. *Game Cultures: Computer Games as New Media*. Maidenhead, England: Open University Press, 2006.

Drucker, Johanna. "Interactive, Algorithmic, Networked: Aesthetics of New Media Art." In *At a Distance: Precursors to Art and Activism on the Internet*, edited by Annmarie Chandler and Norie Neumark. Cambridge: Massachusetts Institute of Technology Press, 2005.

Ellis, John. *Visible Fictions: Cinema, Television, Video*. London: Routledge, 1992.

Fiske, John, and John Hartley. *Reading Television*. London: Routledge, 1989.

Frasca, Gonzalo. "Ludology Meets Narratology: Similitude and Differences between (Video)games and Narrative" (1999). 22 August 2006. http://www.ludology.org/articles/ludology.htm.

Friedman, Ken. Ed. *The Fluxus Reader*. Chichester, England: John Wiley and Sons, 1998.

_____. "Forty Years of Fluxus" (2002). 21 December 2005. http://www.artnotart.com/fluxus/kfriedman-fourtyyears.html.

Fuller, Mary, and Henry Jenkins. "Nintendo and New World Travel Writing: A Dialogue." In *Cybersociety: Computer-Mediated Community and Communication*, edited by Steven Jones, 57–72. London: Sage, 1995.

Galloway, Alexander R. *Gaming: Essays on Algorithmic Culture*. Minneapolis: University of Minnesota Press, 2006.

Gere, Charlie. *Art, Time and Technology*. London: Berg, 2006.

Goodman, Cynthia. "The Digital Frontier from Video to Virtual Reality" (1997). 12 March

2004. http://delivery.acm.org/10.1145/270000/262609/p74-goodman.pdf?key1=262609&key2=5637462011&coll=GUIDE&dl=ACM&CFID=33209770&CFTOKEN=7322589.

Grau, Oliver. *Virtual Art: From Illusion to Immersion.* Trans. Gloria Custance. Leonardo Series. Cambridge: Massachusetts Institute of Technology Press, 2003.

Gunning, Tom. "The Cinema of Attractions: Early Film, Its Spectator and the Avant-Garde." In *Early Cinema: Space, Frame, Narrative,* edited by Thomas Elsaesser and Adam Barker. London: BFI, 1990.

Herman, Leonard. *Phoenix: The Fall and Rise of Home Videogames.* Union, NJ: Rolenta Press, 1997.

Huhtamo, Erkki. "Slots of Fun, Slots of Trouble: An Archaeology of Arcade Gaming" (2005). 21 March 2007. http://www.imagearts.ryerson.ca/michalak/html/MPM022/References/Huhtamo,%20E%20(2005)%20Slots%20of%20Fun,%20Slots%20of%20Trouble.pdf.

Jacobs, Jason. *The Intimate Screen: Early British Television Drama.* Oxford: Clarendon Press, 2000.

Järvinen, Aki. "*Quake* Goes the Environment: Game Aesthetics and Archaeologies." *Digital Creativity* 12:2 (2001): 67–76.

Juul, Jesper. "The Game, the Player, the World: Looking for a Heart of Gameness." In *Level Up: Digital Games Research Conference Proceedings,* edited by Marinka Copier and Joost Raessens. Utrecht: DIGRA/University of Utrecht, 2003. 21 August 2006. http://www.jesperjuul.net/text/gameplayerworld/.

_____. "Games Telling Stories? A Brief Note on Games and Narrative." *Game Studies* 1.1 (2001). 23 March 2007. http://www.gamestudies.org/0101/juul-gts/.

Kearns, Mary Ann. *The Role of Technology in the Art of Nam June Paik: The Social Implications of Television* (1988). 14 November 2005. http://www.experimentaltvcenter.org/history/people/ptext.php3?id=38.

Killer List of Videogames. "Computer Space." (1995–2007). 22 March 2007. http://www.klov.com/game_detail.php?letter=&game_id=7381.

Lowood, Henry. "Videogames in Computer Space: The Complex History of *Pong.*" Unpublished manuscript. 2007.

_____, and Tim Lenoir. "Theaters of War: The Military-Entertainment Complex" (2003). 13 April 2005. http://www.stanford.edu/dept/HPST/TimLenoir/Publications/Lenoir-Lowood_TheatersOfWar.pdf#search=%22lowood%20lenoir%20military%22.

Manovich, Lev. *The Language of New Media.* Cambridge: Massachusetts Institute of Technology Press, 2001.

McCarthy, Anna. *Ambient Television: Visual Culture and Public Space.* London: Duke University Press, 2001.

Newman, James. "The Myth of the Ergodic Videogame." *Game Studies* 2.1 (2002). 21 March 2005. http://www.gamestudies.org/0102/newman/.

Pfaffenbichler, Norbert. "From Panel Painting to Computer Processing." Catalogue essay for the exhibition *Abstraction now.* (2004). 21 March 2006. http://www.abstraction-now.net/catalogue/ABSTRACTION-NOW-EN.pdf.

Popper, Frank. *From Technological to Virtual Art.* Cambridge: Massachusetts Institute of Technology Press, 2007.

Shinkle, Eugenie. "Corporealis Ergo Sum: Rez, Affect, and the End of the Cartesian Subject." dLux media arts (2003). 17 March 2004. http://www.dlux.org.au/plaything/media/eugenie_shinkle_web.pdf.

Smith, Owen. "Fluxus Praxis: An Exploration of Connections, Creativity and Community." In *At a Distance: Precursors to Art and Activism on the Internet,* edited by Annmarie

Chandler and Norie Neumark, 116–139. Cambridge: Massachusetts Institute of Technology Press, 2005.

Spigel, Lynn. *Make Room for TV: Television and the Family Ideal in Postwar America.* Durham, NC: Duke University Press, 1992.

_____. *Welcome to the Dreamhouse: Popular Media and Postwar Suburbs.* Durham, NC: Duke University Press, 2001.

Tancin, Richard. "The Coming of Age of Multimedia in Public Spaces." (2001). 12 December 2004. http://www.tancin.net/download/writings/Multimedia%20Public%20Spaces.pdf.

Wark, McKenzie. "Cyberspace and the Virtual Public." *Australian Humanities Review* (October/November 1999). 27 February 2007. http://www.lib.latrobe.edu.au/AHR/archive/Issue-October-1999/wark2.html.

Williams, Dimitri. (2006) *A (Brief) Social History of Video Games.* https://netfiles.uiuc.edu/dewill/www/research.html. Accessed 23/11/2006.

Williams, Raymond. *Television: Technology and Cultural Form.* London: Fontana, 1974.

Wilson, Jason. "Games, Video Art, Abstraction and the Problem of Attention." *Convergence: The International Journal of Research into New Media Technologies* 10. 3 (2004): 84–101.

Winston, Brian. *Media Technology and Society: A History from the Telegraph to the Internet.* London: Routledge, 1998.

Winter, David. *Pong-Story.* 2001–2006. 23 November 2006. http://pong-story.net.

Wittgenstein, Ludwig. *Philosophical Investigations: The German Text with a Revised English Translation.* 3rd ed. Trans. G.E.M. Anscombe. Oxford: Blackwell, 2001.

Wolf, Mark J. P. "Abstraction in the Video Game." *The Video Game Theory Reader,* edited by Mark J. P. Wolf and Bernard Perron. New York: Routledge, 2003.

_____, and Bernard Perron, eds. *The Video Game Theory Reader.* New York: Routledge, 2003.

Gameography

Computer Space, Nutting Associates 1971.
Odyssey, Magnavox, 1972.
Pong, Atari, 1972.
Qix, Taito 1981.
Space Invaders, Taito, 1978.
Spacewar!, 1961.
Tetris, Atari, 1988.

6

The Navigator's Experience: An Examination of the Spatial in Computer Games

Bernadette Flynn

The following chapter investigates space in computer games. It asks what models might best be utilized to analyze the experience and pleasures of the players' navigation through computer games space. A basic tenet of the approach advanced here is that while computer games are visual worlds, to an extent perceived similarly to other visual media such as film, other traditions of navigation and spatiality can also be useful in gaining a more nuanced understanding of what it is to navigate computer game space. This account therefore seeks to bring existing notions of spectatorship into dialogue with accounts of spatial navigation drawn from other disciplines, including painting, film, and landscape design. To do this, I first need to establish some of the critiques of the traditional Western conception of space. I then introduce the work of thinkers who have presented alternate conceptions of spatial experience, among them Henri Lefebvre, Michel de Certeau, and Maurice Merleau-Ponty. Considering examples from different traditions of garden design — from the formal baroque gardens to the eighteenth-century English landscape gardens and earlier Chinese scholars' gardens — enables us to compare different aesthetic conventions regarding the representation, and movement through space, of the respective subjectivities this engenders. In the final section, using single-player 3D and isometric games as examples, I show how elements of these different cultural and spatial traditions have come together in the computer game player's navigation of virtual games space, considering the significance of this for a model of player experience.

Western Concepts of Space

In the first part of the chapter I trace the way that space has been conceptualized within histories of Western representation and visual illusion. I examine pictorial art, landscape design, and film to identify some trends that have set the context for the way contemporary computer games are understood as spatial systems. A main problem identified is the reduction of computer space to a paradigm that privileges a particularly Western form of the visual as the only measure of space. I examine the development of spatial models in Renaissance pictorial art and outline how these models have in turn dominated how game space has been conceptualized. A number of problems are identified that have marginalized spatiality within computer games, which can be summarized as: first, the rendering of space as empty and static, and second, the positioning of the viewer's eye as the totality of spatial engagement and the subsequent rupture of the kinaesthetic from the visual senses.

Historically, the Western codification of ways of seeing can be identified with the cultural formulations described by the Italian architect Leon Battista Alberti's *construzione legittima* (the legitimate construction) in the fifteenth century. In Alberti's projection of receding horizontals, three-dimensional space is projected onto a two-dimensional picture plane so that the lines of projection meet at an imaginary point on the horizon — the vanishing point. The idea of "the legitimate construction" was to simulate the illusion of looking at a scene through a window with the eye of the physical body. Visual space is thus constructed as geometric proportions based on the technology of sight. Space is polarized into positive and negative space in which objects have positive or solid characteristics with space itself having a negative or empty characteristic as an extended physical void.

Initially a theory of spatial perception, such an idea became inscribed in ways of seeing during the early Renaissance as the eye was trained to read the spatial mathematics and therefore be able to appreciate the harmonic proportions employed by Quattrocento architects. An example of the illusionist painting of the seventeenth century Quattrocento artists includes Fra Andrea Pozzo's painting on the ceiling of the Church of Sant' Ignazio in Rome (1691–1694). In the church the ideal position to view St. Ignatius being welcomed to heaven is from a singular marble yellow floor disc. The illusion of the image is only in correct perspective from the one and only one marked position in physical space. The reception of the image from the marble disc creates an illusion whereby the physical architecture of the church blends into the faux architecture in the painting. Such precise positioning of the body for viewing perspectival painting was instrumental in establishing formal rules for the relationship between the body and the subject. As Margaret Wertheim puts it "Perspectival imagery thereby subjected Western minds to what amounts to a training in conscious awareness of physical space" (113). Seeing space as mathematical perspective that demanded a static contained body fed into Descartes's philosophy on the separation of the mind and the body (Cartesian dualism).[1] Renaissance art not only reinforced ideals of aesthetics and beauty associated with the Golden Mean, but also embedded formal codes associated with an immobile body. Vision was thus reduced to a mental thing detached from the body. As I later outline, this way of thinking the relationship between the body and space became embedded in the ways of experiencing the European landscape garden. The separation between the seeing eye and the inert body became encapsulated in the confined and mute body of the viewer gazing from an upper-story window onto a distant landscape. I will later trace how these ways of thinking the body were reflected in mainstream Western filmmaking and how aspects of these spatial configurations became absorbed into the design of computer game space.

As reinforced by Foucault and Soja this notion of space as empty, static and disembodied has become central to a Western ontology of spatial creation and representation. We can see how this has become the standard for the majority of computer games in which the objects and avatars are made up of 3D geometry placed in an empty and bounded space. In the geometric perspective exemplified in software programs such as *3D Studio Max*, *Lightwave*, or *Maya* (modeling programs used in constructing many 3D game environments), space is defined within familiar Cartesian coordinates. The XYZ system creates polygons and other primitive geometric shapes that forces a notion of space as mathematical division and a container for objects. Working from a grid of lines the Cartesian coordinate system is a particular form of construction that has rendered space as empty and outside the action field. In splitting space into a foreground/background polarity and emphasizing horizon line and depth axis, the body has been excluded from the frame. Such a Cartesian perspectival logic that constitutes the avatar as a mathematical object in empty space is at odds with an avatar body that represents the player's expressionistic engagement with space. At its most extreme then, thinking with and about the body is reduced to a seeing eye or a visioning instrument and space is separated from the main event of gameplay.

Alternative Conceptions of Spatial Experience

This section introduces the work of thinkers who have presented alternative conceptions of spatial experience, among them the important French theorists Maurice Merleau-Ponty, Michel de Certeau, and Henri Lefebvre. These thinkers provide a useful starting point for conceptualizing the spatial as involving bodily participation. The work of Maurice Merleau-Ponty, a French phenomenologist philosopher, is relevant here for its recognition that space must be understood as experiential and bound up with the physicality and material existence of the body in the world. It stands in contrast with René Descartes's dualist ontology of mind and body. Michel de Certeau's contribution as a philosopher and social scientist is to consider space as part of everyday practice. In de Certeau's account of the everyday, he recognizes and analyses the cultural specificity of movement. He describes the way individuals unconsciously navigate everything from city streets to literary texts and argues that this navigation is never wholly determined by homogenous description but open to tactics of everyday usage. Henri Lefebvre, a French Marxist sociologist and philosopher, theorizes space as intrinsically related to the social, something experienced and lived, irreducible to the homogenous space of geometry. These writers describe the physical movement of bodies in real space and the importance of making conscious the lived experience of space. By extension, their work speaks pertinently to the conscious strategy employed by the game player during active gameplay, exploration, and navigation. Inhabiting a space whether it is real or virtual, in the streets, at home, or in a computer game involves investment and produces a strong sense of identification. In this regard the spaces of computer games can be as significant and "real" to a game player as the physical space of the closest city.

I now look at how the work of these theorists can be applied to our understanding of computer game space by explicitly foregrounding the active agency of the gameplayer. In this way the investigation of computer space is located in the context of the dynamic experiential nature of player engagement. Against the familiar reduction of computer-generated spaces to discussions of visuality, Lefebvre's idea of spatiality opens up a broader understanding of space, namely, as a form of praxis that involves spatial practice or performance, representations of space, and spatial experiences. In talking about the virtual space of computer games and the player's kinaesthetic engagement in that space, Lefebvre's concept of space as social and practiced is useful for theorizing players' simultaneously perceptual, symbolic, and performative engagements with this space.

I will now turn to Lefebvre's first category — spatial practice and how this can be applied to the game environment. Often omitted from discussions

Jan Vredeman de Vries drawing of perspective from *Perspective* 1604 edition.

of computer games is that one of the essential ingredients of computer game-play is active exploration of space. A number of writers on the spatial have described activities, such as walking, as a cultural act (see also Solnit). Navigating a terrain is understood as a constellation among bodies, imagination, and space, or, in game terms, the experiential body and the active imaginative engagement of the player responding to the dynamic space of the virtual game world. The players' involvement with geographic orientation and direction requires detailed negotiation of the landscape and close readings of space. Memorizing and mentally mapping the landscape is vital in order for the player to remember where s/he has been, where s/he might be going, and how s/he might return. The negotiation of the spatial grammar of the environment — the navigation of terrain geography, sonic spatial elements, architectural features, and spatial objects is not merely a habit of reading but requires kinaesthetic agency and bodily memory. From this, players perform their spatial journeys, read the landscape as encoded memories, and in turn change the landscape through their actions.

Lefebvre's second category of space refers to representations of space — the aesthetics deployed in designing the game environment. There are a number of representations of space adopted in computer games that relate to different cultural aesthetic traditions and are to some extent built into the geometry of the software or game engine deployed for creating game worlds.

Here I will briefly outline three main systems of representation used in computer games: Euclidian geometry (referred to as 3D), isometric (referred to as either 3/4 perspective or 2.5D) and photorealism (commonly referred to as 2D) (see also Aarseth). A large number of computer games employ the Euclidian attributes of empty isotopic geometric space. *Half-life, Tomb Raider,* or any number of 3D worlds adopt the codes of geometric optics to ensure the formation of a consistent and fully legible space. In this space, geometry is flattened out and confined to the surface of objects in the X/Y/Z plane with the space between objects represented as homogenous and empty.

Axonometry is another representational system used in computer games. As Jan Krikke points out it emerges from a different spatial system — that of classical Chinese perspective.[2] He outlines how Chinese axonometry (*dengjiao toushi* in Chinese) is not based on optical principles and hence has no vanishing point and no optical distortion. In games, the isometric and diametric projections are the most widely used varieties of the axonometric projection. They are also referred to as parallel perspective and 2.5D. Computer game examples that use axonometry include "God's eye view" simulation games such as *The Sims, Age of Empires*, and *Baldur's Gate*. In axonometry structural forms such as houses and carts retain their size and geometry so that parallel pillars remain strictly parallel leaving out any perspectival distortion. Objects

Claude Bragdon's demonstration of isometric principles in *Projective Ornament*, 1915.

are often represented from a skewed direction in order to reveal all three directions (axes) of space in one picture. Ignoring the perspective rules of diminution, figures and objects in the background are similar in size to those in the foreground with little or no shading or contrast on the structures and avatars.

A third representational approach is photorealism, which is used to refer to the likeness of a graphic image to the original object. During the 1990s games such as *The Seventh Guest* and *X-files–The Game* used live characters and sets shot on full motion video against blue screen. Other games took this a step further in creating a simulated image to appear like a photographic representation of the original. Examples include *Riven* and *Myst III: Exile* where traditional filmic or photographic elements are translated into their simulation equivalent. In an effort to emulate camera-originated images, a range of photorealistic strategies are deployed such as mood and naturalistic lighting, complex mise-en-scène, soft focused objects, and lens distortions. Similar to the eye being drawn in film, the players' attention is attracted toward particular objects and on-screen avatars through careful composition, and texture mapping. The players' perceptual absorption in the enclosed topography of the screen is assumed with navigation paths suggested through high levels of photorealistic detail and the seduction of carefully modeled spatial objects.

What do these spatial systems mean for how we read the landscape? In considering navigation as an aspect of exploring computer game space we can investigate how strategies associated with way finding involve the player's experience of orientation. Referencing Lefebvre's third category — the users' experiences — we note that the player's experience of navigation not only engages perception but also invokes it (Champion). Marie-Laure Ryan describes the body in virtual environments as having a sense of being surrounded, a sense of depth, and the possession of a roving point of view bringing together the panorama with Renaissance perspective and a mobile point of view. She frames these as ecologies of representation or spectacle, but they are also ecologies of being or agency. At the point where the player is engaged with the screen space (either as avatar or as cursor) there is a disruption between any Euclidian perspectival logic and that which emerges from the player's spatial experience. The player engaged with the dynamic of the game is both a perceptual and an imagining body. This body, located in a sociocultural context, is framed by its past and potential perceptions. Navigation as a behavior or performance then emerges from a body's relations to a spatial situation and to an environment. To express it another way, adopting Michel de Certeau, the act of walking opens up a place (a limitation of space) to human creativity and articulation, transforming it into "a space of enunciation." For de Certeau, walking is an act of articulating the language of the terrain and, through the improvised movements of the walker, spatial elements are transformed or abandoned. In it, space becomes a practiced place precisely through the activity of walking. By extension, for the gameplayer, it is only through navigation that gameplay articulates the language of the terrain and this terrain then operates as a vocabulary imbued with spatial memories, navigation histories, and embodied experience.

The work of the French phenomenologist philosopher Merleau-Ponty is relevant here for his arguments about the condition of experience. He recognized a corporeality of consciousness and the intentionality of the body. He argues that the body is not only a thing but also a permanent condition of experience. In *The Phenomenology of Perception*, Merleau-Ponty speaks of the body's self image as an attitude directed toward a certain existing or possible task. Resisting the idea of perception as simply a passive reception of visual stimuli, he argues that space cannot be reduced to its ideational representation. As experienced by the lived body, space cannot be simply positional. He describes this not as a spatiality of position, but as a spatiality of situation. The idea of perception as requiring action is most pertinent to computer games. Rather than considering space as only a staging ground for aesthetics, or the occupation of static points of location, such an approach insists that bodily presence is vital for considering how we engage as players. Through the activity of navigation, space is opened up to kinaesthetic engagement with spatial tasks and encounters. From this, the spatial in computer games is conceptualized as a language enacted in embodied practice. The player's self image as one of situation or circumstance is central to their preoccupation with the virtual self and agency in the game world.

Garden Designs as Spatial Systems

The first part of the chapter has traced the way the spatial has been framed as a mode of visualization and outlined how this particular technology of vision has been appropriated in contemporary computer game design. Two key problems emerge from the dominance of Western pictorial art practice and related theories of space: first, the static positioning of the body, which assumes an immobilized viewer and a fixed viewpoint, and second, the rendering of space as empty. The work of spatial theorists has introduced other ways of thinking with and about space. They reintroduce the grammar of the body in a way that is useful for our understanding of player engagement in game space. I now take a detour through garden design to show how space has been framed, visualized, and understood from the perspective of a viewing subject. The seventeenth-century baroque French gardens are taken as a starting place to identify how various codes of viewing established during the Renaissance are reworked in the physical environment of the European garden. This is placed in distinction to the Asian tradition of spatial illusion and receptivity in the Chinese scholar's garden. Such an approach enables us to think about the cultural specificity of different conceptions of space and aesthetic traditions. It demonstrates how different concepts of space structure specific patterns of mobility and positions of subjectivity. This leads to valuable insights for thinking about the relationship between the body/embodiment/kinaesthetic being and space and how these ideas now resurface in a modified form in computer games.

It can be seen how the lineage of viewing practices established in European art extended from the painted landscape to the physical environment of the garden. The spatial structures and cultivated landscapes of the French baroque gardens, with their avenues of clipped hedges and trees, constructed particularly Western pictorial conditions of visuality. At Vaux-le-Vicomte, the baroque garden designed by André Le Notre, imperial views, straight avenues, clipped yews, *parterres de broderie*, and elaborate fountains were employed to produce "a triumphant proclamation of mechanics over nature" (Sharma 338). Sharma notes how the calculated manipulations of scale, distance, and optical angle of Vaux-le-Vicomte used the same mathematical precision that was applied to military artillery and fortifications. As an expression of wealth and power, the baroque garden was designed not for human movement, but for viewing from static elevated positions such as a terrace or window. Based on the symmetry and geometry of architecture, which echoed the symmetry of the perspective grid, nature was to be observed from a fixed position as a fixed subject. For the aristocratic viewer, the garden was interpreted as a landscape painting, marked by its distinction from, rather than its similarity to, nature.

In her work on gardens, spaces, and subjectivity, Eugénie Shinkle points out how the body takes up a particular mode of being within such garden cultures. She outlines how the subject looking onto a distant landscape from the terrace or window is a confined and a mute body cast as something distinct from the self. Given that the formal landscape garden was a luxury few could afford or access, this omniscient "gods-eye view" represented a particular privileged and aristocratic class position. For the aristocratic subject, the body was reduced to a seeing eye of refined visuality that obscured the conditions of the body. However, for the workers required to produce and maintain the gardens, the bodily or visceral experience was quite different. For Nicholas Fouquet, the owner of Vaux-le-Vicomte, it was a place of luxury and diversion and a visual expression of wealth and power. For the 18,000 workers hired to raze a whole village, level hills, plant forests, and divert the course of a river it was a place of hard labor (Sharma).

Privy Garden (Kings Private Garden) Hampton Court (photograph by Bernadette Flynn).

By the late seventeenth and early eighteenth centuries the European "gods-eye view" had evolved to incorporate the idea of the viewer as mobile.

Such landscape schema defined space and structured mobility in relation to particular cultural notions of the body in the garden. For example, the movement of a walker along the straight paths and manicured gardens of Hampton Court was structured as a promenade. Originally laid out for King William III in 1702, the straight paths and symmetrical arrangements of heavily pruned trees in the privy gardens drew the eye into a perspective grid. From the perspective of another walker, this emphasized the spatial trajectory of the figure moving toward the horizon line in the distance. By contrast, movement through the unadorned expanse of water, hills, and trees of Capability Brown's late eighteenth-century Stowe was designed as a wander. This new style of English landscape design was characterized by grass meadows in front of the house, serpentine lakes, follies, encircling carriage drives, belts, and circular clumps of trees. In wandering or strolling through the gardens of Stowe bridges, cascades and lakes were to be appreciated by a highly trained and refined sensibility. The walker set out in the world of a painting where navigation was at the service of the picturesque. In this painting the landscape became the destination and its space the scenery. This form of navigation emphasized a more private individual experience of "naturalized nature" revealed in a series of unique compositions that were structured around ideal views. As Rebecca Solnit reminds us, walking and a taste for landscape were not taken as a given. Landscape connoisseurship was itself considered an art, a sign of refinement and a reflection of character with guides written specifically to explain to the middle classes how to contemplate the landscape as picturesque. As the art of landscape interpretation, like the art of interpreting paintings, developed into an important social skill for the middle classes, modes of navigation organized space into viewing positions and also structured social relations and ways of looking into formal codes.

With an unfolding sense of wonder, the navigation in games such as *Myst III: Exile* can be seen to be similarly at the service of the picturesque. The player navigating through the multinode panoramas is at the mercy of a surfeit of imagery, an over-abundance of trompe l'oeil detail. A reading of the landscape is necessary in order to make sense of the surroundings and identify the challenges built into the geography. There is a way of looking that the player must grasp in order to interpret the scenery as pointers to clues. The player, like the garden visitor, must decode the landscape and the surroundings to find out what the terrain, the spatial objects, and the avatars can offer to enhance gameplay.

That this notion of the picturesque was a particularly Western notion of space can be demonstrated by comparing the formal codes of the European garden with the formal codes of the Chinese scholar's gardens. Chinese scholars or administrators retiring from the emperor's court built retreat gardens as spiritual havens for writing poetry and meditation. The intention of gardens such as *Lingering Garden* and *Mountain Villa with Embracing Beauty* in sixteenth-century Suzhou was to create an environment for contemplation through navigation and meditative pauses. Influenced by Buddhism, Taoism, and occultism, a retirement time spent contemplating the metaphysical universe was seen as the noblest way of life. Designed to create an experience of infinite space within a limited space, the gardens were not intended for visual pleasure but to mirror the depth of the inner spiritual life.

Chinese gardens as "embodied poems and three dimensional pictures" used spatial design to shape the imagination (Hongxun). The poetic gardens are designed to make the small evoke the large in a carefully constructed composition. They are to be experienced by the visitor entering through a gateway and traversing the landscape.

In moving through the physically small space of the gardens the illusion of size and dimensions shifts from different angles. Techniques such as borrowed scenery, leaky windows, and rocky peaks (miniature mountains) are designed to achieve a great sense of freedom and space. The treatment of the

The Circular moon gate frames the Miniature Mountains beyond (photograph by Bernadette Flynn).

The small evoking the large: view over zigzag bridge to pagoda.

Concentration of focus through contrast of light levels and surface texture.

viewing angle creates different points of focus to alter the illusion of space and time and effect consciousness. This shift in the sense of perspective and scale works to destabilize the navigator's reference points. For example, as the visitor moves through the garden, the frame of the moon gate suggests a larger space beyond and a miniature-curved bridge over the artificial mountain stream suggests a large distance traveled over water. The visitor is guided by the design techniques of zigzag bridges, corridors, pavilions, and moon gates to move to specific vantage points for observation and contemplation of unique views. Dusan Pajin makes the comparison between the visitors being led into these different garden scenes to the viewer being led into a composition. The compositions are observed and contemplated gradually, in time, through a succession of scenes that are only ever partially revealed as the navigator moves through the garden. Designed to unfold one after another, they represent the cosmos in miniature and assume a perceptual conscious body aligned with a cosmic reality. This is in contrast to the baroque garden, representing control over nature and assuming a confined body marked by its distinction and separation from nature and the conscious self.

Tracing the ways that the formal codes of the Chinese scholar's gardens were taken up and reinterpreted in the Anglo-Chinese gardens, or chinoiserie, reveals much about Western cultural ideas on spatiality. During the eighteenth century many English gardens were influenced by the design of Chinese gardens.[3] Known as Anglo-Chinese gardens, or chinoiserie, they imitated the complexity and the aesthetic elements of the Chinese garden but bore little resemblance to the cosmos in miniature exemplified by the Chinese scholar's garden. In the chinoiserie, the constructed pastoral scenes of the typical English landscape garden became inundated with the curved banks, pagodas, artificial hills, and stone grottoes of the Chinese garden. The structures integral to the carefully constructed composition of a Chinese garden were reduced to Chinese idiom or landscape "follies." Chinese landscape elements in the chinoiserie became the exotic turned sentimental. Unlike the Chinese scholar's garden, in which navigation was an opportunity for transcendent experiences, navigation in the European garden assumed a privileged point of perspective from which nature is accessed as culture. Movement in the English garden was considered more a mode of visual experience rather than a catalyst for inner reflection. Therefore, it is not surprising that in the translation of Chinese garden elements into the chinoiserie, the important balance between imagination and movement central to the creation of a spiritual sanctuary was replaced with the navigation of the eye and a scenic aesthetics that was intended to demonstrate cultural taste.

These influences can be seen within the construction of game space, where the small evokes the large and where the aesthetic dimension serves to invite the player to step within a carefully constructed composition. The Japanese, like the Europeans, were heavily influence by Chinese gardens, but they interpreted them for their symbolic and abstract qualities. For the Japanese, inspired by Chinese Buddhism and neo–Confucianism, every view has its own point of interest and each view creates a given effect with a minimum of means. From the Chinese landscape, the environment was filled with codes — spiritual, moral, and aesthetic. They required a seeing, navigating body. The diminishing, receding, enlarging strategies used in games can be seen to speak of this body image. In a game like *Ico*, designed and art directed by Fumito Uedo, the codes of way finding invite the player to inhabit space. Moments of contemplation and wonder create a strong connection between spatial habitation and navigation. In *Ico*, decoration is reduced to a minimum with atmosphere being generated from a balance between data density and color (Morris and Hartas 2003). *Ico* has action, adventure, and puzzle elements, but playing the game is not simply about gaining skills at the game level but acquiring aesthetic pleasures associated with the connection between space and bodily engagement. In the dynamics of play, the dimensions and proportions of the game space connect navigation to mobility and imagination. Such a process of navigation, required for deciphering the codes of the landscape, deeply involves the player in the spatial landscape.

Visual Spectatorship in Cinema

It is useful here to briefly trace how the formal codes of viewing the landscape have been taken up and — with some modifications — translated into the spatial configurations of mainstream Western filmmaking practice and reception. Typically, games have been considered in regard to preceding screen media such as film. The evidence from early film indicates that the audience enjoyed film as a visceral experience — as an aspect of mobility and travel (Gunning). A lineage associated with fairgrounds, joyrides, and the experience of vertigo is a part of computer game history that has been subsumed by an emphasis on narrative or formal concerns. Within a decade of the appearance of film, the kinaesthetic sensations associated with film had been replaced by the closed, darkened environment of the cinema and a fully immobilized body. Film came to demand a static form of spectatorship more internal and cognitive than kinaesthetic. Here I will briefly discuss some elements of film space and identify how some elements from screen constructions of space and positions of audience subjectivity have been carried over to the computer game environment.

Engagement with film now requires a different kind of perceptual absorption based on the closed diegetic space of the screen. Like the point of view from an upper-story window onto a Baroque garden, spatial relations in film are expressed through a frontal organization of space. Camera movement is directed by the assumption of the audience's absorption in the characters' movement on screen. This structures navigation around the dimensions of the human form in a flowing movement that is compatible with the navigation of the human eye. In watching the film, the eyes track through mise-en-scène, tracking and dolly movements and conventions of pan, tilt, and styles of framing to reproduce a naturalized view of human perception. Continuity editing conventions further construct a certain type of spatial geography that is consistent with the idealized position of the viewer in front of the garden view. Structured through a dominant line of vision from the perspective of the static viewing subject, formal codes of editing emphasize the depth axis — the relationship between foreground and background or foreground/character and horizon line.

This viewing practice elicits certain modes of looking and conditions particular navigation patterns of eye movement. Film theorists (most notably Laura Mulvey) have critiqued Western cinematic formulations of representation and the rules of audience engagement that are inherent in their construction (see also Mayne, Johnson). She has argued that the cinema structures ways of seeing and mechanisms of looking. Specifically, cinematic codes and their relationship to formative external structures are tailored for particular forms of pleasure relating to the female characters "to-be-looked-at-ness." She describes how cinematic codes create a gaze, a world, and an object that are cut to the measure of male desire that limits the range of pleasurable expectations.[4] Not only is such desire embedded in ideologies of representation that revolve around a specific perception of the subject, but also the concentrated gaze on the subject draws attention away from the expanse of screen space to the more defined space of the "to-be-looked-at" character. From Hollywood cinema, it is evident that this exaggerated "to-be-looked-at-ness" is central to the positioning of computer game avatars. A classic example includes the fetishization of Lara Croft, the central avatar in *Tomb Raider*. Her larger-than-life sexual physiology acts to concentrate the gaze. This scopic focus draws attention away from the broader architectural space and works in opposition to the attention demanded by gameplay (Kennedy).[5]

As scholars of Asian cinema Chris Berry and Mary Farquhar observe, recent Chinese films have a quite different logic of spatiality where there is no notion of a singular dominant line of vision or 180-degree rule. The films of the "fifth generation filmmakers" such as Zhang Yimou (cinematographer on Chen Kaige's *Yellow Earth*, (1984) and director of *Red Shorgum* (1987), *Raise the Red Lantern* (1991), *Ju Dou* (1991)) use long shots, a limited range of colors, available lighting, and nonperspectival use of space. Derived from the Chinese art of the wood block, vertical hanging scroll, and horizontal hand scroll, his films reveal an experience of space that has no vanishing point. There is a favoring of horizontal and vertical axes above all else. Such an idea of space aspires to the Taoist cosmology based on a decentered view from multiple perspectives as differentiated from a Judeo/Christian cosmology based on a single line of vision from an omniscient God. Similar to a Chinese garden, the decentered compositions in the films of Zhang Yimou have a pictorial and spiritual impetus. In much fifth-generation Chinese cinema, characters are abstract figures walking along the horizon line emphasizing the relation of the human figure to the landscape and the link between inner psychic geography and outer visual scenes. Unlike Western cinema, a film such as *Raise the Red Lantern* does not assume a fixed perspective and requires a navigation of the eye that is everywhere all at once. Space therefore is not bounded by the character or objects that occupy space as in Western narrative film but includes the larger sphere of the surrounding space.

While it is too broad a sweep to directly attribute specific techniques to a singular cultural context, I argue that computer games draw on hybrid aesthetic practices. What I want to argue is that games use representational imagery not only from Western art practices but also from Asian art and pictorial traditions. Early Japanese computer games draw on aesthetic traditions familiar to China with the wide use of scrolls and exaggerated horizontal and vertical space. Shigeru Miyamato (creator of classic Japanese games such as *Super Mario Bros* and *The Legend of Zelda*) adopts the distinct morphology of Japanese types and style against a fantasy landscape. *The Legend of Zelda* was principally inspired by Miyamoto's explorations as a young boy in the hillsides surrounding his childhood home in Kyoto, where he ventured into forests with secluded lakes, caves, and rural villages. According to Miyamoto, his Zelda games are an attempt to bring to life a miniature garden for players to explore, which draw on these childhood adventures. Other more contemporary Japanese computer games also have distinctive visual characteristics such as *Parappa the Rapper*, *Space Channel 5*, and *Rez*. However, most contemporary computer games developed in Japan are intended for an international market. As such, they adopt a matrix of aesthetic styles blending anime and manga comic books traditions with more Western photorealistic or perspectival approaches. This is further complicated by the transmedia context of computer game distribution, which tends toward a replication of generic features rather than enabling the emergence of a distinctive directorial style or personal oeuvre.

Over the last hundred years the camera lens has been the primary tool for recording the physical world. Initially associated with a belief in visual neutrality and scientific objectivity, the lens still retains the aura of indexicality — a reference to the real. In the application of computer graphics to create three-dimensional game worlds, a naturalized view of spatial visuality and human perception inherited from this indexical tradition appears to dominate. Certain representational techniques have been absorbed into gaming approaches to the spatial dimension, including camera angles, high-resolution photorealism, simulations of film lighting techniques, water reflections, and depth of field. Depth of field (the amount of distance in front of and behind the point of focus that remains in focus) is a function of the lens. In a close-up shot on a telephoto lens (long lens), the lens is unable to provide deep focus behind the subject (based on how light is bent through a lens). Game interfaces mimic such technical limitations of the two-dimensional planes of the monocular lens, suggesting that the primary subject is still the "to-be-looked-at" character and the primary mode for the player is still the viewer. At the level of representation, many computer game designers hold onto the classic realist style and focus on polygon count and levels of verisimilitude as the holy grail of visuality. Higher levels of verisimilitude, while bringing us closer to the detailed naturalism of other media, such as film, do not necessarily provide higher degree of player immersion or engagement in the game world. Instead, once a level of verisimilitude is reached, it can distract by its distinction from fully motion generated film or photographic imagery. High levels of verisimilitude are not the same as a strong sense of place and atmosphere. In the next section, I expand on this important distinction between representation and the sense of inhabiting an environment that emerges from player performance or manipulation of the environment.

Agency as Spatial Experience

Computer games extend the spatial logic of film in that the images are not only watched but also are moved in, between, and around. The politics of looking and ways of seeing inherited from cinematic aesthetics are extended to point of view, navigation, and forms of embodiment that might be described as gaze and interaction modes. Rather than the characters' movement in film and the film editing conventions of spatial organization, computer gameplay demands the player's immersive presence in the configurations of the computer game world. In navigating in this spatial dimension, the player or the player's avatar is grounded in a form of mobile spectatorship that draws on both the indexical trace of photorealist media and the pleasures of agency offered by game engines. The player engages with spectatorial pleasures relating to the user as reader along with participatory pleasures relating to the user as player. This is most obvious in the shift between the cut scene and gameplay as the player oscillates between the spectatorship position of cinematic audiences and the ludic engagement of gameplay. Markku Eskelinen, for example, sets them up as oppositional with the dominant user function in film as interpretative and the dominant user function in games as configurative. In his analysis, he situates film as an interpretative action based on character identification, narrative structure, and the telling of a story. He situates game playing as a configurative activity that involves the player's strategic operations upon the elements of a game. He is talking here of the ability to manipulate complex systems within continuous loops of intervention, observation, and response. He suggests that these modes cannot be mixed and that interpretive models have no place in a game ecology.

Such a position obscures the close interplay between configurative activity and interpretative activity in many exploratory computer games. In

exploratory games, these activities are interrelated, overlapping, and embedded in player performance. Playing games such as *Myst III: Exile* and *Shenmue* signal how interpretation and configuration are frequently simultaneous
aspects of a spatial dynamic. In these games, reading the landscape in order
to remember where you have been, where you might be going, and how you
might return is vital for good game performance and optimal playing conditions.

The navigational direction in digital gamespace is coded through levels
of photorealism, pictorial systems, spatial detail, and the seduction of objects.
The seduction of objects (avenues, doorways, pick ups) attracts players' toward
or deflects them away from game goals, thereby structuring not only aesthetic
immersion but also the procedural logic of gameplay. In this way the interpretative mode involves the search for hidden meanings alongside the configurative aspect of interpreting puzzles, solving codes, and reading symbols.
Such play then demands the players' immersive presence in the game landscape and engenders a type of contemplation or absorption akin to, but not
identical to, the spectatorship role of sensual absorption in the closed diegetic
space of the film frame described by Mulvey. At the same time, it demands
a level of attention to the procedural logic or action-response-action agency
required to engage in the configurative aspects.

In structuring game challenges and points of view directed toward playability, screen aesthetics are not only bound up with representational elements,
but also intrinsically bound up with game structure. In this way screen visualization is combined with the rules of emergent behavior and procedural
logic. Representational elements inherited from film-based spatiality such as
mise-en-scène, the rule of thirds, deep focus (long-range depth of field to
emphasize the depth plane), combine with representational models generated
by simulation technologies and processes, including programming code, game
principles, and 3D graphics engines. These two sets of rules — the rules of
perspective and the rules of simulation — incorporate different histories and
ideologies of representing as well as modeling navigation experiences. Games
like *Half-Life* and *Grand Theft Auto* are examples of this mix of 3D simulation modeling with film style camera views. These different politics of spatial construction embedded in cultural history structure the rules of play in
game worlds. As such, they directly shape player expectation and the conventions of engagement. Experienced players oscillate seamlessly between iconic
representations of spatial terrain, maps of the landscape, symbolic spatial references, and pictorial and filmic conventions. In exploratory game worlds, the
players direct their behaviors through utilizing the aesthetics of mimetic real-
ism/s while performing in a simulation system. From this, players occupy different situations of subjectivity, and shifts between a subjectivity separated

from the landscape to a more immersed subjectivity are common during game-play across a range of game genres. One form of subjectivity involves being deeply engrossed in winning the game. In being deeply engrossed in the contest of winning and losing, the player's attention is withdrawn from the spatial field and directed elsewhere. Another form of subjectivity is understood as a condition of being deeply involved in the game as an experiential space. This provides a situation of attention to game space that integrates the player in the spatial landscape in a different way. These situations are not always polarized, but they emerge from the complex and multifaceted playing experience. In summary, they bring together playing in a simulation — the agency of interaction — with visual spectatorship — the cinematic gaze in a way that is interdependent and synergistic. As Merleau-Ponty describes it, this is a spatiality of situation, suggesting that the player occupies multiple subject positions and switches between them: one subject position insofar as the player is actively engaged in navigations of a virtual self, and another subject position by virtue of the player's interpretative readings of the spatial landscape and mapping structures of the game world.

Games as Play Spaces

I have been discussing gameplay and the interwoven relationships between configuration and interpretation as interdependent subject and object positions. Turning attention now to how play fits into the discussion of computer games helps clarify the relationship between winning and losing games and more open structures of player engagement. As such, this helps locate our arguments about space in the appropriate context. I now outline the distinction between play and game as addressed by Roger Caillois in his influential taxonomy of play. Caillois makes an important distinction between *ludus* (game) and *paidea* (play) where *ludus* is characterized as rule-governed activity and *paidea* by fantasy and turbulence. For game scholars focusing on what makes games different from narrative texts, the notion of *ludus* (Latin for games) is defined as ontologically central to computer games (Juul, Eskelinen, Frasca). This approach privileges certain types of play, the more ludic (the win/lose conquests) over the more *paidiac* (the more anarchic or rhizomatic). From this context, the spatial is considered as a technology of vision or as a staging context for the gameplay event. This omits the pleasures of spatial performance and imaginative exploration as pleasures in their own right. It also suggests that gameplay operates as a form of systems manipulation separate from and not dependent on spatial engagement. There is also a gendered marginalization of the more anarchic or less structured play located in a division between the soft act of "passive" exploration and interpretation and the hard-core act of "active" gameplay or configuration.

In opening up the debate to a broader range of player pleasures, I would position a number of simulation and exploratory adventure games such as *The Sims*, *Myst III: Exile*, and *Rez* as play spaces rather than game spaces. *The Sims* is a simulation of the day-to-day activities of one or more virtual characters in a suburban household who engage in activities as banal as washing up and sleeping to more dynamic interactions with neighbors. Part of the fun is playing simulated domesticity and seeing what emerges from preprogrammed activities and player interaction. In *Myst III: Exile,* like its predecessors *Myst* and *Riven*, players navigate through imaginary worlds clicking on pre-rendered images.[6] Arguably, navigation through the spectacular worlds of *Myst III: Exile* is one of the main pleasures of engagement irrespective of involvement with the quest challenges. In *Rez* the player soars over nonfigurative, abstract futuristic landscapes to the repetitive beats of trance music. The plot is not really the point but rather immersion in the different senses and stimuli. As play spaces, these environments offer a wider notion of spatial practice and navigational pleasure than a strictly ludological formulation might suggest. As Katie Salen and Eric Zimmerman propose, play is an aspect of a game system outside of the functional structure. They suggest that play allows for free movement within a more rigid system, enabling different types of intervention into the structures of a game and more dynamic participatory experiences. For example, playing in *Myst III: Exile* affords the player a range of spatial pleasures such as moments of wonder, amazement, and intrigue outside of a rigidly imposed rule-bound causality. In many exploratory games such as *Myst III: Exile* (finding and leaving worlds) and *Ico* (the heroic quest) screen space as miniaturized playground becomes both destination and experience. As described by Margaret Morse, the process of miniaturization transforms narrative dimensions into spatial ones: "Miniaturization is a process of interiorization, enclosure, and perfection, one in which the temporal dimensions of narrative or history are transformed into spatial ones, a plenitude of description of seemingly endless details (211)."

Many adventure games operate as a quest for security, for place, for the moment of arrival through transforming the more familiar dimensions of temporality into spatial ones. Spatial immersion and navigation in such geography of place as *Tomahna* and the observatory in *Myst III: Exile* evokes a certain poetics of space — a movement from confinement to multidimensionality — a process of becoming or transformation. Detailed manipulation and close engagement in the environment means that space takes on a more significant meaning than story line or plot development. Structured in multinode panoramas, the navigation within *Myst III: Exile* foregrounds a moving or shifting perspective that moves the focus from the outcomes of events to the process of becoming in those events. Such a use of panoramas and scrolls (from Chinese and Japanese art traditions) illustrates that Euclidian geometric space formulations are not necessarily the most useful for creating experiences of being there — of being a situated body.

Embodied Practice in Games

Computer games offer sumptuously designed spatial environments that draw on both Western and Eastern forms of spatiality to construct different aesthetics and subjectivities. Embedded in these game environments are a matrix of ways of thinking about the player in respect to physical tactile response mechanisms, virtual embodiment, and the cultural and cognitive perceptions of the player. The player is constituted through these spatial environments as an embodied subject. As dynamic environments that respond to player activity, game spaces always involve a particular way of thinking about the body.

Approached in this way the game environment is conceptualized as a spatial dynamic and the player (either as avatar or as cursor) as an embodied subject whose perspective involves the relationship between objects, bodies, and spatial mapping. As Henri Lefebvre's conception of spatial practice suggests, the body is engaged in the experiential, the perceptual, and the imaginary. As a Marxist historian he argues that a dialectical rather than a casual relationship operates between these three modes. In game worlds this relationship between the player's body and space is organized into patterns of meaning, senses, and perceptual experiences that are overlapping and, as Lefebvre argues, linked to the social. As Doreen Massey's work on cultural geography reminds us, socially constructed space is historically and politically constituted. The player engaged with the dynamic of the game is both a perceptual and an imagining body. This body located in a sociocultural context is framed by its past and potential perceptions. Navigation as a behavior or performance then emerges from a body's relations to a spatial situation and to an environment.

Navigation of computer space is a cultural act where social practice, gender, and ideologies of representation are inseparable for the gameplay event. This cultural act is determined by the kinaesthetic being of the player and its access to the spatiality of the digital environment. In relation to Merleau-Ponty, the lived body provides the basis for understanding the manner in which we experience or perceive the world in an embodied rather than abstract understanding of that process. The perceived world and the body form a dialectical relationship in which each is mutually adjusted to the other. Sensation is a communication, or coexistence between body and thing. The body is not a closed mechanism but opens itself to the world. Kinaesthetic engagement of the type described by Merleau-Ponty can be analyzed in relation to a specific instance of spatial practice and here I have selected the first-person shooter game *Half-Life*.

Half-Life uses GoldSrc, a heavily modified Quake game engine. Released as a multiple-player and a single-player version, my focus is on the single-player version. The representational logic is Euclidian and emphasizes the spatial coordinates available for movement. At this level the rigid geometry expresses a certain disjuncture between foreground and background elements of the composition and creates an oddly elongated Z-axis. In *Half-Life* space is an inconvenience, to be traversed with speed and enemies to be destroyed with expediency. The exaggerated lines of visuality suggest a certain force on movement where the body is in the condition of always doing something. This can be described as a subjectivity engrossed in winning the game. The view is straight on with freedom to control camera views. Fuller and Jenkins have associated this force of penetration with narratives of conquest and a "conspicuous consumption of space" (62). In this form of spatial practice, the visualization of the spatial dimension and the experience of movement through that space are related but diverging experiences. There is an oscillation of focus between the environment and the perception of self. The player's body projects itself beyond the present moment into the next moment in a shift between the object of vision and the subjectivity of self. The player moves from the here to the there of potential landing sites guided by direct and peripheral vision of spatial geometry.

Once the rules of the game are mastered the player's attention to the visual interface falls away. In the first-person environment the player inserts him or herself as a nonspecific virtual body. The notion of embodiment is highly abstracted at the level of spatial visuality and thus presents a malleable concept of the body, with a sense of bodily situation emerging experientially through lived space. As the player focuses on game tactics and rapid response, attention to visual treatment, details of composition, or levels of verisimilitude falls away. The interface also includes the physical interface or tool by which the players can act upon the game space. For experienced players, the physical interface also disappears from the player's attention to create a position described by James Newman as "vehicular embodiment." He describes vehicular embodiment as a kinaesthetic experience where the embodied self is mapped onto the mouse or console controller.[7] In *Half-Life* through the complex manipulations of the handset the player can look at horizontal cylindrical panoramas, vertical views up and down, jump, duck, and move forward or back. Through the player learning the experiential space of the game, it becomes more than the represented space — it is a lived space through which the player impacts the world. This operates as a dialogue of engagement through a language of embodied spatial practice. The transference of gameplay kinaesthetics onto the console buttons and joysticks closes the experiential gap between being inside the screen and being at the interface. Instead breath, body, fingers, and visceral sensation are all components of the player's sense of embodied self as they attempt to weave, dodge, and shoot opponents.

Summary: A Way of Thinking Space

This chapter has examined the spatial in computer games. It offers a model of thinking about space from Western and Asian traditions as a key to understanding the multilayered complexity of player engagement. I have argued that a dynamic exploration of space is integral to gameplay and constitutes the player as an active agent (or inhabitant) in the game space. As such, I have outlined a number of overlapping and dynamic aspects of the spatial that need to be considered in our understanding of space. These include: representations of space, the phenomenology of mobility and agency, and the cognitive and imaginative processes emerging from the spatial experience.

Spatial design in computer games reflects histories of spatial engagement as filtered through the cultural framework of screen history and ways of viewing the landscape. Tracing the construction of garden design and film spatiality has shown us that an overemphasis on Western representation has left us with the legacy of a Euclidian hegemony that separates the body from the visible eye and denies the embodiment of the player. In the way that the baroque gardens of Vaux-le-Vicomte swept away the realities of the body, many game studies accounts omit the player's kinaesthetic experience.[8] Games call for the participation of the player and as such are part of a phenomenology of experience that always involves the lived spatial practice of the game player. Relevant to this is the relationship between representational space and bodily navigation — the situation of the body and the kinaesthetic experience of play.

In considering spatial engagement in this way, gameplay is not simply a form of representation or a ludic scenario based on gaining points or winning but a spatial activity that connects to increased perception of surroundings, self, and body. Spatial praxis might then be considered as a process of transformation that operates in a tangential relationship to the procedural logic of gameplay. This is inseparable from the cultural specificity of the player as a socially situated and conditional being. In other words, space operates as a metaphoric, expressive, and sensual language operating in a dialogue with the embodied subjectivity of the player.

Notes

1. René Descartes, considered a leader of Western philosophy (1596–1650), made the claim that mental phenomena are non-physical. He argued that the mind, a thinking thing, can exist apart from its extended body. In this model therefore, the mind is a substance distinct from the body, a substance whose essence is thought.

2. Jan Krikke traces how these techniques used in Chinese scroll paintings were introduced to Europe in the seventeenth century and later taken up in technical drafting, architecture and engineering. Its greatest influence in graphic design came through modernist architects at the Bauhaus and is the basis of CAD systems, modeling in computer games and simulation systems.

3. It should be noted that the influence of Chinese gardens came second hand through accounts given by merchants, Chinese handicrafts, wallpaper and painting. Forty scenes of the Yuan Mingyan (Summer Place) reached England in the 1760s and greatly influenced the design of the Anglo/Chinese gardens or Chinoiserie.

4. Other feminist scholars notably Zoe Sofia and Teresa de Lauretis have pointed out the limitations of Mulvey's application of Lacanian psychoanalytical theory to cinematic pleasure. They argue that the ideal viewer may not be the male and that the gaze can construct oppositional or subversive readings.

5. In a double reference back to film these scopophilic characteristics are central to Lara Croft's cinematic character played by Angelina Jolie in the 1993 adaptation "Lara Croft: Tomb Raider — The Cradle of Life."

6. *Myst* and *Riven* designed by Robyn and Rand Miller and produced by Cyan, Inc were highly successful influential exploratory adventure games.

7. Newman presents the argument that any specific game is not contingent upon the mode of representation, but is principally kinaesthetic. While up to this point I have argued that engagement with the spatial is not only a matter of visuality, I would position representation as an integral component of the spatial dynamic.

8. In the same way that accounts of the exploitative hours of IT workers, the conditions in computer sweatshops, and the types of bodily stresses encountered in long terms gaming are excised in gameplay sessions.

Works Cited

Aarseth, Espen. "Allegories of Space: The Question of Spatiality in Computer Games." In *CyberText Yearbook 2000*, edited by M. Eskelinen and R. Koskimaa, 152–171. Jyvaskyla, Finland: Research Centre for Contemporary Culture, 2001.

Berry, Chris, and Mary Ann Farquhar. "Post-socialist Strategies: An Analysis of Yellow Earth and Black Cannon Incident." In *Cinematic Landscapes: Observations on the Visual Arts and Cinema of China and Japan*, edited by Linda C. Ehrlich and David Desser, 84–100. Austin: University of Texas Press, 1994.

Caillois, Roger. *Man, Play and Games*. Trans. M. Barash. New York: Free Press of Glencloe, 1961.

Champion, Eric. "Explorative Shadow Realms of Uncertain Histories: Intangible Content and Translucent Interaction in New Heritage Projects." Paper presented at New Heritage Conference, Hong Kong, 2006.

De Certeau, Michel. *The Practice of Everyday Life*. Berkeley: University of California Press, 1984.

De Lauretis, Teresa. *Alice Doesn't: Feminism, Semiotics, Cinema*. London: Macmillan, 1984.

Eskelinen, Markku. "The Gaming Situation." *Game Studies* 1.1 (2001). 14 March 2007. http://www.gamestudies.org/0101/eskelinen/.

Frasca, Gonzalo. "Ludology Meets Narratology: Similitude and Differences between (Video) Games and Narrative" (1999). 10 August 2003. http://www.jacaranda.org/frasca/ludology.htm.

Fuller, Mary, and Henry Jenkins. "Nintendo and New World Travel Writing: A Dialogue." In *Cybersociety: Computer-Mediated Communications and Community*, edited by Stephen G. Jones, 57–72. London: Sage, 1995.

Gunning, Tom. "The Cinema of Attractions: Early Film, Its Spectator and the Avant-Garde." In *Early Cinema: Space — Frame — Narrative,* edited by Thomas Elsaesser, 56–62. London: BFI Publishing, 1990.

Hongxun, Yang. *The Classical Gardens of China: History and Design Techniques*. New York: Van Nostrand Reinhold, 1982.

Jenkins, Henry. "Game Design as Narrative Architecture." (2001). 18 January 2003. http://web.mit.edu/21fms/www/faculty/henry3/games&narrative.html.

Johnson, Claire. *Women's Cinema as Counter-Cinema. Notes on Women's Cinema*. London: Society for Education in Film and Television, 1974.

Juul, Jesper. "Games Telling Stories." *Game Studies* 1.1 (2001). 18 January 2003. http://www.gamestudies.org/0101/juul-gts/.

Kennedy, Helen. "Lara Croft: Feminist Icon or Cyberbimbo." *Game Studies* 2.2 (2002). 20 April 2006. http://www.gamestudies.org/0202/kennedy/.

Klevjer, Rune K. "In Defense of Cut Scenes." *Computer Games and Digital Cultures Conference Proceedings*. Tampere, Finland: Tampere University Press, 2002.

Krikke, Jan. "A Chinese Perspective for Cyberspace." (1996). 17 November 2003. http://www.ilas.nl/ilasn/ilasn9/eastasia/krikke.html.

Lefebvre, Henri. *The Production of Space*. Oxford: Blackwell, 1991.

Massey, Doreen. *Space, Place and Gender*. Minneapolis: University of Minnesota Press, 1994.

Mayne, Judith. *The Woman at the Keyhole, Feminism and Women's Cinema*. Bloomington: Indiana University Press, 1990.

Merleau-Ponty, Maurice. *Phenomenology of Perception*. Trans. Colin Smith. London: Routledge, 2000 [1962].

Morris, Dave, and Leo Hartas. *Game Art: The Graphic Art of Computer Games*. New York: Watson-Guptill, 2003.

Morse, Margaret. "The Ontology of Everyday Distraction: The Freeway, the Mall and Television." In *Logics of Television: Essays in Cultural Criticism,* edited by Patricia Mellencamp, 193–221. Bloomington: Indiana University Press, 1990.

Mulvey, Laura. "Visual Pleasure and Narrative Cinema." *Screen* 16.3 (1975): 6–18.

Newman, James. "The Myth of the Ergodic Videogame: Some Thoughts on Player-Character Relationships in Videogames." *Game Studies* 2.1 (2002). 12 July 2003. http://www.gamestudies.org/0102/newman/.

Pajin, Dusan. "Environmental Aesthetics and Chinese Gardens." (1997). 18 January 2003. http://dekart.f.bg.ac.yu/~dpajin/gardens/.

Ryan, Marie-Laure. *Narrative as Virtual Reality, Immersion and Interactivity in Literature and Electronic Media*. Baltimore: Johns Hopkins University Press, 2001.

Salen, Katie, and Eric Zimmerman. *Rules of Play: Game Design Fundamentals*. Cambridge: Massachusetts Institute of Technology Press, 2003.

Sharma, Simon. *Landscape and Memory*. London: HarperCollins, 1995.

Shinkle, Eugénie. "Games, Gardens, and the Anamorphic Subject: Tracing the Body in the Virtual Landscape." *Fineart Forum* 17.8 (2003). 12 December 2003. www.fon eartforum.org/Backissues?Vol_17/faf_v17_n08/reviews/shinkle.html.

Sofia, Zoe. "Masculine Excess and the Metaphorics of Vision: Some Problems of Feminist Film Theory." *Continuum: The Australian Journal of Media and Culture* 2.2 (1989): 116–128.

Soja, Edward. *Postmodern Geographies: The Reassertion of Space in Critical Social Theory*. London: Verso, 1989.

Solnit, Rebecca. *Wanderlust: A History of Walking*. London: Verso, 2001.

Wertheim, Margaret. *Pearly Gates of Cyberspace: A History of Space from Dante to the Internet*. New York: W.W. Norton, 1999.

Gameography

Age of Empires, Ensemble, Microsoft, 2003.

Baldur's Gate, BioWare, Interplay, 1998.

Doom, id Software, 1993.

Final Fantasy X, Square, Square EA, 2001.

Grand Theft Auto III, DMA Design, Rockstar, 2001.

Half-Life, Valve, Sierra, 1988.

Ico, Sony Computer Entertainment, 2001.

The Legend of Zelda, Nintendo, 1986.

Myst, Cyan, Brøderbund, 1993.

Myst III: Exile, Presto, Ubisoft, 2001.

Parrapa the Rapper, NaNaOn-Sha, SCEI, 1996.

Rez, United Game Artists, Sega, 2002

Riven, Cyan/Red Orb, Brøderbund 1997.

The Seventh Guest, Trilobyte, Virgin, 1993.

Shenmue, Sega-AM2, Sega, 2000.

The Sims, Maxis, Electronic Arts, 2000.

Space Channel 5, United Game Artists, Sega, 1999.

Super Mario Bros, Nintendo, 1985.

Tomb Raider, Core Design/Crystal Dynamics, Eidos Interactive, 2006.

The X Files: the Game, Hyperbole, Fox Interactive, 1998.

7

Wargaming and Computer Games: Fun with the Future

Patrick Crogan

This chapter will consider the history of wargaming in light of a broad audiovisual cultural trajectory that computer games evince and advance today. This trajectory is that of the inscription of cultural themes, motifs, and iconography in simulation models whose heritage is drawn in no small part from the military-industrial assumption of the leading role in the advance of technology from the Cold War onward. Computer games exemplify and promote this development of audiovisual culture better than films, television, or other mainstream media forms that rely more on conventional modes of narrative and historical discourse — although its effects are certainly noticeable in these other media, not least in their increasing convergence in the digital integration of all media forms. Wargaming had an important part to play in the military-industrial commandeering of the technoscientific agenda and its legacy is discernible in many genres of contemporary computer games, and not only those directly drawn from wargaming precedents. Electronic computing in general and its progeny, the "information age," can be thought of in no small part as the outcome of this trajectory outward from military research on computer modeling, strategic simulation, and gaming.

Wargaming, however, is much older than the 1940s. As we will see, its emergence as a significant, systematized, component of military training and research dates back to the early 1800s, but its ultimate origins go back much further, merging with that of the prehistoric origins of games generally. As such, the full history and significance of wargaming is an immense subject open to conjecture and speculation about its relation to historical, cultural, and even human biological, evolutionary development. Paying attention to the substantive components of the term, wargaming, namely, war and game, provides an indication of the full scale and scope of the question of the nature and significance of wargaming.

What I propose to do in this chapter is develop a reflection focused more on the recent history of computer wargaming. This focus will be constituted in a kind of dual perspective, one looking forward from the systematic adoption of wargaming practices in the early modern period toward the emergence of the computer age out of the technoscientific revolution of the Second World War, and one backward from contemporary commercial gaming to the emergence of the computer age. I am hoping to answer two related questions: What does the history of wargaming tell us about contemporary computer gaming as a product of the computer age? And what is the nature and appeal of contemporary computer gaming seen from the point of view of this history? My approach will look at the history of wargaming for what it can tell us about the history of modernity, and, above all, the importance of techniques and technologies of calculation and control for that history. Drawing on philosophical accounts of technology, I will propose that wargaming practices represent a pre-formulation of the techniques and principles of modeling so crucial in the development of the electronic digital computer as a simulation machine.

This will then allow me to say something about the nature and the appeal of computer gaming as an inheritor of this impulse toward and technical means of simulating complex environments and scenarios. This inheritance is most apparent in computer games based on conflict. My argument, however, is that the wargame, inasmuch as it anticipated the techniques of, and one might even say, crystallized a model of modeling, has played a constitutive role in the very capacity of computer simulation to program the modeling of all kinds of events and processes, something that describes in general terms most, if not all, contemporary computer gaming.

In relation to the audiovisual cultural trajectory described above, my major claim in this chapter is that the modeling of a situation to explore methods for controlling it interactively describes a computer game's employment of cultural themes, iconography, and content in general, something which is in contrast to that based on the narrative procedures of older mainstream media forms. Narrative involves the retrospective configuration of events-elements, a procedure that serves an interpretative function. This is quite an abstract and schematic description of the difference between computer games and films (and other narrative-based media), or rather film narratives.[1] It is meant to isolate the most fundamental difference between the two forms at a very general level of operation and significance, namely, the different ways each form structures in relation to time. Whatever else they are doing, computer games provide a future-directed modeling of a scenario aimed at either an eventual solution to the games challenges or a creative adaptation of the modeled dynamics, while narrative films relate a constructed sequence of past events for contemplation and interpretation of their significance. It is at this level of temporal engagement of the gamer that I want to consider the significance of the tradition of wargaming for an understanding of computer gaming and gameplay.

Wargaming, Modeling, and Programming

While the use of games in the study and preparation of war has a recordable history stretching back a very long way, the modern tradition of wargaming as a recognized component of military training and planning has its origins in the Prussian *Kriegsspiel* practices of the early 1800s. From there it gained popularity with military classes across Europe and subsequently in the United States and elsewhere. As Andrew Wilson has pointed out in *The Bomb and the Computer: Wargaming from Ancient Chinese Mapboard to Atomic Computer*, modern wargaming needs to be thought of in terms of the rational project of the Enlightenment that is associated with the major philosophical, political and economic transformations affecting Western European societies from this same period. Wilson describes the increase in wargaming activity that ultimately led to its adoption by the Prussian military apparatus, citing the "belief that war was an exact science" and the "quest for 'true principles' to guide its conduct":

In 1780 Helwig, Master of Pages to the Duke of Brunswick, devised a game that for the first time used single pieces to represent whole military units rather than individual soldiers. Five kinds of terrain were represented and could be used to build up a battlefield divided into 1,666 squares. The various arms were given different movement rates, and provision was made for an independent "director" to apply the game rules. The forces on each side included no less than

60 battalions of Grenadiers
25 battalions of Pontoniers
 8 squadrons of Dragoons
10 squadrons of Hussars
10 batteries of Field Artillery
 3 batteries of Siege Artillery
 2 batteries of Mortars [3].

Games such as this, played on a flat table with squares, on a plaster relief model representing different terrain types or on a map with diagrammatic indications of terrain, were the forerunners of Lieutenant von Reisswitz's wargame,

which in 1824 so impressed the Prussian chief of staff, General Karl von Müffling, that he recommended its adoption as part of the military academy's
training and research curriculum. Reisswitz's game was turn-based and had
complex rules, which set out procedures for determining the outcome of individual conflicts between pieces in different circumstances such as relative unit
strength and experience, terrain occupied, and so forth. Conflicts between
pieces were arbitrated by an umpire who applied the rules. This often meant
the rolling of different kinds of dice to introduce an element of chance into
deciding the outcome of a battle. For example, "if Blue, with 200 men,
attacked Red, with 100 men, Blue's chances were taken as two to one and a
die selected with four blue faces and two red" (Wilson, 5).[2] After the outcome was decided, loss tables were used to calculate how many men were put
out of action on each side.

Here at the outset of modern wargaming are the principal features that
Wilson rightly identifies with the worldview of the "Age of Reason," features
that remain discernible in the more recent era of the computer-based evolution and intensification of wargaming practices in both military and commercial contexts. The representational features of the wargame — such as
individual pieces standing in for whole military units, the scaled reduction
of physical space to the dimensions of the game board or miniature terrain-
analog, the formulas for calculating conflict outcomes and losses, the representation of uncertainty and unanticipated factors by means of dice
throws — all these served the purpose of what subsequently became known as
"modeling" in the service of simulation. The ludologist Gonzalo Frasca defines
simulation as follows: "Simulation is the act of modeling a system A by a less
complex system B, which retains some of A's original behavior" (Frasca 2001).

Frasca argues that a key difference between traditional representational
forms (such as the narrative representation of events in time) and a simulation is that representation typically operates from the "bottom up," that is,
from the specific case or situation general reflections are drawn. In the case
of representation in the service of simulation, however, a "top down" process
is in play in which the more general features of a system are modeled and various specific situations can be deduced or examined in an experimental fashion. This projective or experimental characteristic of simulation is crucial to
its appeal to modern military thinkers since Müffling. It is what is at the heart
of wargaming's modernity, namely, its potential to offer a rational basis for
predicting and therefore controlling the future. The model reduces the complexity of the original situation — in this case actual military conflict, and
later the wider context of strategic-political interactions — so that mathematical and statistical calculation can be employed both to determine the outcome of individual wargames and to compare and collate the results from

different wargames. These comparisons suggest the "true principles" of warfare with potential applicability to future conflicts in the real world of "system A."

Leaving aside a critique of the assumptions informing the simplification of "system A" (real war) into "system B" (wargaming model), a critique that has a history as old as wargaming, it is most important here to identify what makes wargaming so characteristic of the modern age.[3] Wargames evince the privileging of rational means for conceiving the world and humanity's involvement in that world. In *Technics and Time 1: The Fault of Epimetheus*, French philosopher of technology Bernard Stiegler cites Martin Heidegger's work on the modern age of technology as one of the most acute analyses of this tendency to seek a measurable determination of the future implicit in the "ratio" of rationality. Rational thought and action allow modern humanity to avoid a head-on confrontation with the inevitable but unpredictable fact of death. He summarizes Heidegger's analysis of the modern age of "calculation" in this fashion:

> The possibility of refusing the horizon of authentic possibility [namely, the horizon of one's own mortality], takes root in "concern" (*Besorgen*), a relation to the future which conceals in the future the opening of all authentic possibility. Concern is constituted by a mode of anticipation which, as foresight, essentially aims to determine possibility, that is, the undetermined. The support of all concern is "equipment" (*das Zeug*), itself the support of the system of references that constructs the significance of the world; and the horizon of anticipation, the originary structure of all worldliness, is the *technical* world — the technicity of the world is what reveals the world "firstly" and most frequently in its *facticity*. Facticity, understood as what makes possible the attempt to determine the indeterminate (to take flight from "the most extreme possibility"), forms the existential root of *calculation* [196].

This is a telling summary of the "concern" motivating the development of technology in the context of our discussion. For Heidegger, in Stiegler's view, the modern impulse to anticipate the future both comes from and is supported by the equipment of the "technical world," which we inhabit and whose meaning is derived from "the system of references" it constructs. This anticipation is expressed in the effort (and hence the belief in the ability) to "determine the indeterminate," that is, to know the future so as to secure oneself from the impact of unknown eventuality. The world as facticity, that is, as what is given to the human as already there, seems to promise this possibility that the possible future can be known and regulated in advance. Calculation is rooted in this promise of the technical world, a promise that for Heidegger is in truth an escape from the encounter with the "most extreme possibility" of the future, namely, one's inevitable but undetermined death.

In relation to wargaming as a phenomenon of the "Age of Reason," this reading of the essential metaphysical ground of modernity takes on the appearance of a justification for wargaming. As a method of training for military officers, wargaming concerns itself directly with the refusal of the horizon of death.[4] It contributes a new technique to the equipment available to improve the conduct of war, that most unpredictable and potentially lethal future possibility. The rules and mathematical formulas, which frame and enable gameplay, are derived from the "facticity" of former conflicts and experiences. The routine playing of the game to develop skills and research general principles for successful military strategy and tactics represents a programmatic employment of wargaming.

Indeed, wargaming could be thought of as an archetype of the modern conception of the program, that is, an organization of the exterior world (including the future as a temporal "outside") by rational, mathematical means. The program projects what is already known and recorded — in the form of technique, tool and more complex technical systems — forward as a means of solving the challenges to be met in the world in the passage of time. The wargaming program anticipates the "invention" of contemporary, computer-based practices of programming simulations via a process of modeling, which rests on the assumption that complex external reality can be conceived as a system with definable borders, interacting elements, and behaviors. A simulation's reduction of "system A" to arrive at "system B" is premised on the programming — "staking-out" in advance as Stiegler says — of the exterior milieu as a system as such (196). For Stiegler, technology is both source and vehicle for this programmatic orientation to the future we have inherited, in this case, in the form of historical records and actual models and techniques of wargaming. It is, he argues, only in and from this milieu of our modern, rational equipment, however, that any questioning of this program can emerge.[5] Computer games bear this potential as well as — indeed, as part of— this legacy of wargaming.

War and Other Games

What then of wargaming in the recent era in which computer programming and simulation become dominant features of the human encounter with existence? In this era (which is our era) the computer is able to simulate other machines by means of mathematical programming languages that enable what Stiegler calls the "largest possible indetermination in the functioning of machines" (80). Computer programming formalizes and generalizes the modeling principles manifested earlier in wargaming. In *The Bomb and the Computer* Wilson relates part of the long and detailed history of the dissemination of wargaming. In the 1940s and 1950s, along with its fellow travelers in the new technoscientific disciplines of Operations Research, Systems Analysis, computer-assisted code-breaking, and Cybernetics, wargaming updated and intensified the "quest for 'true principles'" to guide the conduct of war in its tactical, strategic, and logistical dimensions.[6] Wargaming (more often known as simulation or modeling exercises) was (and is) conducted across all branches of the United States armed services, the U.S. Department of Defense, the Office of the Joint Chiefs of Staff, and by numerous government-supported "think tanks," research centers and defense contractors. On the one hand, this proliferation of wargaming has been accompanied by considerable questioning of its capacity to predict future possibilities with any certainty — in particular, at the level of strategic and strategic-political simulation.[7] On the other hand, this has not impacted significantly on the level of use of simulation and gaming across the military sphere. It is, rather, an index of the extent of simulation practices in the military and indeed in the commercial sector as well as being a function of the close relations between military, academic, and commercial interests across the history of computing and computer simulation.[8]

The cross-fertilization of these three spheres throughout this history of computing has been so extensive as to raise the question of whether they can be legitimately treated as distinct spheres of endeavor at all. Tim Lenoir and Henry Lowood, historians of science and technology who, in cowritten and individual texts, have documented the enormous volume of traffic between military, commercial, and university-led advances in computing, communications, and audio-visual technologies, ponder this question.[9] They examine in their work what has recently been termed the "military-entertainment complex" — an accelerated interchange of personnel and software between the U.S. military organizations, defense contracting firms, defense-funded academic research programs, and commercial gaming and simulation industries that is a key indicator and vehicle of the post–Cold War transformation of the "military-industrial complex" identified in the early 1960s as the outcome of the policy of massive investment in military technoscientific research and development from the 1940s. In "Programming Theaters of War: Gamemakers as Soldiers," Lenoir posits the idea that "a cynic might argue that whereas the military-industrial complex was more or less visible and identifiable during the Cold War, today it is invisibly everywhere, permeating our daily lives" (175).[10]

Wargaming is a key conduit of the dynamic exchanges between military and entertainment innovations and "applications." The influence of amateur and "hobby" wargaming on both the military and the commercial computer games sectors is a clear indicator of this. For instance, Sid Meier, developer of the immensely successful "god game," *Civilization*, had a background in hobby wargaming and had worked for a Baltimore-based defense contractor prior to entering the commercial games industry. His early games for the company he cofounded, Microprose, included several combat flight simulators (*Hellcat Ace, F-19 Stealth Fighter*), wargames (*Conflict in Vietnam, Crusade in Europe*), and a strategy/action combination game based on a submarine simulation (*Silent Service*) (DeMaria and Wilson, 187–188). His preparation for work in commercial gaming is typical of many other designers and developers, many of whom move or have moved between military and nonmilitary employers.

Beyond the direct influence military and defense organizations have had on commercial gaming via the traffic of personnel between the two regimes of simulation programming, it is important to keep in mind the pervasive influence the military-industrial complex has had on the development of computer programming. The American social scientist and historian of technology, Paul Edwards, has documented this history in *The Closed World: Computers and the Politics of Discourse in Cold War America*. Edwards associates early advances in computer development with the impetus in the post–Second World War period toward the conception of global strategic-political events and situations as systems capable of definition, modeling, prediction, and control from a centralized perspective and operational point. "Closed world" discourse is his term for the nexus of strategic-political rhetoric, technoscientific innovation and cultural metaphorics out of which emerged computer culture.[11] He explains the success of digital computing over the then superior analog computing technology of the late 1940s and early 1950s by its appeal to a dream of real-time total control of a whole field of operations, something perceived as imperative in the minds of many military strategists and technoscientific researchers in the context of potential nuclear conflict with the Soviet Union at the speed of jet bomber and missile-borne warhead delivery. As Edwards recounts, computer programming was effectively born as a career and a profession through the large numbers of programmers Rand employed on large military projects, above all on the U.S. Air Force's S.A.G.E (Semi-Automated Ground Environment) air defense system design and implementation (82).

To return to our narrower focus on the two-way traffic between military and nonmilitary computer gaming, the influence of Trevor Dupuy's "Quanti-fied Judgment Model" (QJM) exemplifies the significance of wargaming for both military and commercial computer gaming and simulation. Dupuy was a career soldier with enormous influence in military wargaming. Journalist and historian Thomas B. Allen describes the QJM as follows:

> [Dupuy's] Quantified Judgment Model is known throughout the world of gaming as the QJM. Both professional and amateur war gamers use the QJM, or adaptations of it. The QJM encompasses all of what gamers call the gaming community:

the military establishment, which uses games in the Pentagon and the war colleges and for other types of training; academe, which uses political-military games in international studies; commercial companies that sell board and computer games to the public; and defense firms that use games to develop and sell weapons systems [68].

The Q JM is Dupuy's version of the rules and tables governing the interactions of different units and different weapons systems in different circumstances (including unit strength, "lethality index" of weapons, level of combatant training and morale, terrain occupied, defensive or aggressive posture, and so forth). It was promoted by Dupuy as an improved, more reliable basis for modeling conflict than the "simulated facts" of nuclear wargaming that he argued were pervading military simulation practices (Allen 60). The Q JM was successfully promoted as an improvement in the modeling of war by means of a curtailment of speculative calculation in favor of historically grounded algorithms for conflict simulation and loss estimation — as if the speculative element of such calculation could be definitively excluded from the very project of conflict modeling.

Allen was writing in the 1980s prior to the 1990s explosion of the pc-based computer gaming industry. In "Theaters of War: The Military-Entertainment Complex," Lenoir and Lowood give an account of the acceleration of advances in computer-based military wargaming in the 1970s and 1980s that fed into this rapid development, contributing significantly to the nature and range of game genres and the training of game designers and developers (435–439). In this period military organizations looked to the amateur and commercial wargame community, adopting the game design and programming insights of nonmilitary designers such as James P. Dunnigan of Strategic Publications Inc. to reinvigorate military gaming and simulation practices at the tactical and strategic levels (Lenoir and Lowood 435). This effort was motivated by a desire to move toward a more soldier-friendly gaming practice, one which could be run and managed by military commanders at an operational level, as opposed to the older tradition of simulation training associated with academic researchers, think-tanks, and upper echelon military command.[12] Dupuy's project is wholly in keeping with this motivation. New media artist and cultural theorist, Manuel De Landa, discusses Dupuy's skepticism about the vision entertained by Rand Corporation scientists and their peers of a comprehensive, reliable modeling of war across tactical, strategic and logistical levels (104). Dupuy's efforts at quantifying war were circumscribed by an insistence on the limitations of such calculative processes in the planning and conduct of war. It is perhaps ironic but, in light of Lenoir and Lowood's work, predictable, that in the era of the military-entertainment complex his work on battle simulation would contribute to a massive proliferation

Screenshot from *Panzer General 3D: Assault* showing hex grid (© 1999 Ubisoft Entertainment, all rights reserved. The SSI, Panzer General, Ubisoft and the Ubisoft logo are trademarks of Ubisoft Entertainment in the United States and/or other countries).

and dissemination of computer simulational practices of wargaming and training *in concert with* models of strategic and logistical operations.

The influence on the existing gaming community of the Q JM, along with many other conflict modeling "packages" developed in the 1970s and 1980s, is reflected today across the range of conflict-based commercial game genres.[13] It is most obvious in "classic" turn-based battle games such as the *Panzer General* series, originally designed by another board wargamer, Joel Billings. Here, play takes place on a map covered with a grid of hexagonal shapes. The "hex" grid is a hobbyist innovation (subsequently adopted in many forms of military wargaming) on the traditional square–shaped grid and allows for an improved interaction between multiple units (Allen 96).[14] Movement rates and the algorithms for calculating the results of conflicts typify those developed by Dupuy for the Q JM.

The last iteration of the *Panzer General* series, *Panzer General III*, retains a hex-grid map for gameplay, albeit with improved 3D graphics of military units and conflicts. The major evolution in strategic wargaming has been the shift to real-time strategy gaming, popularized by Westwood's *Command & Conquer* series from 1995. Developer Creative Assembly's *Total War* series combines a real-time battle mode with a turn-based campaign mode incorporating strategic and logistical activities (such as forming alliances, building fortifications, and raising and training military units). Once a conflict is produced from this turn-based activity the player has the option of shifting to the real-time interface to fight it out or allowing the computer to simulate the conflict and automatically generate an outcome. The game combines modeling at two levels, that of strategic/resource management found in turn-based strategy games and battle simulation in real-time. Conflict simulation continues to be modeled in the tradition of the Q JM calculus in which unit arms, strength, fatigue, and morale play a part in deciding the outcome, while the turn-based mode follows *Civilization* in relying on strategic-political simulation practices. Computerized modeling at the strategic-political level originated in the Rand Corporation's "Social Science" and "Economics" divisions, established together in 1948 to enhance the modeling of socioeconomic factors in the anticipation of a logistical duel in which the combatants rushed to attain a position of preemptive dominance via the absolute nuclear weapon (Kaplan 68). That is, they came into existence to help game the arms race. This is the period marked by the acceleration of the dynamic that French theorist of war and technology, Paul Virilio, calls "pure war," in which a logistical orientation to political, strategic-political planning gains ascendancy under the pressure of the threat of absolute nuclear conflict. This logistical dynamic tends to overthrow traditional forms of political and social organization, rendering everything in terms of its potential to be adapted to the needs of the logistical process, from technoscience to cultural and educational practices to entertainment (Virilio and Lotringer).[15] After Virilio, we could say that Rand initiated the "pure wargame," progenitor of logistical and strategic-political gaming practices that flowed from the military-industrial complex to commercial game genres like strategy simulations and "god games."

This generic cross-fertilization in real-time strategy exemplified by the *Total War* series is in keeping with the wider development dynamic of computer game genres in a commercial milieu. The history of Strategic Simulations, Incorporated illustrates the process of dissemination of military wargaming principles across a wider field of game genres. From concentrating on turn-based strategic wargames such as their first release, *Computer Bismarck*, *Guadalcanal Campaign*, and *Kampfgruppe*, SSI moved onto god game simulations (*Rails West*) and role play and fantasy adventure games such as *Questron* and *Advanced Dungeons and Dragons: Pool of Radiance* (DeMaria and Wilson, 158–162). The modeling of system dynamics drawn from the practices of wargaming is a major contributor to all of these programmings of the simulation machine.

Fantasy Roleplay and Adventure gaming is among the most popular of contemporary commercial game genres. The MMOG (Massively Multiplayer Online Game) form of Roleplay gaming earns huge revenues in subscriptions and is a major phenomenon of new media entertainment. A question could be raised about the relevance of the wargaming legacy for such Fantasy gaming. To some extent this genre would seem to imagine a "greenworld" alternative to Edwards's "closed world" of technoscientific, computerized simulation, networking and control. He describes the "greenworld" found in forms of cultural expression such as theater, film and literature as:

> an unbounded natural setting such as a forest, meadow, or glade. Action moves in an uninhibited flow between natural, urban, and other locations and centers around magical, natural forces — mystical powers, animals or natural cataclysms (e.g., *A Midsummer Nights' Dream*). Green-world drama thematizes the restoration of community and cosmic order through the transcendence of rationality, authority, convention and technology. Its archetypal form is the quest, in which characters struggle to integrate (rather than overcome) the world's complexity and multiplicity [13].

This description seems to fit Fantasy Roleplay gaming neatly — unbounded natural settings, magical forces, mystical powers, quests — identifying this genre of computer gaming as the latest iteration of a tradition of alternative visions to a closed world (our programmed contemporary world) designed to anticipate a future of hi-tech war. The fact that these games do not have the same "closed" character as other game genres in terms of the game goals and criteria for completing the game would also support this identification.[16] In this view, Fantasy Roleplay games such as *Everquest* and *The Dark Age of Camelot* seem far removed from the eminently "closed world" games (and spaces) of strategic turn-based simulations, real-time strategy games, not to mention First Person Shooters such as *Doom* or Electronic Arts's *Medal of Honor* series. Key elements of Fantasy Roleplay gaming, however, replay the wargaming legacy: the centrality of modeled conflict using lethality indices (for different weapons, spells, and armament), the potential for tactical and strategic coordination between players; the logistical management of resources (armor, health, spells); skills training ("leveling up") and experiment-based learning. What I would call the wargaming program animates the mystical worlds and monsters in Fantasy MMOGs at the systemic level.[17]

Entertaining the Illusion of Control

Returning to our discussion in the introduction of an audiovisual cultural trajectory exemplified in the contrast between narrative and computer gaming employments of cultural themes, iconography, settings, and so forth, I would state that this account of the dissemination of the wargaming modeling principles across the wider field of computer gaming provides a larger historical context for the shift from a reflective to a programmatic relation to cultural content. This shift, while perfectly consistent with the anticipatory, experimental impulse that animated the war-focused modeling and simulation practices so influential in the postwar birth of the computer age, can be seen as an impulse with a history as old as Western European modernity, at least in this rational, calculative iteration: to regulate and control in advance cultural issues and problems, including those involving violent conflict, by rational, predictable, computable means.[18] As a model of computer gaming, indeed, as a model of modeling, wargaming is applicable to a variety of game types. This would tie in with the claim that war or conflict-based games are not primarily about interpreting historical war, or even war as a cultural or metaphysical theme.[19] That would be the preserve of narrative-based works dealing with war in which reflection on war would be the "value" or primary function. Or at least it would be one major aspect of those forms. The depiction of war as spectacular "special effect" is another longstanding function of war films, something that arguably is held in common with the audiovisual representation of war in computer games.[20] The appeal to the audiovisual "spectacle" of war is, however, something that is not central to all wargames. Consider, for instance, submarine simulations such as *Sub Command: Seawolf*, which downplays spectacle in favor of the rigorous pursuit of the instrument panel interface with the enemy available in the weapon system being simulated. While spectacle per se is not irrelevant to a consideration of what passes between computer wargames and other game genres, it belongs to a wider examination of the relations between war and media.

In terms of what most concerns us here, the question is: what is the wider appeal of the engagement with modeling and simulation that derives from the tradition of wargaming? It is playing with the illusion of control, control, that is, of the model's illusion of a more complex system. Citing Ted Friedman's discussion of *Civilization II*, James Newman argues that ultimately one plays a computer game to learn how to "think like a computer." This involves a relationship between player and gameworld "best considered as an experiential whole that synthesizes action, location, scenario, and not merely as a bond between subject and object within a world" (10). Mastery of this experiential whole amounts to attaining this "synthesizing" perspective in a manner by which the gameworld can be managed to resolve the game challenges. This is something relevant across and indeed beyond specific wargaming genres to all gaming based on modeling an illusionistically satisfying complex system — whether it is fictional, hypothetical, or historical.

As a recreational practice and a form of "entertainment," then, computer games exhibit that curious phenomenon of games and other entertainments in that they can be understood as a modulation of absolutely serious practices. "Entertainment"—from the French root word, *entretenir*, to hold between or suspend—replays and plays with(in) the serious business of modernity, namely, programming the technoscientific regulation of the future. Computer games, the entertainment form of the computer age, suspend the onerous task of managing the determination of the indeterminate, with all its attendant anxieties concerning the shortcomings of the equipment designed to eradicate the unforeseeable, the contingent, and the irreducibly complex. Instead, one can play out mastery of the indeterminate through a game of mastery of the model.

The appeal of computer games lies, perhaps, in both their ability to entertain the illusion of control and their acknowledgment of the illusion as illusion. That is, computer gaming enables a "double-play" in its suspension of the serious mode of information processing. On the one hand, games play out achievement of the imperative to anticipate the future, to attain what Stiegler calls a "synthetic living present" that overcomes the temporal delay of the future and the spatial delay of a distant contingency (225). This is what all the reductions made in the modeling of the more complex "system A" hope to achieve by bringing it within reach spatially and temporally. But what this playing out of a synthesizing mastery of the program perhaps indicates, in the very act of finishing the game, is that its projected goal can, at best, be played at in a modeled world.

Considered in this light as entertaining forms of suspension of technological modernity's project, a project that has war as a determining axis and well-spring of invention, computer games can also offer scope for the reevaluation and differentiation of that project. Suspension interrupts a planned and predicted course of action or sequence of events. However circumscribed, calculated, and regulated this interruption, it provides the possibility of a revision of the original pathway. As suggested above, the suspension can act via the ludic doubling of the serious project of predictive control in a simulated gamespace such as that of a First Person Shooter, a real-time strategy game, a flight simulator, or even a Roleplay game, a doubling that plays with and on the real-life experience of planning and decision making. This has the potential to open up a space (or a moment) of critical reflection or meditation on the gaming context. In this, games resemble other contemporary entertainment forms such as film, television, and literature whose doublings of the serious can also initiate reflection on the contemporary world in which they are enjoyed. And like these other forms, there exists the potential for producers to explore this reflective potential of suspension in game design.

This is the hope expressed by Gonzalo Frasca for the future of cultural forms of expression based on simulation practices (2003).

The diversionary potential of the suspension of the serious can also be realized in the way games are played and played with. This is evinced through player innovations to the scope and nature of gameplay envisaged by game designers. For instance, Espen Aarseth has discussed the invention by his team of players of a novel-winning tactic in a "capture the flag" type of game in the multiplayer mode of *Return to Castle Wolfenstein 2*. The tactic involves profiting from the combination of the ability to obtain a super-boosted jump from blowing yourself up with a grenade and the temporary invulnerability of one's avatar while being "revived" by a medic. Use of this tactic effectively short-circuits the "designed" combat between two teams by allowing the attacking team to advance one player over an obstacle and into a winning position (to capture the enemy flag) so quickly that the other team is unable to react in time (2003, 4). This type of player innovation of gameplay, based on discovering and exploiting bugs or unanticipated functionality from the designed game interface, is one where the game itself is suspended as a serious project — the game as commercial product of the contemporary, corporate technocultural system where designed functionality of the game as consumer good hopes to manage the contingent eventuality of capitalist competition through a sufficiently rapid amortization of the investment in game development.

The player plays with the game's modeling of a more complex system, inventing an exception or modification to the model's operation and redefining it in the process. This type of play can be thought of as a modifying gesture, which changes the game itself, or, from another perspective, differentiates players inasmuch as they can be said to be playing the same game. As Aarseth notes, the whole question of cheating arises in the vicinity of such practices. The real-world issues of moral responsibility, respect for the rights of others to enjoy their leisure time, the injunction to "not spoil the game," and so forth reassert themselves in the face of the challenge to the game's designed, entertaining suspension of real life. A further dimension of the context in which such issues arise is the widespread criticism of commercial game design as being deliberately simplistic or formulaic so as to limit the game's appeal and initiate demand for the next title release. "Cheaters" justify their exploitation of game bugs or "cheat codes" as a way of maximizing the value of their purchase. Furthermore, "cheat codes" and modified gameplay techniques are themselves incorporated by game designers to absorb cheating and innovation into game design/planning processes. The ambiguous and even ambivalent nature of entertainment's modulation of the serious is in evidence here where threats to the enjoyment of playtime manifest the "real stakes" of the game.[21] The operation of the principle regulating the delineation between the "serious" business of life and that which suspends it — just for fun — is itself suspended. This is the permanent danger of and to entertainment forms.

To conclude, computer games both reflect the contemporary cultural-technical milieu in which techniques of simulation and modeling dominate our programming of the future and, as entertainment, represent a privileged potential vector of its diversion. Descendants of the military gaming and simulation processes developed by Western modernity to program the future, computer games offer the possibility of a special contribution to what Stiegler characterizes as the idiosyncratic dynamic of human-technological "evolution." Stiegler names this process "epiphylogenesis" to point to its status as neither a purely biological nor totally technology-driven dynamic (in a purely exterior, rational, or instrumental sense of technology) (159). Its engine is the mutation of the given technical regime and for Stiegler this is at the heart of human development, ethnic difference, and history. While much of the time the design for living inscribed in our technicity is implemented faithfully in/as our existence, the potential for specific, idiosyncratic modification of the given milieu — and of the human-technical "who-what" to come — is always already there along with the design. It depends in no small way on how you and others play.

Notes

1. It should be noted that not all films are narratives, and even narrative films do not only operate as narratives. For instance, war films and other film genres function to provide spectacles of special effects that suspend narration and can relegate narrative operation to a secondary role.

2. The convention of differentiating the two opposing forces in the wargame as Red and Blue continues to this day.

3. Manuel De Landa takes up this topic and this history (84–104).

4. This is not, perhaps, a completely adequate characterization of wargaming as a practice (as opposed to wargaming as a designed activity): Perhaps, and I am speculating here, to play a wargame in the context of military training is a potentially much more ambivalent experience, one which is not only "against" passage into the horizon of one's own mortality, but also "right up against it," very close to an encounter with what eludes, exceeds and undermines the rational, pedagogical framework of the training. Is this ambivalence what resonates in the reflective comments of military personnel concerning the departure of real combat from the training simulation, for instance, in the media coverage of the second Iraqi campaign where commanders were frequently quoted expressing their surprise at the "asymmetrical" response of Iraqi elements to their carefully planned and modeled tactics? With the bloody extension of this asymmetrical campaign beyond the capture of the Iraqi capital (which marked the "official," victorious end of the second Iraq war), the ambivalence of the rational project of military wargaming is, perhaps, increasingly felt by the U.S. forces and their allies. Of course, one (already anticipated, no doubt)

response to this erosion of the certainty of the outcome of "Gulf War 2.0" has been work on improved simulational training more appropriate to this asymmetrical conflict. This is exemplified by Pandemic Studio's *Full Spectrum Warrior* (2004), developed in conjunction with the Institute of Creative Technology at the University of Southern California (funded principally by the U.S. Department of Defense) for use both as a U.S. Army urban warfare training simulation and for commercial release. The military version of the game, a "tactical shooter" in which the player commands two "fire teams" who work in concert to accomplish a variety of missions in the fictitious, despotic Middle Eastern state of "Zekistan," was accessible via unlock codes in the initial commercial release of the game on the X-Box.

5. It is on this point that Stiegler departs from Heidegger's account of technological modernity. To give an adequate account of this departure is beyond the scope of this chapter, but at least a brief summary is in order here inasmuch as it bears on our approach to the computer games that come to us today out of this wargaming past. Stiegler analyses Heidegger's project in detail in the final two chapters of *Technics and Time 1*. His difference from Heidegger, the thinker who addressed the neglected question of technology more than most others in the history of Western philosophy, ultimately resorts to a classic gesture of dispatching it outside the bounds of what is essential to human being. He identifies this gesture in Heidegger's magnum opus, *Being and Time*, with the way Heidegger associates the "inauthentic" temporality which humans ("*Dasein*" in Heidegger's existential analysis) live in their everyday existence with the technical, factical milieu of "world historiality." For Heidegger, argues Stiegler, the authentic encounter with time (that is, that which arises within the horizon of one's mortality) must come from elsewhere. For Stiegler, technology cannot be excluded from consideration of essential human nature, and likewise from thinking the human experience of time, "authentic" or habitual.

6. For an account of the new coordination of military and technoscientific endeavor during the war years of the early 1940s and its evolution in the Cold War period, see Kaplan.

7. See discussion of some of the major critiques of the reliance on strategic simulation practices in Allen, 116–120. Andrew Wilson's history of wargaming, written in the late 1960s, is itself dedicated to an urgent questioning of the enormous influence of wargaming on military strategic decision-making in its contemporary Cold War context. The final chapter, "Vietnam: The Game that Failed," assesses the U.S. military command's grave strategic miscalculation of the Vietnam conflict, sheeting it home in no small part to wargaming and simulation practices out of touch with the real, social, political and geographical situation confronting the combatants.

8. In this regard the recent "discovery" of the potential of computer gaming and simulation for "serious applications" in education and training is indicative of a (perhaps voluntary) amnesia about the origins of commercial computer games and simulations. As with the commercial development of entertainment-based games, the innovations arising from this rising interest in "serious" gaming will no doubt be of considerable interest to military training and education in the future. This is not pre-emptively to consign all potential developments in "serious" (or for that matter entertainment) game design to history as a sub-branch of military R&D. It is important, however, and even critical for a critical discourse per se on computer gaming and simulation, to take account of the dynamics which make these confluences between branches of computer "evolution" intelligible and predictable.

9. See Lenoir and Lowood (2005), and Lenoir (2000, 2003).

10. While Lenoir chooses to distance himself, at least provisionally, from such a claim here, a "cynical" perspective is arguable the only one available to close readers of his

account of the workings of the military-entertainment complex. The questioning which opens up from adopting this perspective concerns the nature and implications of this permeation of daily existence by the dynamic relations driving technoscientific advance, in particular in the realm of audio-visual culture. I am concerned in this chapter, and elsewhere, with contributing to this large and crucial task. Lenoir's work (and Lowood's in their co-written studies), while immensely valuable in providing a rigorous and detailed account of the workings of the military-entertainment complex in terms of histories of government policy, technological innovations, cross-institutional and organizational interchanges and movements of personnel between the military and entertainment (and academic) "Spheres," is somewhat limited in its approach to this further questioning of the critical and cultural ramifications of the situation they document so compellingly. The work of French theorist of war, speed and technology, Paul Virilio, is someone whose pursuit of these questions has been unrelenting. His concept of "pure war" will be discussed briefly further on in this chapter. His book, *War and Cinema: The Logistics of Perception*, is a major contribution to framing the questioning of the broader impact of the long history of exchange between military-inspired or appropriated developments in representational technologies and daily existence.

11. Edwards analyses this nexus or network of discursive, political, logistical and technical interactions in terms of the work of French social and critical theorist, Michel Foucault, on the knowledge/power relations that underpin a particular cultural regime of thought and practice.

12. This conflictual dynamic between operational strategic and tactical levels and the higher levels of military command can be seen in the light of the larger history of the resistance to the policy of centralized and integrated strategic command adopted by the U.S. armed forces in the Cold War era, a policy decision which Edwards analyses in *The Closed World* as being directly related to the promise of total oversight and control associated with networked, digital computing systems (70–73).

13. Other influential modelings of war from this era are the *Strategic Analysis Simulation* (1980), developed by Mark Herman for a Strategic Publications Inc. contract with the U.S. Department of Defense, and Fred McClintic's *McClintic Theater Model* (1980), a new architecture for computer-based wargames which "became the basis for a series of computer-based theater and operational simulations during the 1980s" (Lenoir and Lowood 438).

14. Lenoir and Lowood credit Charles S. Roberts, founding principal of the board wargaming giant, Avalon Hill, with the hex innovation in the 1950s (431).

15. See Crogan for a more extended discussion of Virilio's project in general in relation to contemporary computer gaming.

16. The difference between "closed" game design and what Jesper Juul, drawing on chaos theory, calls "games of emergence" is identified as a key element in what distinguishes multiplayer roleplay gaming from other more objective-oriented games.

17. It is instructive to note here that the first, Fantasy adventure games played via computer networks were developed in the early 1970s by world-encapsulated designers and research assistants across the military-developed ARPANET, precursor of the internet. Making time for leisure amongst the serious business of defense-funded technoscientific research, they devised and began playing *Dungeons and Dragons* type games across their cutting edge computer networks in the Universities and Research Institutes of the military-industrial complex. For an account of the development of the first text-based role-play computer game, *Adventure*, see Aarseth, 1997, 98–99.

18. The anticipatory character of wargaming techniques would be, in Stiegler's view, an inheritance from the anticipatory nature of all technical objects and systems in general (159).

19. Some wargamers would no doubt disagree with this claim, particularly those

who prefer immensely detailed recreations of historical battles. The history of the influence of the "hardcore" amateur wargaming community on military and subsequently, commercial gaming that we have surveyed briefly here is indicative, however, of the wider currency of the predictive, speculative capacities that wargaming has borne in/as its technical heritage from the days of the Prussian *Kriegsspiel* practices.

20. The "family resemblance" between *Medal of Honor: Allied Assault* (Electronic Arts, 2002) and *Saving Private Ryan* (Steven Spielberg, 1998)— Spielberg's company, Dreamworks Interactive, developed *Medal of Honor* before being acquired by EA — is one of the most notable recent instances of this use of war as spectacular "texture" in both games and films.

21. In this regard, and with particular relevance to our theme, see Nieborg for an insightful discussion of the tension between a grass roots gamer culture and the attempted regulation, by the U.S. Army, of player use of their own First Person Shooter game, *America's Army* (2002). He argues that the military developers, in an effort to safeguard the "authenticity" of the game's representation of realistic military training and tactical operations (and hence its original goal as a recruitment and promotional tool), use their considerable resources to circumvent the growth of a culture of "user-created material" including mission design, avatar (skin) modification and so forth. They actively promote, however, tournament and LAN-party activities which are seen to further their goals in developing and maintaining the game online.

Works Cited

Aarseth, Espen. *Cybertext: Perspectives on Ergodic Literature.* Baltimore: The Johns Hopkins University Press, 1997.

_____. "Playing Research: Methodological Approaches to Game Analysis." In *MelbourneDAC 2003 Streamingworlds: 5th International Digital Arts & Culture Conference,* edited by Adrian Miles. Melbourne: RMIT University, 2003.

Allen, Thomas B. *War Games: Inside the Secret World of the Men Who Play at World War III.* London: Heinemann, 1987.

Crogan, Patrick. "Gametime, History, Narrative and Temporality in Microsoft *Combat Flight Simulator 2.*" In *The Video Game Theory Reader,* edited by Mark J. P. Wolf and Bernard Perron. New York: Routledge, 2003.

De Landa, Manuel. *War in the Age of Intelligent Machines.* New York: Zone Books, 1991.

DeMaria, Rusel, and Johnny L. Wilson. *High Score: The Illustrated History of Electronic Games.* New York: McGraw-Hill; Osborne, 2002.

Edwards, Paul. *The Closed World: Computers and the Politics of Discourse in Cold War America.* Cambridge: Massachusetts Institute of Technology Press, 1996.

Frasca, Gonzalo. "Simulation 101: Simulation Versus Representation." (2001). 14 March 2007. http://www.ludology.org/articles/sim1/simulation101.html.

_____. "Simulation versus Narrative: Introduction to Ludology." In *The Video Game Theory Reader,* edited by Mark J. P. Wolf and Bernard Perron. New York: Routledge, 2003.

Juul, Jesper. "The Open and the Closed: Games of Progression and Games of Emergence." In *Computer Games and Digital Cultures Conference Proceedings,* edited by Frans Mäyrä. Tampere, Finland: University of Tampere Press, 2002.

Kaplan, Fred. *The Wizards of Armageddon.* Stanford, CA: Stanford University Press, 1983.

Lenoir, Timothy. "All but War Is Simulation: The Military-Entertainment Complex." *Configurations* 8 (2000): 289–335.

_____. "Programming Theaters of War: Gamemakers as Soldiers." In *Bombs and Bandwidth:*

The Emerging Relationship between Information Technology and Security, edited by Robert Latham. New York: The New Press, 2003.

Lenoir, Timothy, and Henry Lowood. "Theaters of War: The Military-Entertainment Complex." In *Collection—Laboratory—Theater: Scenes of Knowledge in the 17th Century,* edited by Jan Lazardzig, Ludger Schwarte, and Helmar Schramm. New York: Walter de Gruyter, 2005.

Newman, James. "The Myth of the Ergodic Videogame: Some Thoughts on Player-Character Relationships in Videogames." *Game Studies* 2, no. 1 (2002). 14 March 2007. http://www.gamestudies.org/0102/newman/.

Nieborg, David. "Mods, Nay! Tournaments, Jay!" *Fibreculture* 8 ("Gaming Networks" special issue, Eds Chris Chesher, Alice Crawford, and Julian Kücklich) (2006). 14 March 2007. htttp://journal.fibreculture.org.

Stiegler, Bernard. *Technics and Time, 1: The Fault of Epimetheus.* Trans. Richard Beardsworth and George Collins. Stanford, CA: Stanford University Press, 1998.

Virilio, Paul. *War and Cinema: The Logistics of Perception.* Trans. Patrick Camiller. London: Verso, 1989.

Virilio, Paul, and Sylvere Lotringer. *Pure War.* Trans. Mark Polizzotti and Brian O'Keefe. New York: Semiotext(e), 1997.

Wilson, Andrew. *The Bomb and the Computer: Wargaming from Ancient Chinese Mapboard to Atomic Computer.* New York: Delacorte Press, 1968.

Gameography

Advanced Dungeons and Dragons: Pool of Radiance, Strategic Simulations Inc., 1988.
America's Army, U.S. Army, 2002.
Civilization, Microprose, 1991.
Civilization II, Microprose, 1997.
Command & Conquer, Westwood Studios, Virgin Interactive, 1995.
Computer Bismarck, Strategic Simulations Inc., 1980.
Conflict in Vietnam, Microprose, 1985.
Crusade in Europe, Microprose, 1985.
The Dark Age of Camelot, Vivendi, Mythic Entertainment, 2001.
Doom, id Software, 1993.
Everquest, Sony Online Entertainment, Verant Interactive, 1999.
F-19 Stealth Fighter, Microprose, 1989.
Full Spectrum Warrior, THQ, Pandemic Studios, 2004.
Guadalcanal Campaign, Strategic Simulations Inc., 1981.
Hellcat Ace, Microprose, 1984.
Kampfgruppe, Strategic Simulations Inc., 1985.
Medal of Honor: Allied Assault, Electronic Arts, 2015, 2002.
Panzer General, Strategic Simulations Inc., 1992, 1997.
Panzer General III, Mattel Interactive, 2000.
Questron, Strategic Simulations Inc., 1984.
Rails West, Strategic Simulations Inc., 1984.
Return to Castle Wolfenstein 2, Activision, Gray Matter Studios, 2001.
Rome: Total War, Activision, Creative Assembly, 2004.
Shogun: Total War, Electronic Arts, Creative Assembly, 2000.
Silent Service, Microprose, 1985.
Sub Command: Seawolf, Electronic Arts, Sonalysts Combat Simulations, 2001.

8

Gameplay as Thirdspace

Brett Nicholls and Simon Ryan

In Empire the construction of value takes place beyond measure
— Hardt and Negri

Computer gameplay primarily involves reading images on-screen such as spatial cues, maps, and characters; responding to events such as car-crashes or gunfire; discerning the hidden game logic; and attaining a competent skill level with the controller to successfully negotiate the game's challenges. In the latest release in Electronic Arts' *Need for Speed* series, *Need for Speed: Most Wanted* (2005), for example, the underground racing scenario situates players on the streets of a North American metropolis. Mastery involves acquiring and customizing cars to race against rival street racers, outrunning cops, and building up "street cred" to become number one on the "Most Wanted blacklist." In "career mode," the aim of the game is to proceed through fifteen levels. Each level involves challenging a different rival on the "most Wanted Blacklist." Defeating a rival allows players to progress up the list until they reach the top. "Street cred" is earned by evading the police or obtaining "milestones," specific challenges laid out by other racers. Moreover, in order to race players need cars. To acquire cars, players need to earn money through winning races. They also buy and sell cars, and even car parts, in order to accumulate the means to succeed. This accumulation, of course, far outweighs necessity. Players can accumulate a "safe house" full of extremely expensive sports cars, which begin to function as fetish objects. Along with a range of lower end models such as Toyota Supras and Mitsubishi Lancers, a typical "safe house" can contain a V-12 Lamborghini Gallardo, a Lotus Elise, and a Porsche 911 Turbo S. The graphical realism of the game images, their kinaesthetic appeal to virtual street racers, together with the correspondence between game cars and real-world fetish commodities, reveal the game's social and economic location. *Need for Speed* is by no means atypical in this respect: Players develop specific skills and sets of competencies that characterize the activity of gameplay, and the game is structured by a logic of competition and accumulation.

The activity of gameplay and formal game structure have been central concerns in critical engagements with computer games. The repetitive nature of gameplay, for instance, has been utilized to denounce games as symbolically shallow and culturally weak. Conversely, the activity of gameplay, or more accurately "interactivity," has been seized on in celebrations of computer games as signifying a break with the passivity of mass media audiences. One notable exception amidst the either/or structure of this debate is Andrew Darley's *Visual Digital Culture*. Darley argues that computer games, as opposed to cinematic narratives, "tend toward pure diversion, consisting of forms that are immediate and ephemeral in their effect" (6). Darley is not berating computer games here in the name of a "high art" ideal. Rather, his aim is to articulate an aesthetic of gameplay, which he contrasts with an aesthetic of cinema spectatorship. The key focus is the relationship of the player/spectator to the image, which Darley draws up in terms of semiotic depth and the activity of bodies. Though the bodies of cinema spectators remain passive, cinematic narrative allows spectators to actively explore the psychological depth of its characters. In contrast, the bodies of computer game players are very active, but games work upon the surface of signification, and they do not make interpretive demands, or at least not the interpretive demands of cinema. The fast action of gameplay does not allow the time for reflection required in conventional modes of storytelling (such as cinema). To characterize computer games as "pure diversion" is thus to consider play as a surface activity, one that is caught up in an instrumental relationship to the image, its workability as opposed to what Darley terms the "significatory depth" (160) of the cinematic image, its meaningfulness. The upshot of this claim tempers studies of computer games that celebrate gameplay as a break with the power of mass media over a passive audience. Darley contends gamers "are often perceived as being more active than viewers are, yet, this is only true ... in a vicariously 'physical' sense" (163–164). It is precisely this physicality, this activity that demands attention. We accept Darley's claim that gameplay necessitates an instrumental relationship to the image, but we do not consider this as a form of "pure diversion," with the associated uncoupling of computer games from their social, political, and economic environment that his analysis suggests.

Computer Games and the Production of Space

Computer games are a media form at the forefront of the new production of space and spatiality that is itself linked to the emergence of what Michael Hardt and Antonio Negri call "Empire"—the new form of sovereignty that marks technocapitalism and globalization.

> The striated space of modernity constructed *places* that were continually engaged in and founded on a dialectical play with their outsides. The space of imperial sovereignty, in contrast, is smooth. It might appear to be free of the binary divisions or striation of modern boundaries, but really it is crisscrossed by so many fault lines that it only appears as a continuous, uniform space. In this sense, the clearly defined crisis of modernity gives way to an omnicrisis in the imperial world. In this smooth space of Empire, there is no *place* of power — it is both everywhere and nowhere. Empire is an ou-topia, or really a *non-place*. [190].
> The modern dialectic of inside and outside has been replaced by a play of degrees and intensities of hybridity and artificiality [187–188].

Like popular literary texts or films, or other forms of entertainment, computer games function as what the systems' theorist Niklas Luhmann terms "double-sided objects," that is, as objects designed to readily facilitate the transition from real reality to fictional reality: their seeming "inside" is the world of the imagination. As "instruments of forgetting and learning" in the construction of the social memory necessary to ensure the functioning of the mass media system in which they are produced, the schemata operating in and around computer games function to set limits to their conceptual flexibility as digital texts and thus are intended to separate off the reality perceived as the game from the everyday environment for a given period of time without actually uncoupling game and environment altogether. On closer examination, however, the nature of this partial uncoupling of game and environment proves extremely problematic.

The immaterial labor of the entertainment industry produces communication "generally associated with human contact, but that contact can be either actual or virtual" (Hardt and Negri 293). In the case of the mode of entertainment offered by computer games this association with human contact is clearly virtual but the virtual imaginative space of games cannot, even during gameplay, entirely negate the surrounding space. At any moment during a game the "doubling of reality" that Luhmann argues marks any game as an episode (51) can be temporarily or permanently collapsed by contingencies such as an unexpected family event, a competing physiological drive, an equipment failure, or a hurricane. Thus, in the case of *Need for Speed,* in any actual episode of computer gameplay, bodily, social, political, and other environmental dimensions are implicitly co-present.

It is this multidimensional aspect of computer games as complex objects — beyond dialectics yet crisscrossed with fault lines — that leads us to the thinking of Henri Lefebvre and Edward Soja on space. As a form of digital culture, computer games consist of diverse, layered, and heterogeneous images and sounds unfolding in decentered and undermotivated ways. Many celebrate digital culture generally as a fluid and open-ended form that has finally dispensed with the stifling panopticism of industrial capital. But "fluid" does not necessarily mean out of control. Power reconstitutes itself within digital culture and new structures for experience emerge. The "omnicrisis" in the neo-imperial world referred to by Hardt and Negri, whereby sovereignty shifts beyond the auspices of the nation-state to the flows of the global digital economy, demands a reconceptualization of power and, following Lefebvre, such a reconceptualization begins necessarily with space. We see computer games as an important component in this reconceptualization. Games are sites upon which aesthetic and technical practices intersect, offering new ways of organizing the productive practices of technocapitalism.

Lefebvre's *The Production of Space* is a work that moves beyond traditional Hegelian or Marxist dialectical understandings of space, in order to produce new tools for engaging with capitalist society. Lefebvre achieves this by reconstituting traditional binary oppositions, such as that between space as center and periphery, through the introduction of a disruptive and vital third term. His work reconceptualizes spatiality, and produces what Soja calls the "trialectics of spatiality" (30–31, 60–62). As opposed to one-dimensional accounts of space, which tend to privilege either perception or mental concepts, from Lefebvre's difficult and at times abstruse writing we can extract the argument that space is multidimensional in that it is both perceived *and* conceived. Perceived space is socially produced and exists empirically. It can be measured and described; it is the space of what labor produces, together with the structures, pathways and social practices that produced objects bring into being (this computer before me, this building). Conceived space corresponds to the mental concepts and representations that produce our understanding of the world. It consists of discourses about space, signs, and codes. In conceived space, produced objects have social meanings (this computer as marker of high-tech capital, this building as a place of "higher" learning). The everyday practices of subjects in space, their lived experiences, are formed at the intersection and overlapping of both perceived and conceived space. Lived space is, for Lefebvre, "space as directly *lived* through its associated images and symbols, and hence the space of 'inhabitants' and 'users'" (39). Further, the lived experience of the body itself in space, with its practices, routines, pleasures, and pains, has a dimensionality that cannot be reduced to the perceived or the conceived.

Spatiality is thus understood by Lefebvre as a complex "trialectic" that consists of multiple registers: the perceived, the conceived, and the lived. These spaces have been rendered as firstspace (perceived), secondspace (conceived), and lived space, the space that corresponds to what Soja calls "thirdspace." Not to be mistaken for Hegelian dialectics with its three-part scheme, "trialectics" was prompted by Lefebvre's, and others,' discontent with the Stalinist dogma of the Communist Party in France in the early 1950s. We read Lefebvre's work as an attempt to reintensify Marx, to shift the focus of Marxism beyond the struggles of factory workers to the everyday life of subjects living in a world dominated by capitalism (82–83, 340–349). Lefebvre's work points us in the direction of the real subsumption thesis, and strikes a chord with Hardt and Negri's concept of the socialized worker.

We will return to the intersection of Lefebvre and Hardt and Negri in due course. For the present, we want to point out that for Lefebvre this spatial trialectic is uneven and historical. The lived spaces in the fields of medieval Europe, for instance, compared to those in the computer game arcades of twenty-first century Sydney, are different precisely because these lived spaces are situated in different combinations of perceived and conceived space. Any given historical formation is constituted through the intersection of the perceived, the conceived, and the lived. In the capitalist social world, Lefebvre argues — against orthodox Marxism — that conceived space is the dominant space. And if we follow what we have suggested is Lefebvre's reintensified Marxism, in this capitalist context, conceived space as ideology works to reproduce perceived space as the space of capitalist production. In turn, this subsumes everyday practices, producing a harmonious relation between workers, capitalist production, and ideas.

Lived space is by no means a straightforward process: as we have suggested, in its totality it is not reducible to perceived and conceived space. This irreducibility means that thirdspace, to shift to the vocabulary of Soja, is a space of struggle and politics. There is a sense in which lived space is always in tension with perceived and conceived spaces. Thirdspaces can be evasive, excessive, and difficult in the sense that they refuse to be contained within the order of capitalism or any other disciplinary regime. Thirdspaces are thus the locus of struggle, domination, and resistance as capital seeks to penetrate all the spheres of everyday life. As Lefebvre, revisiting *The Production of Space*, writes:

> The organization of centralized, concentrated space serves at one and the same time political power and material production, optimizing profit. Social classes stake a claim to it and disguise themselves in it, in the hierarchy of occupied spaces.... However, a new space *tends* to develop, at the world scale, integrating and disintegrating the national and the local. A process full of contradictions, linked with the

conflict between a division of labor on the planetary level, in the mode of capitalist production — and the effort to create another, more rational world order. This
penetration of and into space has been as historically important as achieving hegemony through the penetration of institutions. A crucial if not the ultimate point
of this penetration: the militarization of space not treated (and for good reason)
here, but which completes the demonstration, on both the planetary and the cosmic scale [Elden, Lebas and Kofman 212].

Computer games are spatial entities in two ways. First, computer games are
actual objects, in the sense that they are run on actual machines with interfaces for users in actual spaces, such as a bedroom at home. Computer games
are produced and take place in socially produced spaces and, as such, they
organize bodies in particular ways. Second, computer games are simulations
of space. In other words, they represent space — cities, landscapes, planets,
and so forth — via a system of signs on the screen.

It would be tempting to argue that the physical space of play and the
virtual space of the game world correspond to perceived (first) and conceived
(second) space in Lefebvre. In this approach, thirdspace emerges as gameplay
itself, in the sense that it is difficult to define. It doesn't exist in the game
itself as object or in the virtual world; it consists in the experiences and practices that are produced through the intersection and overlapping of first and
second space. And, as in Lefebvre, gameplay as thirdness can't be explained
simply through a description of the empirical space of the game or the representational spaces within the game. Gameplay is clearly not reducible to
first and second space. Instead gameplay constitutes a thirdspace with a life
of its own.

Representing the Thirdspace of Gameplay

It is clear that gameplay, as directly lived space, is difficult to represent
or describe. Gameplay is an activity in which lived space collapses into the
lived moment and becomes experience in itself without description or representation. One notable attempt by T. Benjamin Buckley, in his essay "Playing Fields: *Myst*, *Tetris*, and the Production of Simulated Space," goes a long
way toward explaining this difficulty.[1] Marking the distinctness of the space
of gameplay and marking the necessity for a representational shift in regis-
ter, he argues that thirdspace resides in the body of the player:

> let us look for a video game Thirdspace where Lefebvre has hinted it resides: in our
> bodies.... Without the body, there is no production of space.... For this same rea-
> son, it is what the controlled production of space seeks to dominate under a con-
> ceptual regime. However, the body constitutes a barrier between the perception of
> space (which happens at the very limit of the body in space) and its subsequent

practice (which may or may not bend to the constructed space as conceived). To understand the Thirdspace of computer games, and thus complete the triad, we must attempt the impossible and try to speak for the body.

While Buckley insists that the elements of computer games — the machine, the virtual world, and gameplay — can be demarcated clearly in terms of Lefebvre's tripartite scheme, it must be pointed out that computer games as actual objects — machines — are also subject to representations in the sense that there are social meanings attached to the ownership of such objects (owning the latest PC and the latest game), and representations concerning the use of domestic space for leisure activities (as spaces of investment, as spaces subject to building codes, etc.). Similarly, the representational spaces on the screen are also manufactured objects that can be considered as firstspace. The virtual world on screen is a materialized, socially produced space. Game spaces are constructed by game development teams working for game development companies. Indeed, the virtual worlds of computer games require a massive capital investment and a large well-organized labor force. This organization is materialized in the virtual world of the game, around which the bodies of players are organized. The movement of the eyes, for instance, is directly organized by the simulated events on screen in the same way that a body in firstspace must follow a corridor to move through a building.

It is also possible to consider the representational spaces of computer games, gamespace, as secondspace accounts of thirdspace, much in the manner of Soja's book, *Thirdspace: Journeys to Los Angeles and Other Real-and-Imagined Places*, which details instances of thirdness in the city of Los Angeles and in the critical work of Homi Bhabha, Michel Foucault, Donna Haraway, and bell hooks, among others. Games such as Smilebit's *Jetset Radio Future*, with gameplay that is clearly resistant to the represented capitalist city, could be considered as a discourse on thirdspace as resistance.

What we propose is that computer games should be understood as multidimensional and multilayered sites within the context of the capitalist social world. They consist of varying combinations of mechanic interfaces, the representation of worlds, and the practices of playing. So we can draw distinctions between games on the basis of differences in these combinations. The *Eye Toy: Groove* game for PS2, for example, utilizes a camera input device that enables players to see themselves on screen performing tasks upon a range of represented instruments. *Grand Theft Auto: San Andreas*, in the PC version with subwoofer and surround sound, utilizes a keyboard input to a virtual world of the city through which an avatar is directed. In each, the body is organized around sets of practices that are produced through, but are not reducible to, particular spatial combinations. And each game produces a very different game experience because of the varying combinations. Because of the range of possible combinations across spaces, which we have only hinted at here, computer games are an open form of media in the sense that combinations remain unsettled (though many would argue that experimentation is becoming increasingly difficult as the games industry works to rapidly standardize development practices).[2]

This emphasis upon game spatiality, comprised of the dynamic combinations of first, second, and thirdspace, already marks off the study of games from the study of cinema. Cinema is studied almost exclusively as secondspace, where the spectator interprets the images on screen, with little attention given to the standardized firstspace of exhibition. Of course, the spectator is mentally active, making sense of the images and sounds, but the input machinery — bodies in a darkened room — does not change. There is thus no sense in the study of games repeating that branch of film studies that emerged through the pages of the journal *Screen* in the 1970s and 1980s and attacked representational form itself in an attempt to upset the suturing capacity of the realist film form, to produce a politically active mode of spectatorship. In computer games users are already active in a range of ways. We need to consider what kind of activity this is in the context of the multifarious production of gaming space.

In his extensive analysis of new media objects, Lev Manovich has charted the different logical structures that characterize the cognitive activities of computer game players and distinguish their engagement with the screen from that of cinema spectators. He argues that computers have imposed a new ontology onto culture: "a new cultural algorithm: reality-> media -> data -> database" (224–225). In contrast to such digital objects as CD-Roms and HTML websites, games are governed not so much by database logic but by the logic of algorithms and the instruction sets that they enable. Because they function as narratives and not as data structures, computer games and the human activity they invoke correspond with the algorithm and not the database. A considerable part of the player's involvement in gameplay resides in their efforts to reconstruct, or to use Manovich's term, "transcode" features of the algorithms controlling particular events in the game in order to be able to make navigational and other strategic decisions. Although the vast majority of players clearly have no understanding of the actual algorithms in the game or the data structures (arrays, linked lists, graphs, etc.) that they link with, in gameplay they must nonetheless try to reconstruct for themselves the way the algorithms govern the appearance and behavior of objects on the screen. Manovich further distinguishes between two different game types in terms of their modeling of the temporal dynamics of user interaction: games modeled after military simulators like *Doom*, *Quake*, and *Tomb Raider* and interactive narratives like *Myst* or *Lord of the Rings*. Simulator games may take the form of first-person shooters or flight, racing, or other transportation games and are "based on the co-existence of two states of the subject (perception and action) and two states of a screen (transparent and opaque)" (210). The player must act in the transparent space of the continuous illusionistic world and simultaneously take account of the opaque areas of the screen that provide essential data readouts on such matters as navigation, "health," damage, munitions, and logistical support. Interactive narratives, on the other hand, require of the player "temporal oscillation between two distinct states — noninteractive movie-like sequences and interactive gameplay" (210). He argues that this oscillation between different kinds of cognitive activity is related to effects that arise not in the social environment but specifically in the culture produced by the Human Computer Interface itself that demands users engage in forms of "cognitive multitasking":

> Just as any particular software application is embedded, both metaphorically and literally, within the larger framework of the operating system, new media embeds cinema-style illusions with the larger framework of an interactive control surface. Illusion is subordinated to action, depth to surface, window to imaginary universe to control panel. From commanding a dark movie theater, the cinema image, this twentieth-century illusion and therapy machine *par excellence*, becomes just a small window on a computer screen, one stream among many others coming to us through the network, one file among numerous others on our hard drives [211].

Manovich's scheme of perceptual layering and cognitive multitasking in gameplay is consistent with the concept of thirdspace. How players' activity within these embedded layers and surfaces relates to the political economy of thirdspace must be further explored.

One approach to this problem of activity conceives of computer games as a manufactured mass culture that reproduces the assembly-line structure of production within industrial capitalism. Julian Stallabrass articulates this position forcefully, and we cannot fault his demand that we should consider computer games in terms of the operations of capital and the question of labor. A game such as *Max Payne* could be considered in these terms. The game situates players, via the character, Max Payne, in an uncertain visual environment but ultimately with a specific objective. Initially this objective is obscure, but as the player develops a specific skill set in order to survive the encountered obstacles, history opens up a future orientation. The player must thus ride the wave of history, against great odds and with much skill, toward a prescheduled future success. Thirdness in *Max Payne* remains passive; gameplay is subject to the prohibiting algorithm of firstspace. But what is missing from Stallabrass's analysis of games and gameplay are considerations of thirdspace, as well as any sense that games can be sites of struggle and conflict. The player is merely subordinate to the triumph of capital. He argues that the gaming situation is constituted in terms of the neat intersection of the first and second spaces, the "rigid and episodic" (91) structure of machinic interface and the representational preoccupation with "mass carnage" and violence "on a grand scale" (93) that makes up the bulk of titles offered in the gaming market. Gameplay as the result of this intersection of perceived and conceived space is thus rendered passive and subordinate: computer games have been pressed into the service of capital, a fait accompli.

Stallabrass's position means that a game that could be considered politically subversive at the representational level is still fundamentally conservative because the structure of gameplay is subordinate to the machinery of the game code and the interface. And while cinema may still offer the possibility of liberation from the tyranny of what Colin MacCabe called "the classic realist text" through a play upon its form, Stallabrass despairs that the possibility of liberation is already too late for games since they simply complete "the marked trend [in Hollywood] towards producing a visceral and enveloping experience, through extreme close ups, fast cutting and the frequent use of shock" (87).

The Political Economy of Gameplay

A contrast to Stallabrass's hard-line position on the machinic structure of gameplay can be found in a study by Fiske and Watts (1985), who contended that players find spaces of resistance to social control through gameplay. Their line of argument came in response to attacks carried in the popular press in the 1980s on "video parlors" (in the parlance of the time) as "detrimental and addictive" (89) to youth. In the context of industrial capitalism and the assembly-line model of production, in which workers are subjected to the rhythms of industrial machines, gaming machines with games such as *Space Invaders*, *Pac Man*, and *Asteroids* offer the possibility of inverting the relationship between worker and machine. They noted that:

> [w]ith the video game machine, the machinist works not with the machine, but against it — the time his (gender deliberate) 20 or 40 cents buys is extended to the degree that he can resist, work against, the machine. The better the machinist is, the less he pays, and the lower the profit of the owner. This must be a unique phenomenon in capitalism [92].

Unlike Andrew Darley, who maintains that gameplay is a semiotically impoverished form of pure diversion from the social, Fiske and Watts situated the activity of gameplay in an antagonistic relationship to corporate capital and to some extent anticipated the present discussion of gameplay as thirdspace. The pleasure of "beating the machine" translates into the language of resistance.

Gaining time by making twenty cents go for as many levels as possible, rather than feeding the machine with hard-earned cash, equates to a temporal escape from social control.

However, the subversive pleasures to be had on the assembly line of Fordist models of production, which is precisely how Fiske and Watts (and Stallabrass) view the videogame arcade, need to be rethought in the present context of post–Fordist economies. Even though Fiske and Watts attempt to situate gameplay socially, politically, and economically, they don't in fact move beyond Darley's idea of gameplay as pure diversion. In their account, gaining time against the machine is a diversion away from the political reality of life in industrial capitalism. The pleasure of inversion, whereby the player works against rather than for the game machine, is precisely an aesthetic space operating within the dominance of capital:

> It is resistance against the subordination produced by a capitalist technocracy, but not against the society itself. The games provide opportunities for resisting that subordination by inverting, not rejecting, social relations, and thus the oppositional meanings and subjectivities are articulated with and within the dominant frame [103].

Within post–Fordist economies such spaces of resistance need to be rethought. The Western Australian "video parlor," "Timezone," that was the object of the popular press's attack and Fiske and Watts' defense, some twenty years later remains a profitable franchise in Singapore, India, Indonesia, the Philippines, Australia, and New Zealand. Players haven't been that successful in "beating the machine" and bankrupting the owners. It could be that "beating the machine" should be considered as merely the rhetoric of technocapitalism with its insistence upon innovation.

A more adequate approach to the problem of the spatial discourse inherent in player activity has been articulated by Tiziana Terranova in the much cited essay, "Free Labor: Producing Culture for the Digital Economy." Terranova's essay shifts the focus of the discussion on the processes of labor in digital environments beyond Stallabrass's and Fiske and Watts's insistence upon Fordist accounts of labor to post–Fordist accounts. Her concept of "free labor" directly engages with the activities of computer gaming. For Terranova the "freeing" of workers from the factory, as factory production goes offshore in search of cheap and nonunionized labor, produces a surplus of labor that is able to be "translated into productive activities that are pleasurably embraced and at the same time often shamelessly exploited" (37) by technocapitalism. Game development teams, for instance, routinely incorporate the free labor of gamers through different forms of feedback in the development process. The labor of gamers in this context is both willing and unpaid.[3] But this double sense of free labor means, contra Stallabrass and Fiske and Watts, that the digital economy for Terranova should not be understood in any way as a confrontation between workers and capital. Terranova states:

> The digital economy is an important area of experimentation with value and free cultural/affective labor. It is about specific forms of production (Web design, multimedia production, digital services, and so on), but is also about forms of labor we do not immediately recognize as such: chat, real-life stories, mailing lists, amateur newsletters, and so on. These types of cultural and technical labor are not produced by capitalism in any direct, cause-and-effect fashion; that is, they have not developed simply as an answer to the economic needs of capital. However, they have developed in relation to the expansion of the cultural industries and are part of a process of economic experimentation with the creation of monetary value out of knowledge/culture/affect [38].

In this view, the forms of immaterial labor associated with the digital economy are intertwined with, and inseparable from, developments in technology and capital. The nature of this intertwining, a sort of mutual dependence, leads to the argument that digital machines offer new forms of communication and community and, at the same time, possibilities for new forms of exploitation. She writes:

> The question is not so much whether to love or to hate technology, but an attempt to understand whether the Internet [and other digital technology] embodies a continuation of capital or a break with it. As I have argued in this essay, it does neither. It is rather a mutation that is totally immanent to late capitalism, not so much a break as an intensification, and therefore a mutation, of a widespread cultural and economic logic [54].

Terranova's insistence upon immanence, the mutual dependence of workers and capital, and mutation is of limited use in engaging with the exploitation that marks free labor. This is because the argument doesn't really break with conservative economics, which would claim that capital needs workers just as workers need capital. All that this amounts to is that capital is at the center of working life. We argue instead that the digital economy amounts to nothing less than a confrontation between workers and capital. Nick Dyer-Witheford offers a concise description of the autonomist position that expresses this view: "Far from being a passive object of capitalist designs, the worker," he writes, "is in fact the *active* subject of production, the wellspring of the skills, innovation, and cooperation on which capital depends." As a consequence of this dependency, he continues, capital "attempts to incorporate labor as an object, a component in its cycle of value extraction, so much *labor power*" (65). Indeed a wide array of games exist that build career structures and financial success into gameplay. These are games that perpetuate the meritocracy through which capital is reinforced as ideology. *Sim City, Singstar, Nascar 06, NHL 06,* and *Nintendogs* are recent examples. While ranging across genres, all draw upon the familiar structure of productive labor within the circuits of accumulative capital.

We view computer games as a site of value extraction, precisely because computer games contest what constitutes productive activity. What we are left with after Stallabrass, Fiske and Watts, and Terranova are important questions: is it the case that gameplay as thirdness is always prohibited space? In other words, is it the case that no matter how we engage with the game world onscreen as representation, as secondspace, the demands of gameplay mean that it must function ultimately as firstspace? If we answer yes to both of these questions, the lived experience of gameplay, thirdness, is always dominated and passive. Buckley is acutely aware of this problem. Yet against Stallabrass's position, and to a lesser extent Fiske and Watts, he insists that gameplay, as lived experience, as thirdness, still holds out the possibility for "new space that is fraught with desires and contestations of space." This is a space of contention that, he continues, "can be turned against dominating conceptions and productions of space to provoke imaginative new kinds of spatiality, or *counterspaces.*" We concur with this view, and with his insistence upon bodily experience. But we would wish to take this phenomenological account of thirdspace further to the sociopolitical domain, to argue that computer game thirdspace needs to be understood as a locus for the struggle and politics that mark technocapitalism. If we follow Lefebvre's insistence, that all three aspects of space operate simultaneously, with historically specific degrees of intensity across this simultaneous operation, computer games are a media form that opens up for inspection, provides a locus, and marks a moment in which the multidimensional aspects of space that characterize experience and practices within technocapitalism come to the fore. In short, computer games are discourses on space that are as central to capitalist society today as cinema was to vision in the capitalist society of the twentieth century.

In response to recent developments within the games industry, especially the rapid and seemingly relentless concentration of the computer games industry into a global, vertically integrated system of production, publishing, and marketing since the failure of Sega's *Dreamcast* launch in the games console war of 1999, we have modified our earlier, more optimistic position on the thirdspace of computer games.[4] This space now appears considerably less indeterminate and uncontainable than it did when we investigated Smilebit's Xbox game, *Jet Set Radio Future* (2002) and located in that game forms of counterspace that related closely to Soja's concept of the "marginal sites" at the boundaries of capitalism.[5] Certainly the scandal of cyberbeing — its ontological indeterminacy in actual gameplay, the hovering of players between "as" and "as if" states and structures — persists in the way the process of the breaking down of categories once held to be stable still operates in computer games. But there is mounting evidence of the games industry's determination to subject the potentially subversive indeterminacy of computer gameplay to an "apparatus of capture" and thus collapse vital distinctions between the actual social, economic, legal, and political environment that producers and players inhabit and the virtual game worlds that are promoted as a zone of aesthetic free play. The sense of scandal around any revolutionary force latent in the new visual regime of computer games is now dissolving and settles instead on the speed with which the seemingly open frontier of virtual game space is undergoing a process of reterritorialization.

The structural profile and high level of capital investment evident in the games industry since the mid–1990s have grown to the extent that computer games can now be seen to function as a new-media formation, which exhibits a number of the characteristics delineated by Luhmann as the markers of the general system of the mass media. Established game categories, genre divisions, and general rules of orientation for actual gameplay help to generate and reproduce the schema that aid a mass-media mode of comprehensibility. Comprehensibility has a high value in the communication system of mass media and is "best guaranteed by the schemata which the media themselves have already generated" (110). The already massive scale of the industry is clearly evident in the current chapter in the history of the "console wars," which is marked by intense competition between the industry's big three, Microsoft, Sony, and Nintendo, to successfully release their new consoles and thus dominate a games market that is soon expected to eclipse the music industry in annual value. By 2009 the global market for console and PC games will, it is reliably estimated, be worth between US$20 and US$25 billion per annum.[6]

Given the scale of this market, gameplay is a precarious and highly contested practice in capitalist society today. The struggle within computer game thirdspace is a struggle against the prohibiting tendencies of firstspace and the codes of secondspace. So the "objects" against which the user struggles in thirdspace are precisely the perceived and the conceived spaces of the game. In short, if we follow Lefebvre, to be liberated would be to alter the machinery and the representations of the game itself, or at the very least, to play against the grain of representational space, to "drift" in the Situationist sense. What is crucial about games is that the player must physically and mentally participate in the production of space. And this production becomes the most acute when the player actively overturns the representational world of the game through "hacking." The massive investment in anti-hacking software and hardware design shows that computer games are both a protected commodity form and sites for capitalist assumptions concerning legitimate gaming activity. The semantic shift within the term "hacker," from a positive counter-cultural term to a term that marks criminal activity, is evidence of capital's (for the most part successful) attempts to dominate thirdspace.

Indeed, the "hacker" ethic bears all the hallmarks of Lefebvre's/Soja's sociopolitical accounts of thirdspace. As described by Pekka Himanen, "the hacker ethic" with its resistance to the private ownership of intellectual property through open information sharing is a *work ethic* and a *money ethic* that challenges the Protestant work ethic that Max Weber argues has been central in capitalist society.

We are inclined to accept Hardt and Negri's conclusion that capitalism is increasingly immanent rather than transcendent and "tends towards a smooth space defined by uncoded flows, flexibility, continual modulation and tendential equalization" (327). Under such conditions, the global distribution and consumption of computer games as the "ideal type of commodity" (Kline et al. 75) in an informational economy serves to enhance the smoothing of global social space through their promotion of player's temporal flexibility and spatial mobility most especially in online gaming.[7]

For capitalism, the games industry's potentially limitless capacity, particularly in online games, to produce the virtual space that enables gameplay, constitutes the production of a synthetic form of *Land* that can then be captured by rent or by outright purchase.[8] In the case of online games, players rent access to virtual Land from the publisher for a monthly fee. Alone or with other players they compete for occupancy rights. Edward Castranova's study of the economy of online gaming has analyzed and quantified the trade in the "unreal estate" and other game properties that may be purchased from other players, some of whom are professional traders who derive income from their activities. For the state there is the promise of harvesting tax from the profits of those players engaged in the online trading of game properties, over and above the taxation already imposed on the profits of the industry itself. Instead of the fertility, the presence of valuable resources, or the desirable location that signals the profitability of sites in the real-world economy, the marker of value in this new space is the level of playability accruing around points of intensity in the territory of a particular game. At least since 2003, high prices have been paid for virtual properties in key locations in games like *Everquest, Dark Ages of Camelot,* and *Project Entropia.*[9]

Although computer games players do not usually think of their activity as anything other than a highly engaging leisure pursuit in which they and many of their peers freely engage, as the investigations of Hardt and Negri, Klein, Dyer-Witheford, de Peuter; Graham, and others demonstrate, in the post–Fordist economies characteristic of contemporary capitalism, social relations arising from computer-based or digital modes of production (Hardt and Negri 291) are undergoing a profound transformation that is bringing into ever sharper focus Adorno's nascent sense that leisure time in the America of the 1940s was already becoming in part a "shadowy continuation of labor"

(168). To examine the possible erosion of the boundaries between play and work in computer gaming, it is necessary to identify distinguishing characteristics of each mode of human activity. Crucial to any attempt to demarcate the limits of play from labor in computer games culture at the level of ordinary language are at least the following two considerations: (1) play is a voluntary activity that is not productive of economic value; and (2) labor signifies the engagement of living bodies in socially recognized value-creating practices, an engagement that in postindustrial societies is currently almost totally reduced to the recognition of the production of economic value. It is widely recognized in games culture that player feedback enhances game design and is recognized by the industry as an important element of their asset base. Kline et al. cite Alvin Toffler's definition of the "prosumer" or the producer /consumer in their account of the way player activity is harnessed by the games industry to develop and market computer games. They recognize five industry processes that effectively convert play into labor (202):

(1) the marriage of gaming with market research;
(2) the "laboratory" model of interactive entertainment centers;
(3) the use of game testers and expert gamers by major manufacturers;
(4) the use of shareware and player editing to add value to games;
(5) the role of gaming culture as a training-and-recruitment arena for the industry.

We can add to this concept of prosumer labor the possibly coercive form of social currency that accrues to gamers identified in Herz and Macedonia's analysis of what they term "the social ecology of games." They expose the importance in the activities of computer games players of the social dynamics of status, identity, and affiliation that normally govern interpersonal relations (6). The kudos within the games community that accrues to the winners of online tournaments and the opportunities for dedicated players to display on densely populated Internet fan sites their authoring or editing skills in the form of games patches, and other tradable virtual game assets such as avatars and their equipment or even an entire game level are hugely motivating to individuals and groups. Particularly in the case of teenage boys, participation in computer games has become an important element in peer group affiliation to the extent that nongamers can sometimes suffer a marked sense of social exclusion. Further, multiplayer virtual environments like those that can be experienced in first-person shooter games such as *Quake, Arena,* and *Unreal Tournament* (now predominantly played in teams rather than solo) require complex in-game artificial intelligence programming to simulate the actions of actual combat opponents. Some of the most sophisticated AI plug-ins for commercial games (such as *ReaperBot* for *Quake*) have been authored by gamers themselves and have subsequently been built into later releases of the games. Such player AI modifications also inevitably find their way into the combat simulation games authorized by the U.S. Department of Defense, which has since the mid–1980s commissioned for training purposes several versions of commercially available games that have been specifically modified to incorporate actual combat zones and the technical specifications of military air, sea, land, transport, and weaponry. In 1999 the U.S. Army set up the Institute for Creative Technology at the University of Southern California with the explicit aim of exploring further the military use of computer games technology and content. Games manufacturers profit considerably from such well tried and tested innovations while the military system also benefits from the vast collective experience of players whose desire to excel in simulated combat often pushes the envelope of possible programmable responses well beyond the parameters first envisioned and encoded by games designers. Evidence from this quarter underscores James Der Derian's analysis of the emergence of what he identifies in *Virtuous War* (2001) as MIMENET, the "military-industrial-media-entertainment-network."

According to Castranova, capitalism's advance toward the collapse of the distinctions between game as discrete episode of imaginative play and game as extension of the real-world economic, social, and political environment (199–200) is already well underway. It is not just that game avatars and properties can be bought and sold for real money. The hacking of this virtual property has become a real-world crime. The Korean police now prosecute hackers who "steal" property from players (191).[10] The coupling of real-world legal codes to the game code of such synthetic worlds — Castranova prefers the descriptor "synthetic" to "virtual"— co-opts aesthetic free play by attributing actual economic value and property rights to activities conducted in online game worlds, dissolving the distinction between the hacking of games and other forms of cyber crime. In a further violation of Huizinga's principle (cited by Castranova) — that a game ceases to be a game as soon as it has moral consequences — we note that a recent development in the market enables affluent players of several MMORPGs to purchase from poorer piece-workers in less developed economies, through such trading sites as *eBay*, the tens or even hundreds of hours of leveling-up required to participate in advanced gameplay (Thompson). A British journalist, Tony Thompson, recorded the low pay and primitive working conditions — UK£2.80 for ten hours work in the back room of a run-down apartment in a small Romanian town — experienced by digital laborers in a small company subcontracted to the Northern California company Gamersloot.net. The contracting company charges players £250 (approximately) for instant "promotion" in their listed online game worlds. Such abusive labor practices have attracted the concern of NGOs opposed to the global proliferation of sweated labor such as London's *No Sweat* (Lee).

The activities of players in a number of tactical, transport, and weapons simulation scenarios undoubtedly promotes skills that are useful to tertiary forms of labor in both civil and military occupations at a higher level of cognitive engagement than that required for the routine manipulation of symbols common to many lower paid workers in the digital economy. Participation in gameplay enables male players in particular to engage in the simulation of violent or otherwise socially disruptive forms of affective behavior that if actualized would immediately be condemned as criminal or at least delinquent in civil and military spheres. In this mode, first person-shooter games and other action games function as a channel for the working off of affective behavior that the disciplinary regime regards as unproductive. From this point of view games act as a safety valve for superfluous emotions and aggressive drives in post–Fordist digital economies where many of the more physical aspects of engagement with the environment are no longer required except in voluntary recreational pursuits or in the arena of professional sports.[11]

As mass entertainment, games constitute a recent transformation in the process of distraction that seeks to conceal the very real violence of capitalism. The irony here is that in certain modalities of cyberbeing such as those entered into by the players of the more violent first-person shooter and military games or of such popular titles as *Max Payne* and *Grand Theft Auto 3 San Andreas*, the violence of capitalism itself has never been made more transparent. By requiring players' avatars to engage frequently in simulated acts of threatening behavior, coercion, or outright violence for the purpose of gaining dominance over other game characters/players and their territory, capitalism cynically instantiates for profit its own inherent violence. Active engagement with these digital technical images functions simultaneously as distraction from, and virtual enactment of, this violence. Players' experience of gaining control over a virtual textual world may ease the widespread fear of criminal or military violence or of being excluded from participation in the social nexus of capital through unemployment and the descent into poverty resulting from neo-liberalism's relentless attack on the welfare state; but constantly recycling fearful military and criminal scenarios also serves to exacerbate this fear.

The unremitting harshness of the radically depoliticized urban space represented in the virtual San Andreas State of *GTA San Andreas* (2004) provides a case in point. This city space of this game contrasts sharply with the politicized counterspace of *Jet Set Radio Future*. In *JSRF* teenage skaters battle as a subcultural group to regain the openness of urban territory as they fight the takeover of the city by Gouji, the downtown corporate boss of the

Rokkaku Group, and his henchmen who are backed up by the Rokkaku police. As a clear model of an ideologically contested and thus positively unsettled space, the future Tokyo of *JSRF* exemplifies Lefebvrian/Sojaean thirdspace. The cell-shaded graphic style of *JSRF* resists graphic realism and simulation and at the character level, where the player is actant, the cartoon rendering avoids specificity in social type, nationality, or ethnicity in way that enables players to identify with a character type, as opposed to playing a specific game role. In contrast, players of *GTA San Andreas*— a game that is celebrated by the industry and its fans for its embrace of graphic realism —find their avatar's identity and environment precisely delineated. San Andreas and Los Santos, "a city tearing itself apart with gang trouble, drugs and corruption, where filmstars and millionaires do their best to avoid the dealers and gangbangers," evoke unmistakable associations with California and Los Angeles, as a virtual urban hell that has arisen out of the cybernetic fault line that links in the designers' and players' imagination these two urban environments. Players of *GTA San Andreas* have no choice but to enter into the character and predicament of the gangster Carl Johnson who is visually and socially presented as an African American struggling to survive as a member of the virtual underclass of San Andreas. The fact that Carl Johnson's physical appearance, fitness, and skill level is open to customization and development through gameplay does nothing to alter his social marginality as an African-American gangster. The meanness of the streets of "Los Santos with its celebrity and sprawling ghettos, San Fiero with its eclectic artist community, and Las Venturas with the glitz and glamour of casinos" where the only available means of advancement open to CJ is through violence, drug dealing, and other criminal activities, marks the space of this game as a site of complete capture: players encounter no ideological alternative to a Hobbesean "war of all against all."[12]

The form of subjectivity invoked by engagement with the game avatar presupposes the necessity of responding to threat only by flight or violence. The rule of law is only present as the oppressive and unreasoning power of the police. The sense of community is reduced to loyalty to what remains of CJ's family: everyone else is an actual or potential enemy. The "almost endless" possibilities for gameplay referred to by a reviewer do not include release from oppression by the disciplinary regime or any possibility of redemption.[13] Players face only the choice of indulging in CJ's potential for outright mayhem and pathological violence or utilizing his force in a more calculated and "productive" manner to gain control over others.

The instruction booklet included with the game takes the form of a Local Business Advertiser's Guide. While it contains the usual statutory declarations, "Getting Started" instructions and productions credits, it consists mainly of fictional advertisements for goods and services available to CJ in the San Andreas area but also includes plugs for the real gangsta rap and hip-hop artists who contributed to the game's soundtrack. The games industry appears to be aware of the leakage in the system of commodity exchange that occurs when players' attention is directed only into fictional worlds and is already experimenting with extending control over the economic life of the game by blurring the boundaries between real-world and virtual-world patterns of consumption. Castranova describes one possible outcome for gameplay of this trend toward convergence:

> As meaning seeps into these play spaces, their status as play spaces will erode. As their status as play spaces erodes, the laws, expectations, and norms of contemporary Earth society will increasingly dominate the atmosphere. When Earth's culture dominates, the game will be over, the fantasy will be punctured and the illusion will be ended for good. Taxes will be paid. The rich and poor will dance the same macabre dance of mutual mistrust that they do on Earth, with no relief, no rewriting of beginnings, and no chance to opt out and start over. The art that once framed an immersive imaginary experience will be retracted back to the walls of the space, and the people will go back to looking at it rather than living it. Living there will no longer be any different from living here, and a great opportunity to play the game of human life under different, fantastical rules will have been lost [2004: 196].

If Castranova's suspicion is correct, the sense of temporary release from the anxiety in the real-world environment currently available to both affluent and economically marginal players may be relatively short-lived: the compensatory pleasures of succeeding in virtual game arenas may soon be replaced by pressure to pay for the "right" to compete for status and rewards in a new zone of economic life. In the closely guarded world of online games, the less well-off player of a ripped copy of the game who formerly enjoyed at no cost the same experience becomes no more than a squatter who has no legal right to occupy the virtual space of play. She will be hunted down and expelled.

For Lefebvre: "the social relations of production have a social existence to the extent that they have a spatial existence; they project themselves into space, becoming inscribed there, and in the process producing space itself" (129). Does it not then logically follow that as capital moves to colonize the cybernetic circuits of the digital, this spatial existence of the social relations of production will flow into the virtual space of computer games? Cybernetic circuits operate not according to predetermined "game rules" but in terms of evolving feedback loops that distinguish between information and noninformation. In terms of Luhmann's understanding of the system of the mass media, games are "episodes." They are not "transitions to another way of living" (51). For Luhmann, games have temporal limits that mark them off from the environment without negating it. Of course, in keeping with the concept of thirdspace, everything that exists does so simultaneously. The game always contains, in each of its operations, references to the real reality that exists at the same time. With any move it marks itself as a game; and it can collapse at any moment if things suddenly get serious. [...] The continuation of the game requires that the boundaries be kept under constant surveillance" [52].

But computer games are situated in thirdspace somewhere between traditional concepts of games and mass entertainment. And for Luhmann a key difference between games and entertainment is that "entertainment is by no means unreal (in the sense of not being there)" (52). Instead of the formal prescribed rules of conventional games or sports, in entertainment the "double-sided objects that facilitate the transition from real reality to fictional reality" are driven by information. In entertainment as opposed to traditional games, the boundaries between the real and the fictional are far more slippery: "not everything should be fictional, especially when the story is told as a fiction" (52). To form the memory that enables engagement with the computer game narrative, players refer not to set rules but to items of information that are "constantly and recursively linked together in a network" (52). It is precisely in the networking of the cybernetic circuits that operate in thirdspace that capitalism in the form of the games industry structures computer gameplay. This structuring operates as an apparatus of capture, extracting value from gameplay. This process of extraction confirms Lefebvre and Soja's view of thirdspace as a politically contested space and appears finally to contradict Luhmann's observation that games are episodes and "not transitions to another way of life" (51).

Notes

1. See also Miklaucic, Nicholls and Ryan.
2. At the time of writing the average size of a game development team has risen from around 15 in 2003 to between 20 and 25 members. The start-up capital required to take a game to the point of launching a marketable prototype is already in excess of US$20 million. Data supplied in seminar on Game Production by Daniel Sanchez-Crespo, CEO, Novarama Technology, Barcelona, hosted by the University of Otago Games Development Club, April 6, 2004.
3. See Banks.
4. Sega's *Dreamcast* console, released in 1999 and still regarded by its fans as the best console of the 128-bit generation, was pushed out of the market by Sony's *PlayStation 2*. Sega suffered massive losses and withdrew from console production altogether, leaving the field to the triumvirate of Sony, Microsoft and Nintendo. See Kline, Dyer-Witheford and de Peuter, 173–176.
5. See Nicholls and Ryan.
6. This is an average of figures taken from recent media reports. See, for example, a report on the future value of online games by Williams.
7. The translation of the space of gameplay from such Fordist and pre–Fordist

public spaces such as the street, the park, the stadium or the beach to the virtual space of the game is occurring against the background of a corresponding decline in traditional public space.

8. The term is to be understood here in Deleuze and Guattari's sense as the assemblage that emerges when territories are superseded and the possibility of ground rent appears. 440–441.

9. Julian Dibbell reports on the purchase by a Wonder Bread delivery man of a house in Everquest on *eBay* for US$750. Since then there have been many reports in the world press of purchases of much greater value.

10. Castranova cites the research of F. Gregory Lastowka and Dan Hunter into the legal status of virtual poverty.

11. Even much of contemporary military activity draws on immaterial forms of labor. As a key element in the digital visual regime, we maintain that computer games also impose on players Foucault's immanent disciplinary strategies within the horizontal circuits of control that as consumer discipline, military discipline etc are a concomitant of capitalism's desire to both regulate and derive value from "errant" affective behavior.

12. Although CJ's life as a gangster is not without its visceral pleasures, material, emotional and social rewards, from the game's back-story it is already clear that whatever he undertakes and no matter how successful he is, he is condemned to remain in the underclass: "Five years ago Carl Johnson escaped from the pressures of life in Los Santos. [...] Now, it's the early 90s. Carl's got to go home. His mother has been murdered, his family has fallen apart and his childhood friends are all heading towards disaster. CJ is forced to go on a journey that takes him across the entire State of San Andreas, to save his family and take control of the streets" (*Grand Theft Auto San Andreas* [back cover]; San Andreas: Local Business Advertiser's Guide [back cover].

13. The reviewer, h0stile, writes: "Well, the possibilities you'll get are almost endless and they range from a small bicycle and a few bikes to XX [sic] types of cars (including low-riders), pick-ups, police cars, ambulances, you name it. You can activate the special missions by pressing the "2" key (pimp, vigilante) and they'll bring you even more cash, as it's rather hard to get it these days. You should be aware of the fact that San Andreas is a little bit more difficult than Vice City, as your wanted level seems to grow faster and your life to empty in pretty much the same way. On the other hand, the cars get visually damaged even if you scratch them and it's just frustrating to tune a car and see it explode three minutes afterwards. One way for quick cash is conquering territories and killing rival bands members [sic], but they usually walk in groups and if you unleash a war, then you must face multiple waves of enemies. In the first case, just try to drive over them and kill them instantly. It's a quicker and a smoother method. Later on, when you'll reach a four or five stars wanted level, you'll just wonder how they were able to hire so many policemen. Well, I never found out how. I was busy shooting and driving away from them" ("*Grand Theft Auto San Andreas* Review").

Works Cited

Adorno, Theodor. *The Culture Industry*. Ed. J. M. Bernstein. London: Routledge, 1991.
Banks, John. "Gamers as Co-creators: Enlisting the Virtual Audience — A Report from the Net Face." In *Critical Readings: Media and Audiences,* edited by Virginia Nightingale and Karen Ross, 268–278. London: Open University Press, 2003.
Buckley, Benjamin T. "Playing Fields: Myst, Tetris, and the Production of Simulated

Space." *Serious Discussion of All Things Ludological* (2004). 5 August 2005. http://www.academic-gamers.org/articles.shtml?playing_fields.htm.

Castranova, Edward. "On Virtual Economies." *CESinfo Working Paper Series* 752 (2002). 14 March 2007. http://ssrn.com/abstract=338500.

_____. "The Right to Play." *New York Law School Review* 49.1 (2004): 185–210. 14 March 2007. http://ssrn.com/abstract=733486.

_____. "Virtual Worlds: A First Hand Account of Market and Society on the Cyberian Frontier." *CESifo Working Paper Series* 618 (2001). 14 March 2007. http://ssrn.com/abstract=294828.

Darley, Andrew. *Digital and Visual Culture: Surface Play and Spectacle in New Media Genres.* London: Routledge, 2000.

Deleuze, Gilles, and Felix Guattari. *A Thousand Plateaus: Capitalism and Schizophrenia.* Trans. Brian Massumi. Minneapolis: University of Minnesota Press, 1987.

Der Derian, James. *Virtuous War: Mapping the Military-Industrial-Media-Entertainment Network.* Boulder, CO: Westview Press, 2001.

Dibbel, Julian. "The Unreal Estate Boom." *Wired* 11.01 (2003). 14 March 2007. http:www.wired.com/wired/archive/11.01/gaming.html?pg=1&topic=&topic_set=.

Dyer-Witherford, Nick. *Cyber-Marx: Cycles and Circuits of Struggle in High-Technology Capitalism.* Urbana: University of Illinois Press, 1999.

Elden, Stuart, Elizabeth Lebas, and Eleonore Kofman, eds. *Henri Lefebvre: Key Writings.* New York: Continuum, 2003.

Fiske, John, and Jon Watts. "Video Games: Inverted Pleasures." *Australian Journal of Cultural Studies* 3.1 (1985): 89–104.

Grand Theft Auto San Andreas. Rockstar North (2004) back cover (PS2 version) and San Andreas: Local Business Advertiser's Guide (Instruction Booklet).

"*Grand Theft Auto San Andreas* Review" (2005). 14 March 2007. http://www.computergames.ro/site/p/articles/o/review/lng/en/artid/677/grand_theft_auto_san_andreas.html.

Hardt, Michael, and Antonio Negri. *Empire.* Cambridge, MA: Harvard University Press, 2000.

Herz, J. C., and Michael R. Macedonia. "Computer Games and the Military: Two Views." *Defense Horizons* 11 (2002). 14 March 2007. http://www.ndu.edu/inss/DefHor/DH11/DH11.htm.

Himanen, Pekka. *The Hacker Ethic and the Spirit of the Information Age.* London: Secker and Warburg, 2001.

Kline, Stephen, N. Dyer-Witherford, and G. de Peuter. *Digital Play: The Interaction of Technology, Culture, and Marketing.* Montreal: McGill-Queen's University Press, 2003.

Lee, Eric. "Virtual Worlds, Real Exploitation." *No Sweat* (2005). 29 March 2005. http://www.nosweat.org.uk//article.php?sid=1242

Lefebvre, Henri. *The Production of Space.* Blackwell: Oxford, 1991 [1974].

Luhmann, Niklas. *The Reality of the Mass Media.* Trans. K. Cross. Stanford, CA: Stanford University Press, 2000.

MacCabe, Colin. "Realism and the Cinema." *Screen* 15.2 (1974): 7–27.

Manovich, Lev. The Language of New Media. Cambridge: Massachusetts Institute of Technology Press, 2001.

Miklaucic, Shawn. "Virtual Real(i)ty: SimCity and the Production of Urban Cyberspace." *Game Research: The Art Business and Science of Computer Games* (2001). http://www.game-research.com/art_simcity.asp

Nicholls, Brett, and Simon C. Ryan. "Game, Space and the Politics of Cyberplay." *fineart forum* 17. 8. (2003). 14 March 2007. http://www.msstate.edu/Fineart_Online/Backissues/Vol_17/faf_v17_n08/reviews/nicholls.html.

Soja, Edward W. *Thirdspace: Journeys to Los Angeles and Other Real-and-Imagined Places*. Cambridge, MA: Blackwell, 1996.

Stallabrass, Julian. *Gargantua: Manufactured Mass Culture*. London: Verso, 1996.

Terranova, Tiziana. "Free Labor: Producing Culture for the Digital Economy." *Social Text* 63, 18.2 (2000): 33–58.

Thompson, Tony. "They Play Games for 10 hours — and Earn £2.80 in a 'Virtual Sweatshop.'" *Observer*. 13 March 2005.

Williams, Leigh. "Global Online Games Market Worth €8bn by 2009." *Digital Media News for Europe* (5 August 2004). 14 March 2007. http://www.dmeurope.com/default.asp?ArticleID=2508.

Gameography

Asteroids, Atari, 1979.
Dark Ages of Camelot, Mythic Entertainment, 2001.
Everquest, Verant Interactive, 1999.
Eye Toy: Groove, Sony Computer Entertainment, 2003.
Grand Theft Auto: San Andreas, Rockstar Games, 2004.
Jetset Radio Future, Smilebit, 2002.
Max Payne, Remedy Entertainment, 2001.
Myst, Cyan, 1993.
Nascar 06: Total Team Control, Electronic Arts, 2005.
Need For Speed: Most Wanted, Electronic Arts, 2005.
NHL 06, Electronic Arts, 2005.
Nintendogs: Dachshund and Friends, Nintendo, 2006.
Pac-Man, Namco, 1980.
Project Entropia, MindArk, 1995.
Quake III: Arena, id Software, 1999.
Sim City, Maxis, 1989.
SingStar, Sony Computer Entertainment, 2004.
Space Invaders, Taito, 1978.
Tetris, Elorg, 1985.
Unreal Tournament, Epic Games, 1999.

About the Contributors

Patrick Crogan spent his childhood playing wargames. His research into war, computer games and technoculture amounts to an extended self-analysis of his (and our) militarized subjectivity. He teaches film, media and cultural studies at the University of the West of England, and he has published work on games, film, media, and technology in journals and anthologies, including *Angelaki, Theory, Culture & Society, Film-Philosophy, Paul Virilio: From Modernism to Hypermodernism and Beyond,* and *The Videogame Theory Reader.*

Bernadette Flynn is a lecturer at the Griffith Film School at Griffith University where she teaches in screen media and game studies. As a researcher in new media theory and production she focuses on embodied subjectivity in interaction spaces. Her work has been published in journals and books on archaeology, digital heritage, and computer games. A recent project is the application of spatial visualization systems to a prehistoric cultural heritage site located in Malta. This includes exploring how phenomenological approaches from spatial knowledge systems can communicate ideas about the past.

Seth Giddings is senior lecturer in digital media and critical theory in the School of Cultural Studies at the University of the West of England. He researches the relationships between technology and culture, most recently video games and videogame play as everyday technoculture. This research takes both written and moving image form. He has written on digital cinema, animation, and new media art, and he also teaches media production, with particular interests in the theory and practice of interactive media and the digital moving image. He is a coauthor of *New Media: A Critical Introduction* (Routledge, 2003).

Joyce Goggin is associate professor in literature, film, and new media at the University of Amsterdam. She holds degrees from the University of Toronto and Université de Montréal, where she wrote a dissertation on card games in twentieth-century fiction. She previously taught in Canada, and at the University of Leiden.

Helen W. Kennedy is senior lecturer, MA award leader and chair of the Play Research Group in the School of Cultural Studies, University of the West of England. She has spoken at a number of both academic and industry conferences on the role of women in computer games and computer games culture. She was co-organizer of the first U.K. international conference in computer games in 2001 entitled "Game Cultures" and helped to establish the Play Research Group at the University of the West of England, which organized an international symposium entitled "Power Up: Computer Games, Play and Ideology" in 2003 and hosted a second symposium on technology and agency in relation to computer games — "Playful Subjects" 2005. She is coauthor of *Games Cultures: Computer Games as New Media* (McGraw Hill/Open University Press, 2006).

Julian Kücklich is a Ph.D. student at the University of Ulster in Coleraine (Northern Ireland), where he is currently working on a dissertation on the rhetorics of play in the new media. He holds a Magister Artium in German and American literature from Ludwigs-Maximilian University (LMU) in Munich, Germany, and he is the author of a thesis on literary theory and computer games. His publications in the field of digital games include articles in *Game Studies, Philologie im Netz,* and *Dichtung Digital,* reviews in *Game Research* and *Medienobservationen,* and chapters in the forthcoming collections *Understanding Digital Games* and *Orienting Systems: The Official Strategy Guide for Video Game Studies.* Together with Aphra Kerr, Pat Brereton, and Roddy Flynn he has authored a report on the *New Media, New Pleasures?* research project, in which he was involved as a Marie Curie Fellow at Dublin City University in the academic year 2003-2004. A member of the Digital Games Research Association (DiGRA) since its inception in 2002, he is an active member of the games research community, and he has presented his work at a number of conferences related to the field, such as COSIGN (Amsterdam 2001), Computer Games and Digital Cultures (Tampere 2002), and Level Up (Utrecht 2003). He maintains an information website for the German games research community, playability.de, and blogs at *http://particlestream.motime.com.*

Brett Nicholls is a lecturer in the Department of Media, Film, and Communication at the University of Otago in New Zealand. His current research spans the political economy of the media, critical theory, and games studies.

Simon Ryan is a senior lecturer in the Department of Languages and

Cultures at the University of Otago, New Zealand. He teaches and researches in German and European studies, digital culture, and German cinema. His most recent publications include articles on the spatiality and political economy of computer games and a study of the perils of assimilation in Kafka's "The Metamorphosis." He is currently researching the impact of network culture on narratives of city life.

Melanie Swalwell's research centers on the intersections between aesthetics, new media arts, and digital games. Her writing has been published in journals and anthologies, including *Convergence, Reconstruction, Vectors, Journal of Visual Culture,* and *Videogames and Art* (Intellect, 2007). She leads the NZTronix project, which is researching the history and preservation needs of early digital games in New Zealand (www.nztronix.org.nz). Other work addresses the development of LAN gaming. Melanie lectures in the Media Studies Program at Victoria University of Wellington.

Jason Wilson has a range of international publications in videogame studies, on topics including early video games and independent game design. His Ph.D. research in Australia dealt with the aesthetics of early video games. He is a research associate in creative industries at Queensland University of Technology.

INDEX